m

Good-byes and Other Messages

Books By Whitney Balliett

The Sound of Surprise

Dinosaurs in the Morning

Such Sweet Thunder

Super-Drummer: A Profile of Buddy Rich

Ecstasy at the Onion

Alec Wilder and His Friends

New York Notes

Improvising

Night Creature

Jelly Roll, Jabbo, and Fats

American Musicians

American Singers

Barney, Bradley, and Max

Goodbyes and Other Messages

Goodbyes and Other Messages

A Journal of Jazz, 1981–1990

WHITNEY BALLIETT

New York   Oxford
OXFORD UNIVERSITY PRESS
1991

Oxford University Press

Oxford   New York   Toronto
Delhi   Bombay   Calcutta   Madras   Karachi
Petaling Jaya   Singapore   Hong Kong   Tokyo
Nairobi   Dar es Salaam   Cape Town
Melbourne   Auckland

and associated companies in
Berlin   Ibadan

Copyright © 1991 by Whitney Balliett

Published by Oxford University Press, Inc.,
200 Madison Avenue, New York, New York 10016

Oxford is a registered trademark of Oxford University Press

Library of Congress Cataloging-in-Publication Data
Balliett, Whitney.
Goodbyes and other messages : a journal of jazz,
1981–1990 / Whitney Balliett.
p. cm.   Includes index.
ISBN 0–19–503757–X
1. Jazz—New York (N.Y.)—1981–1990—History and criticism.
I. Title.   ML3508.8.N5B34   1991
781.65'09747'109048—dc20   90–23721   MN

With the exception of "The Sound of Jazz" and "Romantic Agony,"
all the material in this book first appeared
in *The New Yorker*—but often in rather different form.

9 8 7 6 5 4 3 2 1

Printed in the United States of America
on acid-free paper

For those players
who are gone,
those who are here,
and those to come.

Note

This book contains many of the shorter pieces I have done on jazz for *The New Yorker* during the past decade. "The Sound of Jazz" and "Romantic Agony" have not appeared anywhere before, however, and I have done considerable editing and distilling throughout. (Self-parody and self-plagiarism, both unwitting, are the bugaboos of aging writers.) The book is still another of the informal chronicles of the music that I began publishing in 1959. Not surprisingly, it has over a dozen obituaries—thus its title. And there are numerous other backward looks, jazz now being in a recollective stage. I have only touched on the avant-garde and on the young hard-bop players who have come along recently. The avant-garde is thirty and no longer avant, and the new hard-boppers seem to me neos rather than originals. There is no index, but the principal figures in the book are listed in the table of contents.

New York City   W. B.
1991

Contents

1990

1981

The New Red Norvo Trio

Red Norvo formed his famous trio of vibraphone, guitar, and bass in 1949, and kept it together for seven years. It included the guitarists Mundell Lowe, Tal Farlow, and Jimmy Raney, and the bassists Red Kelly, Red Mitchell, Clyde Lombardi, and Charles Mingus. Norvo once talked about its early days, at his home in California: "I got the idea for my trio after I'd moved out here. I figured a group with just vibes and guitar and bass could go into almost any place on the Coast, which would mean I could spend more time at home. Naturally, what happened was that our first booking was into Philly. We were playing opposite Slim Gaillard, who was swinging hard and making a lot of noise, and I felt naked. I wanted to know, what do you *do* behind a guitar solo with a vibraharp? Use two mallets? Four mallets? What? It was awful. But by the last couple of days it began to unfold for me a little. Then we went to New York, and one night I stopped in to eat at Billy Reed's Little Club, where they had this sissy group. The guitarist, whom I didn't know, played sixteen bars of something that spun my head. Mundell Lowe was on guitar with me, and he wanted to stay in New York, but he said he knew a guitarist who would be just right, and I told him I'd heard one who would be just right, too. I insisted Mundell hear my man and Mundell insisted I hear his man, and you know what happened—they turned out to be the same guy, Tal Farlow. I took the trio to Hawaii, and when we got back to the Haig, here in Los Angeles, my bass player wanted to leave, and one night Jimmy Rowles came in and asked me if I remembered the bass player I had used when we backed Billie Holiday in Frisco a while back. I said I did—Charlie Mingus. We called all around Frisco, and no one knew where he was, and finally we found him here—carrying mail. He wasn't playing at all, and he was big. I'd watch him sit down and eat a quart of ice cream . . . But he went down in weight with us, and by the time we opened [in New York] he was fine. He could play those jet tempos that most drummers can't touch, and he was a beautiful soloist."

The best of the small bands in jazz—among them the Creole Jazz Band, the Basie, Goodman, and Ellington groups, the John Kirby band, the Norvo trio, the Modern Jazz Quartet—have shared a loose density, an unbreakable collective sense, a lyrical bent. The Norvo group, made up of two stringed instruments and a hybrid percussion instrument, all with delicate timbres and all inclining toward the treble registers, went a little farther. Its music was closer to thought than to action, to spirit than to flesh. The trio stripped its music to the essentials of melody and rhythm and improvisation, almost eliminating the barriers between musician and listener. The music seemed to emanate from the listener himself. The trio played with great gentleness. Even when it hustled, it suggested rather than stated, pointed rather than pushed. Few of its numbers gave the impression of having a beginning, a middle, and an end. This was marvellous trickery, for each piece was meticulously structured. From the first note, the listener was caught, and he remained caught until the final note. The ensembles were in unison or in harmony and were generally elaborate variations on the melody. Guitar solos were backed by the bassist and by Norvo chords, played offbeat or behind the beat, and bass solos rested on on-the-beat guitar chords, which achieved a soft railroad click-click-click. The guitarist and bassist would give Norvo four-to-the-bar support, or the guitarist would circle him with admiring offbeat chords. Sometimes the closing ensemble repeated the opening one, and sometimes it offered a new variation on the melody. Being rhythmically perfect, the trio loved hard tempos—the very fast, the serenely slow—and it rarely spent much time in between. It was great fun to watch, mostly because of Norvo, a fugitive from the vaudeville of the twenties, who likes to make O mouths, pop eyes, and assorted manic movements.

For years, people have been after Norvo to reorganize his trio, and at last he has. Tal Farlow, who has been in semi-retirement, is on guitar, and Steve Novosel, from Washington, D.C., is on bass. Norvo has taken the group into Michael's Pub. In many ways, the new trio is better than the old one. The old one was a meteor: it always got where it was going in the fastest, most direct way. The new trio meanders a little and favors easier tempos. The old trio, in spite of its gentleness, was all muscle, while the new one is unclenched and relaxed. Best, the new trio has discarded—or perhaps simply forgotten—the bebop finery of the old group, which, in the mode of the time, was decked out in Charlie Parker melodic lines, flatted ninth chords, and ensembles that were so tightly woven in the Parker manner that they were opaque. The new trio's ensembles are looser, the solos are longer, and Norvo and Farlow indulge in the sort of counterpoint that was once at the heart of jazz. (Norvo first began fooling with the device fifteen years ago, with the pianist Dave McKenna.) On opening night, during the middle sections of "All of Me" and "How About You?," Novosel lay out, and Farlow and Norvo, suspended in midair, developed exquisite melodic lines that at once pushed past and embraced one another—the great paradoxical magic of counterpoint. And on "How About You?" Novosel joined Norvo and Farlow after their chorus, and three voices floated through the room. Farlow was one of the first guitarists to be influenced by Charlie Parker, and in the forties he invariably used five notes where one would have done. He is statelier now. Silence appears, and stands on its own. His solos think and move in peaceful and deliberate ways. They are the poems of a middle-aged man. All Norvo need do is match the standard of beauty he established for himself forty years ago. And he does. Here are the ducking runs, the crystalline melodic pools, the winglike tremolos, the crowding, cheeky chords, the soothing momentum. There was much graceful music on opening night—in Norvo's and Farlow's contrapuntal excursions; in Norvo's kid-glove opening and closing choruses on "We'll Be

Together Again," both done ad lib and a cappella; in his sunrise solo on "All of Me"; in his four-mallet figure behind Farlow on "The Jitterbug Waltz," a kind of shadowing ground figure; and in Farlow's fleeing, smiling solo on the fast "Fascinating Rhythm." Brilliance sometimes blinds; Norvo, Farlow, and Novosel light the way.

Down the River _____

FRIDAY: George Wein has sold his Newport soul to the Brown & Williamson tobacco company. The original Newport Jazz Festival, which included an incomparable list of performers (Pee Wee Russell, Bobby Hackett, Lee Wiley, Jo Jones, Lester Young, Buck Clayton, Dizzy Gillespie, Billie Holiday, Lennie Tristano, and the fledgling Modern Jazz Quartet, with Horace Silver on piano), has become, in its twenty-seventh year, the Kool Jazz Festival New York. Brown & Williamson will pay Wein an undisclosed amount over the next five years for having removed the name Newport (also the name of a rival mentholated cigarette, of course), and it will assume all advertising and promotional costs of the festival. (This all becomes a gallimaufry when we are also told that Wein, in order to protect his copyright on the name Newport Jazz Festival, will hold a two-concert Newport Jazz Festival in Newport in August.) Wein states in the program that his deal with Brown & Williamson will enable the festival to continue. More likely, it will help the festival to continue its self-competing giantism (this year hundreds of musicians will perform over ten days in fifty events at fourteen locations in New York and New Jersey, and some of the events will last twelve hours and involve simultaneous performances), its repetitiveness (a dozen events being held this year are variants of events given before), and its deepening unimaginativeness.

The festival, in its tawdry new clothes, began this afternoon, in Carnegie Recital Hall, with an unaccompanied concert by the pianist Cedar Walton. He played three standards, three Duke Ellington tunes, a couple of Bud Powell numbers, and some of his own material. Walton is a clear, robust, declarative pianist, who speaks with the tongues of Art Tatum, Powell, and Lennie Tristano. But this afternoon, without rhythmic support, he donned protective rhapsodic robes. His arpeggios rose and fell, and he kept breaking them in unexpected, Bud Powell places. These ceaseless contrary motions caused Walton to slip and slide rhythmically, and they also hid the fact that, at his ease with a bassist in a night club, he is a joyous and swinging pianist.

Walton was better at the evening concert in Carnegie Hall. This was a celebration for the old drummer Art Blakey that was carried forward by Blakey's present group and by such alumni as Walton, Walter Davis, Johnny Griffin, Jackie McLean, Freddie Hubbard, Bill Hardman, Donald Byrd, and Curtis Fuller. It was hard-bop heaven again. (Blakey formed his first Jazz Messengers in 1954.) There were the dull unison ensembles, the interminable solos, and Blakey's toneless thunderclap drumming. But it was good to hear Hardman's hilly phrasing (so intense beside Hubbard's glassy vacuity), and to hear how far Griffin, who has lived in Europe for many years, has moved from where Don Byas stopped. The sound system nearly destroyed the evening. The piano sounded like china being unpacked and the ensembles like a hennery when a fox gets in.

SATURDAY: The pianist Joanne Brackeen, tall and narrow and stooped, appeared in Carnegie Recital Hall this afternoon in a blouse and skirt and an immense Virginia Woolf straw hat. She did half a dozen numbers, all of them unidentifiable but presumably hers, and they varied from silken Debussy barges to hardboiled Keith Jarrett fantasies. Rhythm and melody were implied. It was a mannered music also marked by Cecil Taylor avalanches and bellying McCoy Tyner chords. The straw hat seemed disembodied after a time, and it never stopped bobbing and swaying and tipping.

There was a long, loose history of Chicago jazz at Carnegie Hall this evening. A swing group led by the bass trumpeter Cy Touff and including Norman Murphy on trumpet, Franz Jackson on tenor saxophone, Marty Grosz on guitar, Truck Parham on bass, and Barrett Deems on drums played four easy, elated numbers. Touff's flat-faced playing contrasted nicely with Murphy's sweet, round tone and Jackson's Ben Webster lyricism. Next came a surprising duet by two members of the Association for the Advancement of Creative Musicians—the reedman Roscoe Mitchell, who works with the Art Ensemble of Chicago, and the trumpeter Hugh Regan. They did one ten-minute number, which was made up of long-held treble notes, some in unison and some in a freakish bagpipe harmony, broken here and there by scratching sounds, steamboat whistles, and bird tremolos. It was funny, needling, free music. There was booing, and several people fled the hall, their fingers in their ears. Time fell back thirty years for a bebop set by the trumpeter and reedman Ira Sullivan, who had Lee Konitz on alto saxophone, Chris Anderson on piano, Victor Sproles on bass, and Wilbur Campbell on drums. There was good ensemble lobbing by Sullivan and Konitz, and Campbell revealed that he is an alert, driving bebop drummer. Then back twenty more years, to around 1930. Art Hodes played a solo version of "St. Louis Blues," which moved from deep-blue left-hand chords to stride figures, and he and Parham accompanied Mama Yancey for three numbers. She is in her mid-eighties and came onstage in a wheelchair, but her dry, sad voice was intact. She sang "Trouble in Mind" and "Make Me a Pallet on the Floor," and Hodes was there at every turn with tremolos and low-register rumbles. He rocked the hall. The tenor saxophonist Von Freeman (father of the tenor saxophonist Chico Freeman) moved us up to the fifties with a hard-bop group that had Paul Serrano on trumpet, Sproles, and Campbell. Von Freeman is a curious saxophonist. He likes dying notes and notes that sound as if they were split, and his tone is reedy and diffuse. Sonny Rollins is always passing by. Then back to 1930 for good. Jimmy McPartland and Wild Bill Davison (together and separately), assisted by Frank Chace on clarinet, Jim Beebe on trombone, and a rhythm section of Hodes, Parham, Grosz, and Don DeMicheal on drums, went through seven Chicago anthems, including "Sugar," "Royal Garden Blues," "Big Butter and Egg Man," and "China Boy." McPartland hustled (he sang on one number), and Davison rooted and growled and champed. The concert was produced by Harriet Choice, and the singer Joe Williams read a script she had prepared as if he were a Latin teacher intoning a first-year student's composition. At the very beginning of the evening, he also demonstrated the melismatic street cry he used as a kid when he hawked the Chicago *Defender.*

SUNDAY: Duos are cheaper to hire than trios or quartets, and in the past ten or fifteen years they have become the most fashionable jazz ensemble. Their members have discovered that the form, which involves counterpoint, soloing, unison and harmonic playing, accompanying, and intense listening, is as challenging as any in jazz. They have also discovered that a successful duo must balance. The players must be equally gifted, they must relish each other's work, and their instruments must be complementary. Multi-noted instruments (guitar with guitar, piano with piano) work well, and so do different single-noted instruments (alto saxophone with tenor saxophone, trumpet with trombone), and one single-noted instrument (tenor saxophone) with one multi-noted instrument (guitar). But identical single-noted instruments (two trumpets, two trombones), hobbled by similar tones and timbres, do not. A program of duets—seven in all—was assembled by Dan Morgenstern at Carnegie Hall tonight, and only one really worked. This was made up of the guitarists Wayne Wright and Marty Grosz. Wright, a Django Reinhardt admirer, favors quavery single-note lines, while Grosz uses a chordal attack. They offset each other's solos, and they have worked together enough to have found each other's nooks and crannies. They did "It Don't Mean a Thing If It Ain't Got That Swing," Reinhardt's "Tears,"

"Goody Goody," and a three-part piece written down in the thirties by the guitarists Dick McDonough and Carl Kress. Red Rodney and Ira Sullivan played their trumpets and flügelhorns, Zoot Sims and Lee Konitz played their soprano saxophones, and Major Holley and Slam Stewart sang and played their basses. Herbie Hancock on acoustic piano and the bassist Ron Carter turned out to be Hancock accompanied by Carter. The same imbalance was true of the singer Carol Sloane and her pianist, Norman Simmons. The final group, made up of Milt Jackson and John Lewis, sounded exactly like what it was—the top half of the Modern Jazz Quartet. Herewith some foolproof duos for concerts to come: Zoot Sims and Bucky Pizzarelli; Jim Hall and Michael Moore; Red Norvo and Dave McKenna; Dick Wellstood and Ralph Sutton; Ellis Larkins and Joe Wilder.

MONDAY: We listen to jazz to be surprised. Tonight, at an allstar concert at Carnegie Hall, we waited a long time. Set after set went by, consisting of the likes of John Bunch, Eddie Bert, Al Grey, Kenny Burrell, Frank Foster, Dave Brubeck, Bobby Rosengarden, and Gerry Mulligan, and then it happened. Ellis Larkins, accompanied by the bassist Billy Popp, played two unamplified blues—one slow and one in medium tempo. The first, Larkins' own "Happiness Boy Chaser," was an ingenious arrangement of right-hand riffs that circled around over an ostinato bass, rose in a delicate crescendo, and subsided. The second, Mercer Ellington's "Things Ain't What They Used to Be," deepened the subtle blue mood established in the first number. Here were Larkins' zephyr touch, his rueful ease, his hidden, spinning arpeggios, his cumulative rhythm. He enthralled us, and nothing that followed (Dizzy Gillespie, Clark Terry, Machito, Cecil Payne, Benny Powell, Billy Taylor, Jimmy Rowles, Zoot Sims, Mel Tormé, Joe Albany, Kenny Davern) diminished his hold.

TUESDAY: Two groups played at Avery Fisher Hall tonight— the Red Norvo Trio, which was meant to be the crowd-quieter, and the Chick Corea Quartet, which was meant to be the main draw. But there was a dazzling turnaround. The evening, to all intents and purposes, ended with Norvo. He insisted that his group be heard without amplification, and its treble, lattice-work music could be heard everywhere. Norvo's trio, with Tal Farlow on guitar and Steve Novosel on bass, was reconstituted three weeks ago (he disbanded his first trio in 1956), and it is now close to perfection. The ensembles breathe, the accompanying is clairvoyant, Farlow has his chops back, and Novosel is braver. There were wonders in every one of its ten numbers: Farlow's double-time solo on "Here's That Rainy Day"; Norvo's serene, belling, hymnlike a-cappella version of Bix Beiderbecke's "Candlelight"; Norvo and Farlow's twining but parallel counterpoint on "The One I Love" and "Fascinating Rhythm"; and all of Fats Waller's "Jitterbug Waltz," a tricky, irresistible tune that seems to force jazz musicians to surpass themselves.

Chick Corea changes his musical address every year or so. Having abandoned Electronic Heights, in Fusion City, he introduced a group tonight that included a hard-bop tenor saxophonist (Joe Henderson), an aging avant-garde bassist (Gary Peacock), and a bebop drummer (Roy Haynes). And he himself played acoustic piano. The music, partly written, partly improvised, was romantic, motionless, and eclectic (tatters of free jazz, acres of hard bop). No one seemed to be who he was. Peacock, that lyrical speedster, had a barbarous sound and used a lot of whining notes. Haynes, a champion chatterer, sounded bored. And Corea never got much beyond several two-handed high-register glisses. But what else could he do? He, too, had been out front during Norvo's set.

WEDNESDAY: It no longer matters whether Art Tatum was a great jazz pianist. He was a magnificent hybrid, caught somewhere between Vladimir Horowitz, on the classical side, and Lee Sims, on the popular side, and he changed the course of jazz with his rococo, million-noted, arpeggioed attack. Charlie Parker heard him as a young man, and so did Bud Powell and Lennie Tristano and Don Byas and John Coltrane. We are still swimming in his florid sea. Tonight, at Town Hall, the pianists Billy

Taylor and Dick Hyman gave a joint lecture on Tatum, and they illustrated their remarks by performing separately and together and by bringing on such pianists as Jaki Byard, Dick Wellstood, Adam Makowicz, John Lewis, Ellis Larkins, and Barry Harris. They also sat in, separately, with the old Art Tatum Trio—Tiny Grimes on guitar and Slam Stewart on bass. The presence of some of their exemplars was puzzling. There is very little of Tatum in John Lewis, and Byard's Tatum is watery. Wellstood and Harris are a generation removed: Wellstood mirrors one of Tatum's idols, Fats Waller, and Harris one of Tatum's descendants, Bud Powell. The best of tonight's illustrators was Hyman himself. (Taylor is too diffuse, Larkins brings us mainly Tatum's touch, and Makowicz is close to an unintentional caricature.) Hyman's "Body and Soul" with the trio was faultless, and so was his solo reading of the Thad Jones-Alec Wilder "A Child Is Born." All that he lacks is Tatum's pneumatic touch and his ability to make you gasp. A series of duets—Byard and Lewis, Harris and Taylor, Wellstood and Hyman, Larkins and Makowicz—followed. The winners were Wellstood and Hyman with a stride version of "If Dreams Come True." They matched that look-out! quality that Tatum took on when he shifted into a stride bass at a fast tempo and blew the house down. There are only two film clips of Tatum in action; both were shown tonight. The first is a snippet from a "March of Time" newsreel, and the second is from a jam-session sequence in a feature film called "The Fabulous Dorseys." But one hears and sees more in it of Charlie Barnet and Ziggy Elman and Ray Bauduc than of Tatum.

THURSDAY: The lack of decent movie footage on early jazz music was due to racism and ignorance. (How would Samuel Goldwyn have known in 1933 that Louis Armstrong was playing the most lyrical and original music in the United States when Olin Downes, the *Times'* music critic, didn't know either?) Bessie Smith and Charlie Parker appear only once on film, and the brief glimpses we have of Bix Beiderbecke and Chick Webb are useless. There is no known footage of Fletcher Henderson, King Oliver, Jelly Roll Morton, or Charlie Christian. What does exist from the twenties and thirties and forties (television has done far better than Hollywood) is almost accidental: generally hoked-up "jam sessions" from feature films (one has Wingy Manone on trumpet, Joe Venuti on violin, Les Paul on guitar, Jess Stacy on piano, and Abe Lyman on drums), newsreel clips, and cheap shorts made as fillers to be shown between the cartoon and the newsreel. (The first honest, serious attempt to capture jazz in the movies was Gjon Mili's 1944 "Jammin' the Blues.") The film collector David Chertok showed thirty-four of these oddities at Town Hall tonight, and all were of big bands. The earliest was from 1933 (Claude Hopkins playing "Careless Love" in a huge barbershop, with Edmond Hall on alto saxophone), and the most recent was from the late forties (Woody Herman's "Lemon Drop"). In between, we saw Charlie Barnet playing "Cherokee" in a field next to a tepee; Bob Crosby doing "Sugarfoot Stomp" in a baggage car; and Gene Krupa playing a frantic, yeah-man "Leave Us Leap." But we also saw the 1943 Duke Ellington band doing two numbers with Ben Webster, Tricky Sam Nanton, Ray Nance, and Johnny Hodges; Sidney De Paris, still in his Louis Armstrong shoes, soloing with Don Redman in 1934; the 1936 Jimmie Lunceford band doing "Nagasaki"; and a brief solo by Don Fagerquist on Les Brown's "I've Got My Love to Keep Me Warm." There was good singing along the way by Frank Sinatra, Helen Forrest, Peggy Lee, Billy Eckstine, Fran Warren, Helen O'Connell, Sister Rosetta Tharpe, and Louis Armstrong, who did "I Can't Give You Anything But Love" in a bartender's jacket.

FRIDAY: The late-afternoon piano concerts in Carnegie Recital Hall continue to be uneven. Ram Ramirez, who wrote "Lover Man" and plays composer's piano, did a Duke Ellington medley and a medley of songs associated with Billie Holiday, a couple of blues, some Gershwin, a tune by Richie Wyands, and "Lover Man." He is a loose-kneed swing pianist who has listened to Red Garland and Erroll Garner. Albert Dailey offered half a dozen harmonic castles, built of arpeggios, loud pedal, rubato, and portmanteau chords, and concealing in their dungeons such songs as "Emily" and "What Is This Thing Called Love?" Dorothy Donegan, a vaudevillian who plays Art Tatum piano, made her corkscrew faces and played her usual concatenation of "Tea for Two," "Rhapsody in Blue," and "The Man I Love," all the while using rubber tempos, interpolation, stride piano, and white water arpeggios. And this afternoon Ross Tompkins, who went West with the "Tonight Show" band ten years ago, followed in the ad-lib footsteps of Walton, Brackeen, and Dailey. He is a fine jazz pianist, and it's too bad that, on this rare trip East, he didn't show us that.

At an afternoon concert at the 1970 Newport Festival, Bill Cosby presented a Los Angeles band that he called Badfoot Brown and the Bunions Bradford Marching and Funeral Band. It was made up of a tenor saxophonist, a trombonist, two Fender bassists, three guitarists, two pianists, an organist, and two drummers. Its principal number lasted forty-five minutes and was a sly, blueslike survey of modern jazz, done up with endless breaks and tempo changes, duets, mountainous crescendos, and a vocal of "White Christmas" interrupted several times by drum solos. The piece swung massively, and it remains indelible. Tonight, Cosby brought B. B. King, Arnett Cobb, Nat Adderley, Jimmy Smith, and Mickey Roker into Carnegie Hall to play the blues. They played slow blues, medium blues, and fast blues, but the group never found its heart. Cosby himself delivered the best music—a parody of a blues singer who can't get off a word unless it has at least a dozen notes in it. A study in melismatic madness, it cut so close to the bone it shook up B. B. King.

SATURDAY: All-female jazz events are voluntary acts of segregation and seeming admissions that only through numbers can women equal men in jazz. But women have long been equal to men in jazz. Men have dominated its instrumental side, but women have dominated its vocal side. A syllogism could even be fashioned: the human voice is the greatest instrument; women are the greatest jazz singers; therefore, women are the greatest jazz instrumentalists. Who has surpassed Billie Holiday's sense of rhythmic placement? Who has scaled the melodic peaks and plumbed the melodic depths of Sarah Vaughan? Who has matched the majesty of Bessie Smith? So "Women Blow Their Own Horns," a concert put together by Rosetta Reitz at Carnegie Hall tonight, was needless. And it was not an all-female event anyway—Melba Liston's band had three men, and Dizzy Gillespie and Clark Terry wandered on and off during the evening. The Willene Barton quintet began the concert, with two old-fashioned jump numbers and a slow "As Time Goes By." The leader, sawing her tenor saxophone up and down, appeared to be cutting her way through her music. Dorothy Donegan did a coherent "An Affair to Remember," then opened her "Tea for Two" box and let her flying arpeggios out. Melba Liston, who was in Dizzy Gillespie's big band in the fifties, played four numbers, two of them in the sort of barely moving tempos that dance bands used to sink into late at night. Britt Woodman, the old Ellington trombonist, was with her, along with a fine tenor saxophonist named Erica Lindsay. The rest of the evening was a kind of jam session, with Marian McPartland or Dorothy Donegan on piano, Mary Osborne on guitar, Jean Fineberg on tenor saxophone, Lucille Dixon on bass, and Barbara Merjan on drums. Gillespie and Terry leafed through their solos.

SUNDAY: Miles Davis, absent from jazz for the past five years or so, turned up for two shows at Avery Fisher Hall tonight with a reedman (Bill Evans), a rock guitarist (Mike Stern), a Fender bassist (Marcus Miller), a percussionist (Nino Cinellu), and a drummer (Al Foster) and, for the hour that the first show lasted, pretended he was in *Apocalypse Now*. Davis was dressed for the trip. He had on a fisherman's cap, a dark jacket, which he kept taking off, a singlet, gray pipestem pants, and clogs. It was night, and the darkness was broken by a searchlight that followed Davis as he stumped from side to side of the boat; sat on a stool in front of Foster's drums, his back to the audience; raised his fist and brought it down to turn the ship of sound in a new direction; played one of his brief solos (sixteen or twenty bars at the longest), his back bent almost double, so that the bell of his horn was inches from the floor; and sipped from a cup brought by a deckhand. The heavy-metal roar of guitar, bass, and drums was almost always present, and to make himself heard Davis had a small microphone fastened to his trumpet. His muted solos rose clearly above the din, and when he took out his mute and let loose an open-horn blast the crocodiles on the banks jumped. Davis played one non-stop number, which was unidentified and unidentifiable. Evans soloed on soprano and tenor saxophone, the guitarist soloed, and the percussionist soloed. The tempos changed ceaselessly, and so did the rhythm. Davis's chops are in good shape, but he played the same solo again and again. It went like this: an ascending shriek (Dizzy Gillespie, 1945) followed by a scurrying downward run; a second, lower shriek; silence; another run, broken off abruptly in the Bud Powell manner; silence; a three-note cluster, the last note flatted and held for a measure or two; silence; an upward run; and a closing six-note cluster. When the boat reached Kurtz's hideaway, Davis turned to the audience for the first time, and *waved*, as if to let us know that he is just one of us after all and that what we had been watching—it was a visual music—was only imaginary.

This afternoon, at the last of three concerts given during the week at the Guggenheim Museum, the drummer Louis Hayes appeared with Frank Strozier on alto saxophone, Harold Mabern on piano, and Jimmy Rowser on bass. Strozier came up from Memphis in the fifties with the late trumpeter Booker Little, the tenor saxophonist George Coleman, and Mabern, and he is one of the most original of Charlie Parker's second wave of admirers. The group played five numbers. The finest was a long, intense "My Funny Valentine." It had formidable opening and closing cadenzas by Strozier and an in-tempo solo, full of Parker runs, Strozier's peculiar high-register pipings, and his way of shaping a phrase—a descending six-note figure, say—and playing it over and over, each time with slight variations.

TUESDAY: Having a jazz festival at all in New York is like shipping artichokes to Castroville. The thirty or more jazz night clubs in the city celebrate the music continuously. During the past year or so, we have heard Jabbo Smith, the Lee Konitz Nonet, Lee Konitz and Gil Evans in a duo, Art Hodes, the Red Norvo Trio, Ralph Sutton, the George Coleman Octet, Warne Marsh, and endless piano-and-bass duos. Now still another duo, made up of Dick Hyman and the California pianist Roger Kellaway, has turned up at Michael's Pub. Hyman and Kellaway first played as a duo at one of Dick Gibson's Colorado jazz parties. Hyman, with his long, pale face and white, flickering fingers, is an academic Art Tatum, while Kellaway, bearded and stubby-fingered, is an academic Oscar Peterson. (Both men are also gifted composers and arrangers.) They balance. Hyman's touch is light and self-effacing, while Kellaway digs in—sometimes he splats the upper register with his right elbow. Hyman suggests and Kellaway points, Hyman outlines and Kellaway itemizes. Hyman, got up tonight in a dark-blue blazer and tie, swayed from side to side at the keyboard, while Kellaway, in an electric-blue velvet jacket, light-colored trousers, and a yellow open-neck shirt, bent over tightly or, when he got off a good one, reared back. Duo pianists can be relentless, crowding the air and making an endlessly quarrelling music. But Hyman and Kellaway step aside when the other takes off. On "Yesterdays," Kellaway played octave melodic lines in both hands and Hyman laid down drifting, applauding tremolos. Hyman unrolled into-the-wind arpeggios in "Get Happy" and Kellaway rocked around in his lowest register. They made rhythm machines out of "Get Happy" and an Albert Ammons boogie-woogie number and out of a slow "Just a Closer Walk with Thee." On a very fast "Blue Skies," they sat at the same keyboard and switched places every other chorus. Their hands advanced, bowed, retreated, advanced, bowed, retreated, and the sound was as thick as thunder. On a medium-tempo "Remembering You" (Kellaway's song, and the closing theme of "All in the Family"), they did two-handed octave figures and in the last chorus created brilliant counterpoint, their right hands making voices that wound around and around, never touching, never separating.

New Bird _____

The lurid, secret, phantasmagoric shape of Charlie Parker's life has not made him easy to write about. He bulges out of the fiction he appears in, and is surrealistic in his two biographies. He was a legend when he was alive, and the legend has grown. He is now a demigod—a wizard primitive musician who is widely thought of as the greatest jazz improviser, a super-dropout who seemingly outwitted society by almost completely skirting it, a Gargantua whose appetites destroyed him. The newest attempt to get him down in a book comes from France, and it is a surprising one. It is called *To Bird with Love* (Editions Wizlov), and consists largely of giant photographs—over two hundred and fifty of them—that have been assembled by Parker's widow, Chan, who lives in France, and by Francis Paudras, a French graphic artist. It is a monolithic book. There are blowups of Parker's head that are the same size as Parker's head. Indeed, all the pictures—they bleed off the page—give the impression of being life-size. (The book measures ten and a half inches by fifteen, weighs seven pounds, and has over four hundred pages.) Scattered among the pictures are reproductions of Parker ephemera and Parker's "papers": his driver's license, stamped with traffic violations; letters, cards, and notes; contracts and telegrams; a pawn ticket (a hundred dollars for his alto saxophone—dated seven weeks before his death). The book is arranged chronologically and becomes, as the images and papers accumulate, his life. But, alas, the book presupposes considerable knowledge of that life. Many photographs have no captions or information of any kind. Some have semi-poetic effusions supplied by Chan Parker: facing pictures of Parker with his arm around fellow-musicians are labelled "Those touched became profound by the passage," and a double-page spread of Parker's head is captioned "Exhale the melody exquisite, inhale a cry of anguish, a plea for acceptance and understanding."

Here, for the sake of reference, are the bones of Parker's life: He was born in 1920 in a suburb of Kansas City and raised by his mother, Addie Boyley, in the city proper. His father, a vaudevillian and Pullman chef, disappeared when he was eleven. Parker did well in grammar school, but then his life began to accelerate. By the time he was sixteen, he had dropped out of high school (he'd been a freshman for three years), he was married and had a child, he was a professional alto saxophonist and a member of the musicians' union. And he was on his way to becoming a drug addict. At seventeen, he went briefly to Chicago and New York, where he heard Art Tatum, whose teeming melodic lines became a permanent part of his musical furniture. He joined Jay McShann's Kansas City band when he was nineteen, and stayed with McShann off and on for three years. He rooted around in Harlem for a time after that, then went with Earl Hines' band and with Billy Eckstine's all-star bebop band. He made his first important recordings in 1944, and late in 1945 he went to Los Angeles with Dizzy Gillespie in a band that included Milt Jackson, Al Haig, and Ray Brown. (It was the first bebop band to cross the Rockies, and it had the same effect as the arrival of the Spaniards: the natives were incredulous.) But, constantly souped up with drugs and alcohol, he collapsed, and midway in 1946 he was committed to Camarillo State Hospital. In the biography *Bird Lives!*, Ross Russell quotes a doctor who took care of Parker:

A man living from moment to moment. A man living for the pleasure principle, music, food, sex, drugs, kicks, his per-

*sonality arrested at an infantile level. A man with almost no
feeling of guilt and only the smallest, most atrophied nub of
conscience. One of the army of psychopaths supplying the
populations of prisons and mental institutions. Except for his
music, a potential member of that population. But with
Charlie Parker it is the music factor that makes all the difference. That's really the only reason we're interested in him.
The reason we're willing to stop our own lives and clean up
his messes. People like Charlie require somebody like
that . . .*

Parker was released, in buoyant shape, in 1947, but by the
time he reappeared in New York later that year he was down and
out again. He went to France in 1949 and to Scandinavia in 1950.
During the last five years of his life (he died March 12, 1955), he
disintegrated steadily but continued to work, sometimes brilliantly (the famous Massey Hall concert in Toronto in 1953,
with Dizzy Gillespie, Bud Powell, Charles Mingus, and Max
Roach). His last job in New York, or anywhere, took place over
the weekend of March 4 and 5, 1955, at Birdland, with Kenny
Dorham, Bud Powell, Mingus, and Art Blakey. On the second
night, Powell got drunk, insulted Parker, and walked off the
bandstand. Parker shouted Powell's name endlessly through the
microphone, but Powell refused to come back. The club emp-
tied, and Parker left and got drunk himself. Four days later, he
set out for an engagement at George Wein's Storyville, in
Boston, and on the way stopped off at the apartment of Baroness
Pannonica de Koenigswarter, in the Stanhope Hotel, on Fifth
Avenue at Eighty-first Street. He had a seizure, and three days
later died there, aged thirty-four.

Some of the photographs in *To Bird with Love* are famous
shots taken by William Gottlieb and Gjon Mili and Robert
Parent, but many appear to be snapshots rescued from albums
and drawers and wallets. Here is Parker rehearsing in some hall
with an experimental big band led by the arranger Gene Roland
and including Zoot Sims, Al Cohn, Jimmy Knepper, and Eddie
Bert; Parker in a double-breasted chalk-stripe suit standing

ceremoniously beside Duke Ellington; Parker on a Paris stage with Sidney Bechet, Bernard Peiffer, and Don Byas; Parker's mother, worn, bemused, kindly; Parker's childhood home, its windows gone, and surrounded by saplings and overgrown shrubs; and a derelict three-story brick building in Kansas City that once housed a night club called Subway, where Parker worked with Jay McShann and Jesse Price when he was seventeen. Ross Russell quotes McShann on Parker's already sneaky ways: "He was a strange kid, very aggressive and wise. He liked to play practical jokes. And he was always borrowing money, a couple of dollars that you'd never get back." The pictures in the last hundred or so pages of the book are often dismal. Parker is overweight, his eyes are unfocussed, he looks beat and dejected. Most frightening of all are three double-page photographs taken on the bandstand at Birdland during Parker's final engagement there. In the first, a huge Parker leans over to say something to Bud Powell, who, seated at the piano, has mad blank-white eyes. In the second, Powell, still mad-looking, plays while Art Blakey stares angrily at him. In the last picture, Powell is out of sight, Mingus has vanished, and Parker, fat and sweating, plays, backed by Blakey. All three pictures have a dark, hellish cast: demons are loose.

There are rare glimpses of a jazz musician's backstage life in *To Bird with Love*, particularly in a couple of exchanges of letters between irate night-club managers and the musicians' union and between a defensive Parker and the musicians' union. Toward the end of his life, Parker often behaved poorly on the job or failed to show up at all. The manager of the Latin Quarter, in Montreal, writes to an officer of the musicians' union in New York:

Now for [the musicians'] appearance. When they arrived at the club, they looked anything but musicians, at least, those [we] have been in the habit of engaging. They were shabbily dressed, torn shirts, even on Mr. Parker's back; they were unshaven, dirty looking and not fit to be presented to any public.

Parker's answer to the union official is calm and even stately:

For explanation: It is an over night ride on a train from New York to Montreal, and the men who arrived in the early evening went immediately, as soon as they got off the train, to the Latin Quarter to ascertain what the requirements of the engagement were, and naturally, this being in the neighborhood of 7:30 in the evening, and we not scheduled to play until 10:00 o'clock, and having ridden all day on a very dirty train, all of us certainly admit we were definitely not dressed to make a professional appearance . . . When we appeared . . . at the prescribed time of 10:00 P.M., my entire band wore dark blue suits, were cleanly shaven, and were ready to perform in a professional manner.

Six months later, Parker apparently misbehaved at the Tiffany Club, in Los Angeles. The manager writes to the same long-suffering union official in New York:

Mr. Parker played four sets instead of five, consisting of 17-14-18-20 minutes each. During these short sessions, Mr. Parker played very little. He leaned on the piano and weaved from side to side, obviously intoxicated. His eyes were shut for three and four minutes at a time and he didn't play a note. He sweat profusely, and wiped his brow with his fore finger and thrust sweat to the floor, unbecoming to a performer. His stage behavior was the most deplorable I have ever witnessed. Patrons laughed and giggled and wondered what next.

Parker will have none of it:

His comments about my behavior on the stage are purely a matter of personal opinion and conjecture. All I can say is that the people seemed satisfied with my performance and applauded the performance.

Parker, however, lost out; the union decreed that he pay the Tiffany Club five hundred dollars in damages.

Duke Ellington

Refused admittance to the Broadway musical stage except for the short-lived *Beggar's Holiday*, done with John Latouche in 1946, Duke Ellington created his own musical theatre. This was not surprising, for he was, with his ornate courtesy, his cool, sharp humor, his sometimes arcane dress, and his tinted, mocking speech, intensely theatrical—and so was his often programmatic composing. *Jump for Joy*, produced in Los Angeles in 1941, and *My People*, produced in Chicago in 1963, were elaborate revues in which the music dominated the acts. (That is also the case in the current *Sophisticated Ladies*, despite the highly touted dancing and singing.) *A Drum Is a Woman* was a fantasy written in the mid-fifties for television. *The River* was an almost Bunyanesque allegory done for American Ballet Theatre in 1970. And his so-called Sacred Concerts were unique extravaganzas that were premièred at Grace Cathedral, San Francisco, in 1965, at the Cathedral of St. John the Divine, New York, in 1968, and at Westminster Abbey, in 1973, not long before he died. The Sacred Concerts came to seem to him the most important things he had written. "I am not concerned with what it costs," he wrote of the first Sacred Concert in his autobiography, *Music Is My Mistress*. "I want the best of everything possible. I want the best musicians, the best singers and coaches—amateurs or professionals—and I want them to give the best they have. I want all the help I can get and to say that I hope I am good enough to say because this is the performance of all performances—God willing." Ellington's Sacred Concerts never matched the dimensions of Berlioz's Requiem (four brass bands, full orchestra with sixteen kettledrums, a five-hundred-voice choir), but he did his best to fill the empyreal spaces of the cathedrals and churches and temples he worked in. His band was the base, and to it he added choirs, the cathedral organ, male and female vocal soloists, narration, and dancers, tap and ballet. The results were uneven. Some of the songs had the density and fervor of religious music. Others were romantic, and even lachrymose: they sentimentalized God, possibly making Him an adjunct of Ellington's revered mother. Some of the dancing was showy and superfluous, and so were some of the band instrumentals (long drum solos). The performers were erratic, and varied from the sublime (the Swedish soprano Alice Babs, the tap dancer Bunny Briggs, the band itself) to the melodramatic (the singers Jon Hendricks and Tony Watkins, and the dancer-choreographer Geoffrey Holder). But it was spectacular when everything came together.

This happened in the "David Danced Before the Lord" done at the Fifth Avenue Presbyterian Church in December of 1965. There, in full aural and visual flower, was Ellington's vision. The number, which was recorded during the concert, begins with a short, annunicatory band chord, and this is immediately followed by Briggs dancing fast, light steps. He continues by himself for sixteen measures, and drops into rangy half-time steps. (He dances throughout the number, which lasts six minutes.) The saxophones play the lovely steplike thirty-two-bar melody (originally "Come Sunday"), which, like a lullaby, covers less than an octave and a half and is built on sequential notes. It is played in half time to the dancing, and this sets up an exhilarating rhythmic tension. A choir chants the words over the band, which further enriches the rhythms, and in the next chorus the choir hums the melody while the band plays countermelodic figures—beautiful little flags of the sort that Ellington ran up again and again in his best work. The band falls silent, and the choir chants for a chorus, backed by Ellington and the rhythm section. (Don't forget the continuing rattling, clicking, stomping drone of Briggs' feet, and how, every once in a while, he throws in wild, offbeat, two-footed steps, which jar everything around him.) The choir rests, and Ellington and Briggs do a charging duet for a chorus. Then the choir hums the melody again, there's a pause, and Briggs gives an electrifying shout, which is answered by sixteen bars of ensemble band shouts. At the same time, the drummer (Louis Bellson) solos, the choir chants, and a clarinettist sails into the stratosphere. This mad five-tiered float careers along for eight bars, and— bang!—Briggs dances out into the sun by himself for several easy measures, and the piece comes to rest with a final band chord.

Part of Ellington's third Sacred Concert was given a trial American run at Queens College in 1975, and recently it was announced that it would be played in its entirety at the Cathedral of St. John the Divine. But, for whatever reasons, the concert was limited to snippets from all three concerts, which were done by a troupe that included the Mercer Ellington band, the Byrne Camp Chorale, the soloists McHenry Boatwright, Alpha Brawner-Floyd, Anita Moore, Tony Bennett, and Phyllis Hyman, the tap dancer Honi Coles, an Alvin Ailey group, and Douglas Fairbanks, Jr., as narrator. (Fairbanks' Hollywood-English accent fitted Ellington's New York biblical words uncommonly well.) Nine numbers from the third Sacred Concert were played (about half of the whole), and they sounded much like the earlier concerts. But there were good moments: David Young's tenor-saxophone solo, backed by the chorale, in "The Brotherhood"; the chorale singing "Alleluia" softer and softer, accompanied only by a bass; and Joe Temperley's a-cappella baritone-saxophone solo on "The Majesty of God" (Temperley's tone is strikingly close to Harry Carney's, but it lacks Carney's great *bottom*), and the succeeding quiet, ascending organ chords from the band. "David Danced Before the Lord" was among the ten numbers taken from the earlier concerts, but it was short and choppy. Coles never had a chance to get his momentum going, and the towering last chorus was omitted. Boatwright and Brawner-Floyd were lugubrious and often off pitch, while Hyman and Moore, who did gospel songs, and Bennett, who did a fine Ellington song called "Somebody Cares," swung.

It was strange not having Ellington there. He was at his best at his Sacred Concerts, and he somehow managed to make their disparate parts blend. In *Music Is My Mistress*, he unwittingly told us how: "As I travel from place to place . . . taking rhythm to the dancers, harmony to the romantic, melody to the nostalgic, gratitude to the listener . . . receiving praise, applause, and handshakes, and at the same time doing the thing I like to do, I feel that I am most fortunate because I know that God has blessed my timing, without which nothing could have happened." He left us his music, but he took the timing.

Ellington's Sacred Concerts were, in their way, sometimes ludicrously inflated imitations of the thirty or more masterpieces he set down between 1940 and 1942 for Victor Records. It is still not altogether clear why this exuberant flowering took place. The surrounding musical soil was sandy, and the Ellington band itself had been going through dry times. The rhythm section was inert, the arrangements often had a staccato, old-fashioned sound (toy-soldier muted trumpets, ornate saxophone writing), and the ensemble playing was imprecise. Even such fine numbers as "Riding on a Blue Note," "Blue Light," "Barney Goin' Easy," and "Portrait of the Lion" seemed inconclusive. In 1939, things began to stir. The composer and arranger Billy Strayhorn joined the band, and by the end of the year he began to take hold. Ellington left his old, tenacious manager, Irving Mills, and went with the William Morris agency. He also left Brunswick Records, whose sound was closed and soupy, and signed with Victor, whose sound was clear and open. The band made a heartening European tour (black jazz musicians were already going to Europe to be revitalized; indeed, they were often overwhelmed by applause and kindness), and the bassist Jimmy Blanton and the tenor saxophonist Ben Webster became part of the band. Blanton, who was just twenty-one, was the first modern bassist. He had a big tone and unshakable time, and he was the first bassist capable of "melodic" improvising. He woke the band up rhythmically. Webster was thirty, and he had been with Ellington briefly, as well as with Andy Kirk, Fletcher Henderson, Cab Calloway, Benny Carter, and Teddy Wilson. ("I always had a yen for Ben," Ellington says in his autobiography.) All the big black bands except Ellington's had tenor-saxophone stars. Basie had Lester Young and Herschel Evans; Andy Kirk had Dick Wilson; Fletcher Henderson had Coleman Hawkins; Cab Calloway had Chu Berry. But Ellington's major saxophone soloist had been the alto and soprano saxophonist Johnny Hodges. Webster enriched the band tonally, and he brought it new intensity and emotion. In return, Ellington built "Cotton Tail" and "Just A-Settin' and

A-Rockin'" around Webster, and gave him an invaluable opportunity to sit beside Hodges in the saxophone section and absorb
him. Within a year or so, Webster, already on the verge of being
first-rate, was the equal of Young and Hawkins. So the band was
complete. On trumpets were Wallace Jones, Rex Stewart, and
Cootie Williams (replaced late in 1940 by Ray Nance); on
trombones Juan Tizol, Lawrence Brown, and Tricky Sam Nanton; on reeds Otto Hardwicke, Barney Bigard, Ben Webster,
Johnny Hodges, and Harry Carney; and in the rhythm section
Ellington on piano, Fred Guy on guitar, Jimmy Blanton on bass,
and Sonny Greer on drums.

Ellington's 1940–42 masterpieces have strong jazz characteristics—improvised or partly improvised solos, jazz timbres
(plunger mutes, growls, instrumental tonal peculiarities), and a
regular sounded beat. They also have classical characteristics—
fixed solos (originally improvised solos, which gradually became set), concertolike forms, and complex scoring, some of it
rivalling Berlioz's. And they were entirely original in their
instrumental combinations and in their odd, often surprising
structures. Ellington used the twelve-bar blues and the thirty-
two-bar a-a-b-a song form, but he decorated them with introductions and codas, with interludes and transitions, with key
changes, with dissonance. Much of the time, his materials
appeared to dictate his forms. "Sepia Panorama" has an "arch"
form. The first chorus lasts twelve bars, the second chorus lasts
sixteen bars, the third lasts eight, and the fourth twelve; the
fifth chorus repeats the fourth chorus, the sixth repeats the
third, the seventh repeats part of the second, and in the eighth
we are back at the first chorus. "Concerto for Cootie" has an
eight-bar introduction, and the first chorus is thirty-six bars
long (two ten-bar sections and two eight-bar sections). A two-
bar transition leads into the second chorus, which is sixteen
bars. There is an eight-bar recapitulation of the first ten bars of
the first chorus and an eight-bar coda. Ellington (and, increasingly, Strayhorn) wrote most of the materials. Ellington had
considerable help from his sidemen, who would contribute a
melody here and a bridge there, and who often groused about not

getting more credit (to say nothing of royalties). He also re-worked chestnuts like "Chloe" and "The Sidewalks of New York," and occasionally he built a new structure on old chords: "In a Mellotone" was based on "Rose Room," and "Cotton Tail" on "I Got Rhythm." He wrote several different kinds of pieces. There were programmatic or descriptive pieces, like "Just A-Settin' and A-Rockin'," "Harlem Airshaft," and "Dusk." There were tone poems, like "Blue Serge." There were rhythmic exercises, like "The Giddybug Gallop," "Ko-Ko," and "Jumpin' Punkins." There were plain old blues, like "Across the Track Blues" and "C Jam Blues." And there were miniature concertos, like "Concerto for Cootie" and "Jack the Bear."

How does one of these Concertos go? Here is "Ko-Ko," a minor blues and no relation of Charlie Parker's "Ko-Ko," made five years later. It starts *in medias res*. Sonny Greer gives a couple of quick timpani beats, and Carney goes immediately into a chuffing sustained note in his low register—his house-moving register—and is backed by the trombone section, possibly salted with one trumpet. The introduction lasts eight bars. In the first chorus, which is twelve bars, Juan Tizol plays an ingenious six-note figure that is pursued closely by the reed section in such a way that it sounds like a continuation of Tizol's figure. Tizol starts the sentence and the reeds finish it. In the next two choruses, twelve measures apiece, Tricky Sam Nanton, using a plunger mute, solos against offbeat muted trumpets and the reed section, which plays a sighing three-note figure. Greer punctuates on his tomtoms. In the fourth chorus, also twelve bars, the reeds repeat the figure they used in the first chorus, and the trumpet section supplies "ooh-wa"s. Ellington himself surfaces from behind, throwing runs and chords into the air. The twelve-bar fifth chorus is climactic. The trumpet section plays a repeated long-held note (one of the trumpets, probably Williams, uses a plunger mute) while the saxophone section, broken into two groups, plays accented figures and a melody parallel to the trumpets. The dissonance is almost overpowering. Then the reeds and trombones slide into an eight-bar interlude, pausing for several two-bar breaks by Blanton. In the seventh chorus, the trumpets again play long-held notes, and the saxophones play a countermelody. Carney returns in the final chorus with his very low chuffing note, backed by the trombones. The reeds climb abruptly into view and disappear into a closing full-band chord. The atmosphere of the number is rough and hustling. There are few treble sounds, and there is little delicacy. The piece bullies. It sets out to be abrasive *and* lyrical, and it succeeds. It is also almost completely an ensemble piece—a kind of concerto for orchestra.

All this is by way of saying that the Smithsonian Collection (the record label of the Smithsonian) is well along in its Ellington reissue project, begun six years ago. Four albums have been released—"Duke Ellington 1938," "Duke Ellington 1939," "Duke Ellington 1940," and now "Duke Ellington 1941." Each of the first two albums has thirty titles and two alternate takes, and although Ellington's strengths are evident, nothing prepares us for what happens at the start of the 1940 album. This includes twenty-eight selections and four alternate takes. At least seven numbers are mediocre, but weak Ellington was superior to almost everything else in popular music. The four duets that Ellington did with Jimmy Blanton (how fine for the young Blanton, how selfless of Ellington) are in the album, and there are two takes of "Mr. J. B. Blues." The 1941 album has twenty-four selections and eight alternates, and it has even more lacklustre material. Fourteen of the numbers are radio transcriptions made around the same time as the Victor sides, and they don't add much to our Ellington knowledge. How much better to have put in the ten or eleven classic sides—one is the surging "Main Stem"—Ellington made in 1942 before a union-imposed recording ban, which lasted into 1944, brought his great creative splurge to an end. But there are tracks from two "soundies," which were three-minute films made for jukeboxes equipped with tiny screens. The first is a furious (but truncated) "Cotton Tail" and the second is an easy "C Jam Blues" notable for the longest drum solo (twelve bars) that Greer, an infrequent soloist, ever recorded with Ellington. He rarely used the muffling pads on his snare drum or tomtoms, and he kept his drumheads very tight. The result was a sharp, ringing tone. His solo is staccato and rocking. It crackles. It is played mostly on his snare drum, although he inserts one fast round-the-set explosion. The 1940 and 1941 albums include the rattling swing of "Jack the Bear," "A Portrait of Bert Williams," "In a Mellotone," and "Jumpin' Punkins," which has a lot of two-bar Greer breaks; the tonal depths of "Dusk" and "Blue Serge"; the almost ecstatic shout by what sounds like the full band between Hodges' solos on "Never No Lament"; Cootie Williams' fury on "Harlem Airshaft" and his acidulous preaching on "Never No Lament"; all of Ben Webster's solos, and particularly his classic statement on "Blue Serge," with its growling near the end; and the sly, affecting work of Tricky Sam Nanton, who was in frequent evidence in 1940 and 1941.

Reunion

The Modern Jazz Quartet—those who considered it delicate and marginal notwithstanding—was at the heart of jazz in the sixties. Its members—John Lewis on piano, Milt Jackson on vibraharp, Percy Heath on bass, and Connie Kay on drums—grew up under the grand masters of swing (Count Basie, Duke Ellington, Roy Eldridge, Ben Webster, Coleman Hawkins, Lester Young, Art Tatum, Jimmy Blanton, Lionel Hampton, and Sidney Catlett). They also grew up alongside the founders of bebop (Charlie Parker, Dizzy Gillespie, Bud Powell, Thelonious Monk, and Kenny Clarke). The swing musicians taught them the beauties of straight melodic playing. They taught them chordal and melodic improvisation, rhythmic precision, musical taste, how to swing, and what the work ethic was. They taught them, without ever saying so, that jazz is an art, and that being a jazz musician can be ennobling. With the exception of Jackson, the members of the quartet did not absorb as much from their bebop peers. They learned the new harmonic and rhythmic vocabulary of bebop, and they studied its exuberance and flashiness. They marvelled, as everyone did, at the improvisational depth and daring of Parker and Gillespie and, to a lesser extent, Bud Powell. But they eventually rejected bebop's garrulity, which was brought on in large part by the arrival of the L.P. recording, with its forty-five-minute time limit. (Lewis once said of the quartet's beginnings, "There were things wrong in the music around us that we all agreed on, and some of them were long, long solos and that formula on a tune of everybody playing the melody in the first chorus, followed by a string of solos, and then the melody again.") They also rejected its tonal harshness and its harmonic tyranny—the endless, competitive "running of the changes" that bebop improvisers loved. But Jackson embraced Parker and Gillespie and their principles. Lionel Hampton had taught him the fundamentals of swinging, and Jackson added Parker's and Gillespie's speed and fluidity. Lewis never moved much beyond Basie and Webster and Young, and Heath and Kay never abandoned Blanton and Catlett. So the quartet had three feet in swing and one foot in bebop, and it was far more conservative than it seemed when it came up, in the early fifties. What gave it the deceptive glow of newness was its odd, largely accidental instrumentation (Lewis, Jackson, and Ray Brown, its original bassist, were part of Gillespie's big band before they decided to play on their own) and its use of Baroque devices and materials—the fugue, the rondo, and Lewis's "Italian" compositions. It was a swing group aerated by the imaginations of Parker and Gillespie—an up-to-date outgrowth of the Benny Goodman small groups, the King Cole Trio, and the Red Norvo Trio.

The quartet was not alone at the center of the music. It was flanked by Thelonious Monk (his compositions, his quartets, his brilliant pickup recordings for the Riverside label) and by Charles Mingus (his ceaseless experiments with instrumental combinations and with improvisational modes—in particular, collective improvising). But in 1973 this triumvirate began to disappear. Mingus, hampered by illness, became increasingly ineffectual, and Monk went into a mysterious retreat and stopped performing. Then, in 1974, the quartet, which had been in existence for twenty-two years, disbanded. It reassembled in 1976 for two brief Midwestern tours. A week or so ago, reassembled again, it capped a two-week tour of Japan and San Francisco with a concert in Avery Fisher Hall. The concert was a beauty, and Lewis made it clear, once and for all, that he is far from being Jackson's improvisational inferior. It was often said in the sixties that Jackson was wasted on the quartet. He *is* an exceptional improviser, who constantly circumvents the metallic properties of his instrument. He is a rhapsodic melodist who uses surging Charlie Parker lines that pitch up and down his keyboard. He has a strong sense of dynamics, and he has unlimited ideas. Lewis, on the other hand, is the soul of brevity. The unofficial leader of the quartet and its chief composer and arranger, he is probably the most undervalued pianist of his generation. He has said that, in the main, horn players, not pianists, shaped his style, and this must be true, for the only pianist clearly audible in his work is Count Basie. He uses few notes, and he plays with a relentless rhythmic intensity. He does this with repeated notes, with simple repeated riffs, with occasional legato tempo dips, and with monosyllabic on-the-beat single-note figures. He is as lyrical a player as Jackson, but he implies his lyricism, while Jackson broadcasts his. Lewis's best solos develop an irresistible rhythmic momentum, and when he rises into the upper registers, where he often ends his solos, he seems to tap the sky.

Lewis was in rare condition at Avery Fisher Hall. There was none of the stiffness and pompous simplicity that sometimes affect his improvisations. Again and again, in such numbers as "Odds Against Tomorrow," "The Cylinder," "Billie's Bounce," and "Willow Weep for Me," he was full of ease and swing and freshness. (Jazz musicians have often pointed out that they play best when they are exhausted. The quartet, after its Japanese marathon, flew directly to San Francisco, where it gave two concerts in one day; then it took off for New York, and arrived at Avery Fisher from the airport.) Jackson never falls below excellence, and he poured out solo after passionate solo, especially in "What's New?," " 'Round Midnight," "The Martyr," and "Willow Weep for Me." Lewis lent Jackson his customary sterling support, with offbeat chords, with applauding declarative figures, and with polite counterpoint. Neither Heath nor Kay solos much; their beauties lie in the self-effacing way they hold up Lewis and Jackson—in the velvet they provide for the jewels.

1982

Monk

The pianist and composer Thelonious Monk, who died last week, at the age of sixty-four, was an utterly original man who liked to pretend he was an eccentric. Indeed, he used eccentricity as a shield to fend off a world that he frequently found alien, and even hostile. A tall, dark, bearish, inward-shining man, he wore odd hats and dark glasses with bamboo frames when he played. His body moved continuously. At the keyboard, he swayed back and forth and from side to side, his feet flapping like flounders on the floor. While his sidemen soloed, he stood by the piano and danced, turning in slow, genial circles, his elbows out like wings, his knees slightly bent, his fingers snapping on the after-beat. His motions celebrated what he and his musicians played: Watch, these are the shapes of my music. His compositions and his playing were of a piece. His improvisations were molten Monk compositions, and his compositions were frozen Monk improvisations. His medium- and up-tempo tunes are stop-and-go rhythmic structures. Their melodic lines, which often hinge on flatted notes, tend to be spare and direct, but they are written with strangely placed rests and unexpected accents. They move irregularly through sudden intervals and ritards and broken rhythms. His balladlike tunes are altogether different. They are art songs, which move slowly and three-dimensionally. They are carved sound. (Monk's song titles— "Crepuscule with Nellie," "Epistrophy," "Ruby, My Dear," "Well You Needn't," "Rhythm-a-ning," "Hackensack"—are as striking as the songs themselves. But none beat his extraordinary name, Thelonious Sphere Monk, which surpasses such euphonies as Stringfellow Barr and Twyla Tharp.) His improvisations were attempts to disguise his love of melody. He clothed whatever he played with spindly runs, flatted notes, flatted chords, repeated single notes, yawning silences, and zigzag rhythms. Sometimes he pounded the keyboard with his right elbow. His style protected him not only from his love of melody but from his love of the older pianists he grew out of—Duke Ellington and the stride pianists. All peered out from inside his solos, but he let them escape only as parody.

Monk hid behind his music so well that we know little of him. He was brought from North Carolina when he was little, he eventually settled in the West Sixties, and he lived there until his building was torn down. He married the Nellie of his song title, and he had two children, one of whom became a drummer. He began appearing in New York night clubs around 1940, but he achieved little recognition until the late fifties. (He was often lumped with Charlie Parker and Dizzy Gillespie; however, he did not have much in common with them outside of certain harmonic inventions.) Part of the reason for Monk's slow blooming was his iconoclastic music, and part was the fact that he was unable to perform in New York night clubs from 1951 to 1957—the time when Charles Mingus and the Modern Jazz Quartet and Gerry Mulligan were becoming famous. (The police had lifted his cabaret card, because he had been found sitting in a car in which narcotics were concealed.) But when he returned to the scene, he suddenly seemed to be everywhere—on record after exceptional record, at concerts and festivals, at the old Five Spot and the Vanguard and the Jazz Gallery. He filled us with his noble, funny, generous music.

Then, in 1973, he vanished again. There were rumors that he was ill and had been taken in by his old friend and mentor the Baroness Nica de Koenigswarter, who lives in a big house in Weehawken, New Jersey. The rumors turned out to be true, and this is what the Baroness had to say about Monk before he died: "No doctor has put his finger on what is wrong with him, and he has had every medical test under the sun. He's not unhappy, and his mind works very well. He knows what is going on in the world, and I don't know how, because he doesn't read the newspapers and he only watches a little telly. He's withdrawn, that's all. It's as though he had gone into retreat. He takes walks several times a week, and Nellie comes over from New York almost every day to cook for him. He began to withdraw in 1973, and he hasn't touched the piano since 1976. He has one twenty or thirty feet from his bed, so to speak, but he never goes near it. When Barry Harris visits, he practices on it, and he'll ask Monk what the correct changes to 'Ruby, My Dear' are, and Monk will tell him. Charlie Rouse, his old tenor saxophonist, came to see him on his birthday the other day, but Monk isn't really interested in seeing anyone. The strange thing is he looks beautiful. He has never *said* that he won't play the piano again. He suddenly went into this, so maybe he'll suddenly come out."

But Monk must have known he wouldn't. His last public appearance, at the Newport Jazz Festival of 1976, was painful. His playing was mechanical and uncertain, and, astonishingly, his great Gothic style had fallen away.

Sonny Greer

The longer Duke Ellington's musicians stayed in his band, the younger they seemed to become. Perhaps this Fountain of Youth effect came about from their having to keep up with Ellington's voluminous composing, from their constantly having to cope with new music. Perhaps it stemmed from their inborn originality: many were great American primitive artists. Perhaps it could be explained by the mystique of elegance and excellence that bound them together. Sonny Greer, Johnny Hodges, Lawrence Brown, Cootie Williams, Harry Carney, Ray Nance, Russell Procope, Ellington himself—all invariably looked ten or twenty years younger than they were. This was particularly true of Greer, who, seemingly in his fifties, died a little while ago at the age of seventy-eight.

Greer had been a co-founder of the Ellington band, in the early twenties, and he remained Ellington's drummer and unofficial co-captain for almost thirty years. (Worn out by being on the road and by Ellington's relentless brass, he left the band in 1951 with a splinter group headed by Hodges and including Lawrence Brown. Hodges and Brown returned to the band permanently several years later, but Greer never went back.) Greer's appearance and his playing were inseparable, and they helped to establish the band's high tone and cool assurance. He was a thin, handsome, dapper, concave man with a wide smile and a smooth cap of black hair. His eyes, which he often popped, matched his hair, and he had a drummer's long fingers. His rich, quick speech gave him an Ancient Mariner insistence. Greer came up in the vaudeville tradition, and he was a consummate showman. He encircled himself in the thirties and forties with a forest of white drums that included a snare drum, tomtoms, a bass drum, and timpani. These were lit by cymbals, chimes, and gongs, and decorated by temple blocks, wood blocks, and cowbells. He even had a vibraphone. Often dressed in white, he sat at the center of this gleaming array and, his trunk motionless, allowed his Shivalike arms to dart among his cymbals and drums. He would snap his head from side to side on the beat, his chin slightly lifted, and smile brilliantly. He would lunge at a cymbal or spin a stick into the air. He would loose a heavy mock frown. He was an incomparable accompanist, who would launch a Ben Webster tenor-saxophone solo by tapping a cowbell, fill an ensemble pause with a couple of eighth notes on a timpani, make his Chinese cymbal hiss beneath a Tricky Sam Nanton muted-trombone solo, place easy, clicking, pushing rimshots on the afterbeat behind a Rex Stewart cornet solo. He cooled the band when it grew frenzied, and heated it when it was too cool. He once described his methods: "I learned how to keep my drums crisp, to tune them so they had an even, clear sound. I knew about showmanship, about how audiences eat it up—that it ain't what you do but how you do it. Things like hitting three rimshots and opening and closing one side of my jacket in time. I always strove for finesse. I always tried to shade, and make everything sound beautiful. It was my job to keep the band in level time, to keep slow tempos from going down and fast tempos from going up. Those things meant more to me than solos, which I rarely took."

Greer was born William Alexander Greer, Jr., in Long Branch, New Jersey. His father was an electrician with the Pennsylvania Railroad, and his mother was a modiste. He had an older sister and a younger sister and brother. He didn't waste a minute of his childhood. He caddied, peddled fish, delivered newspapers, became a master pool player, and learned how to sing and play the drums. He said that he had learned most of his music from a tall, elegant drummer named Eugene (Peggy) Holland, who once played the Keith Theatre in Long Branch for two weeks with J. Rosamond Johnson. Ellington, sly and jocose, saw Greer's beginnings as a drummer somewhat differently. He wrote in *Music Is My Mistress*, "Instead of following in his father's footsteps, Greer . . . [banged] on his mother's pots and pans, and he developed his own style of drumming from those bim-banging beginnings. . . . A natural supporting artist with his pots and pans, he kept time with horses trotting, people sweeping, and people digging ditches. He didn't indulge in such activities himself, but he kept time with those who did . . . and he dug the value of teamwork all the way back. By adding his own embellishments, he developed what was later to be his forte. Everything in his life, I think, has always been done in a happy way, even though not according to Hoyle." What Ellington meant at the end of his tribute was that Greer was an old-fashioned opportunist, who always had his eyes peeled, his tongue ready, his cue in hand. He developed a set of homilies that supported his view of life:

When you're getting ready to lie, don't smile.

Pool is like the violin—you've got to play an hour every day.

Bread cast upon the sea comes back buttered toast.

I always had an ambition to make money and not have money make me.

If there are three people going that way and only two people this way, then there must be more happening that way than this way, so I'm going that way, too.

Retired people lie under a tree and play checkers, and first thing you know they're gone.

So Greer didn't retire. (He lived on the West Side, with his wife, Millicent, a Cotton Club dancer he was married to for over fifty years. They had a daughter and grandchildren, great-grandchildren, and even great-great-grandchildren.) From the mid-seventies on, he played dates with his friend Brooks Kerr, a pianist and Ellington scholar, and with the Ellington clarinettist and alto saxophonist Russell Procope. After Procope died, Greer and Kerr kept going. He sat at his drums in the same erect, poised way he had when he was with Ellington, and it was not hard (at Gregory's or the West End Café, or at some private party) to summon up from Greer's playing alone the rest of the band.

Dizzy Gillespie and Bill Coleman

Excerpts from three concerts given by Dizzy Gillespie and the Mitchell-Ruff Duo (Dwike Mitchell on piano, Willie Ruff on bass and horn) during the past decade or so have been released by Book-of-the-Month Records as "Dizzy Gillespie—Live." The concerts were held at Dartmouth in 1970, at Yale in 1974, and at Town Hall in 1980. The album reveals that Gillespie, who will be sixty-five years old this fall, can still play with fire. He pictured himself as an iron man in his recent autobiography, and he appears to be right.

When Gillespie came up, in the mid-forties, his style was an intricate and explosive composite of Roy Eldridge, Charlie Parker, Charlie Shavers, and Art Tatum. It was dense and rococo. Each solo billowed, and each, with its cascade of notes, got where it was going as fast as possible. Gillespie *ran*. He liked to spell out on the piano the new augmented chords—for the benefit of himself and other musicians—and he would then build his solos out of them, using combinations of notes that only Charlie Parker had dared before. He liked to knock down the bar lines, in the manner of Art Tatum, and let his phrases tumble on for six or eight measures. He liked to shock. In a chorus of medium-tempo blues, he might begin with a high-register blast, followed by a resounding silence. He would then play a snatch of the melody in a soft, vibratoless half time, and slide into a descending double-time run, pause, and work out a climbing, zigzag figure. More silence, followed by a high two-note yell, a run, and a low, slow closing whole note. All Gillespie's solos offered hair-raising melodic flights and masterly rhythmic inventions. Half-time passages slipped into on-the-beat figures, which gave way to double time, which dropped to half time, which then sped up to full time. His solos swung, and it did not matter if in his haste he split notes, missed them, or allowed his tone to shriek.

Gillespie's playing has slowed to a fast walk. His trademarks—staccato, undulating connective phrases; upper-register excursions; serpentine runs; fat, blinding opening notes—are intact, but he surrounds them with new effects. He uses more silence (sometimes three or four beats go by between phrases), and his playing is gentler and quieter; he no longer has to shout for attention, the way he did in the forties. His phrasing is simpler. Quarter notes do for eighth or sixteenth notes, and he registers them firmly in the air before moving on. Much of Gillespie's playing used to be almost subliminal; now it is fully visible. He reverts to the melody more than he once did, perhaps to make sure he is on course. He also, curiously enough, reverts to two trumpet players who have never been associated with him—Red Allen and Rex Stewart. He must have listened to them in the late thirties, and perhaps it has taken this long for what he heard to surface. He uses richly spaced, low-register Allen notes, and even reproduces the fluttering tremolo that Allen opens his solo with on "A Sheridan Square." He has also adopted Stewart's famous half-valved notes—an effect that is achieved by pressing a trumpet valve partway down and blowing a note that is slightly below the one sounded when the valve is released. It is a pleasing effect: the first note, squeezed and thin, becomes rounded as the valve rises. It is like passing through a low doorway into a high-ceilinged room. Aging brass players take a while to warm up, and when Gillespie is sufficiently heated he can get off passages of great brilliance and éclat. He is, after so many years, still king.

The Book-of-the-Month album has twenty-one numbers. Four are by Mitchell and Ruff, one is a Mitchell piano solo, one is a funny, buck-dancing Gillespie solo on the Jew's harp, one is a Gillespie-Ruff duet, and the rest are by the three men. Both Mitchell, who is fifty-two, and Ruff, who is two years younger, have had musical training, and they are not the sort of chamber-jazz musicians Gillespie generally plays with. Ruff is a good Charlie Mingus bassist and a virtuoso horn player, and Mitchell is a florid, occasionally impassioned Art Tatum admirer who favors the loud pedal. They work well with Gillespie, partly out of admiration and partly because they stay out of his way. (Ruff plays horn with Gillespie on just three numbers, and the duets are tentative.) Gillespie, also unencumbered by a drummer, is free to fly, and he does. He produces half a dozen careful, muted choruses at the beginning of "Blues People," which is Charlie Parker's "Now's the Time," and returns at the close for five open-horn choruses, complete with a breakneck upper-register passage. He does the verse of "My Man" ad-lib, gracing the melody with added notes and new harmonies, and then jumps into a sparkling medium-tempo solo that at first suggests Charlie Shavers. "Lover Man" is taken out of tempo all the way through, and is a winding, complex melodic study. (Many bebop trumpet players never mastered the art of playing slow melody). More than half the album is given over to the 1980 Town Hall concert. There is an ad-lib Gillespie rendition of "I Remember Clifford," and on his own "Ow!," based on the chords of "I Got Rhythm," he delivers an open-horn solo that crowds the listener to the ropes. On "Conception," the three men, starting off without any theme or tempo, wander around in their shirt-sleeves. Ruff plays horn, and he and Gillespie solo well and do some counterpoint; all three reach the finish line more or less together. A very slow version of "Mood Indigo" threatens to fall apart even before it gets going but is rescued midway through the first chorus when Gillespie, improvising on the second theme, goes into a sudden, left-hand open-horn descending passage. It fools with time. It is intense and casual and lyrical and surprising. It swings, and is altogether beautiful.

It is not too late to celebrate the elusive and magical trumpeter Bill Coleman, who died late last summer, at the age of seventy-seven. He lived with his Swiss wife in a small farm-house in the village of Cadeillan, in southwestern France. Born near Paris, Kentucky, he spent almost half his life in France, where, he said, no one ever called him "nigger." He first went abroad in 1933, with Lucky Millinder, and he went back again and again, until the Second World War drove him home. He was in constant demand here, and he worked with Teddy Wilson, Benny Carter, Fats Waller, John Kirby, Andy Kirk, Noble Sissle, and Sy Oliver. Between 1942 and 1944, he settled in New York, where he either led or appeared in trios with the pianists Ellis Larkins and Mary Lou Williams. He also turned up in Wilson's sextet at Café Society Uptown (Emmett Berry, Edmond Hall, Benny Morton, Johnny Williams, Sid Catlett), and at the Sunday-afternoon jam sessions at Jimmy Ryan's. In 1948, the war over and his racial patience exhausted, he went back to France for good.

Coleman's early recordings, made here and in France in the thirties with Fats Waller and Django Reinhardt and Dickie Wells, were always hard to come by, and the same is true of the scattered sessions he did in the forties, with Wells and Lester Young, with Mary Lou Williams, and with Nat Cole and Coleman Hawkins. So little of Coleman exists here that it might not be an exaggeration to say that scarcely two or three hundred people in America knew who he was when he died. But those admirers champion him, for he was one of the great jazz trumpeters.

Like most players of his generation, he listened to Louis Armstrong. He also listened to the dulcet-toned Joe Smith, and to the heretical Jabbo Smith, who came to New York when Coleman did, in the late twenties. Coleman's playing, like Coleman himself, was never still. He preferred the middle registers, and he moved constantly from one end of them to the other. He played with a dancing lyricism, but he played with such delicacy that he gave the impression of shying away from his notes. He came at them from slightly below or above, sounded them, and was gone, his vibrato barely stirring the air. Few jazz improvisers know how to construct sequential solos, but Coleman's had a rare logic. He never lost the melodic thread he was weaving, and when he finished a solo there was nothing extraneous, nothing missing. It rested complete in the mind.

Coleman did well enough in France. He generally worked as much as he needed to, and he recorded frequently. He was made a Chevalier de l'Ordre National du Mérite, and he dictated his memoirs to his wife, who, failing to find an English or American publisher, translated them into French and had them published. He played almost to the time he died, and his playing didn't change much. It slowed down, it flattened out. Would that he had not been driven away. He was always missed.

Good Tidings _____

Old and New Dreams, made up of Dewey Redman on tenor saxophone and musette, Don Cherry on pocket trumpet and piano, Charlie Haden on bass, and Ed Blackwell on drums, suggests the Hot Five without Louis Armstrong, the Red Hot Peppers without Jelly Roll Morton. Barring Redman, it is the same quartet that Ornette Coleman had at the Five Spot Café in the winter of 1960. That group, more or less intact until Coleman disbanded it in 1962, was first reassembled, with Redman standing in for Coleman, on a 1976 recording called "Old and New Dreams" (after a Redman number in the album). The recording was acclaimed, and in 1978 the four men decided to become a working group. They wanted to celebrate Coleman's compositions, and they wanted, as Coleman protégés, to reinvestigate his old adventures and discoveries. (Redman grew up in Fort Worth with Coleman and has played with him frequently.) What made Coleman's Five Spot quartet so startling was its leader's passionate and unshakable belief in what he was doing (a new kind of improvisation, based on mood, melody, and certain tonal centers and rhythms) and the blazing, headlong way he and his musicians carried it out. They travelled fast across ground that only a few jazz musicians had seen, and that none had explored. The quartet, which had a hounding tension, was exhausting. The listener first had to clear away the verbiage that almost immediately engulfed it (brickbats or messianic superlatives). Then he had to learn *not* to listen for chords, conventional melody, keys, chorus structures, or expected rhythmic turns. He had to do some virgin listening. The group was not nearly as madcap as it seemed. Its improvisations were strongly attached to Coleman's muscular melodies, the rhythmic pulse was strong, if not always stated or steady, and the collective playing loosely resembled early New Orleans polyphony. Old and New Dreams is aptly named; its music is a series of meditations, carried out with striking calm, on the old Coleman quartet. Redman is an earthy Coleman whose rhythm-and-blues origins show. Sometimes his solos wander and sometimes he plays with logic and great feeling. Cherry has changed. During his Five Spot days, he sounded shrill and inconclusive; his solos went against the grain of the music. Since then, he has broadened his technique, and he has experimented with the folk music of Europe, Africa, and India. He has replaced uncertainty

47

and implication with a declarative ease. Haden was from the first a passionate impulsive player. He has avoided the current bass fads (sliding, sing-song notes, wooden tone, empty technical displays), and he has developed his melodic sense. He has become a hornlike voice in the group. Blackwell, a native of New Orleans, is a funny, melodic drummer. No matter what tempo he is playing, he sits behind his drums—his dark glasses halfway down his nose, his elbows loose, his shoulders rounded, his hands hayforks—as if he were ambling down a country road. He gets a lot of melodic continuity out of his snare and cymbals and tomtoms, and much of what he does as an accompanist and as a soloist is based on New Orleans marching-band drumming.

Most of the time at Lush Life, Old and New Dreams sounded like an adventurous edition of Art Blakey's Jazz Messengers. The melody was stated in unison or in rough counterpoint by the horns, there were long solos, and the melody was restated. There was little of the collective interplay of Coleman's quartet, and the solos were approachable and often highly melodic. Cherry alternated outpourings of notes with brief melodies, and his tone was sure and sweet. Redman steamed, and Haden and Blackwell developed immense, marching rhythms. It's a wonder they had the strength. The room was full, and there was little ventilation. The temperature on the bandstand must have been in the high eighties. Jazz musicians, more often than not, are still hired hands.

Teddy Wilson _____

Teddy Wilson still presides when he sits at the piano. He will be seventy this year, but all is in place—the ramrod back, the flat hands, the square elbows held close to the sides, the slightly raised chin, the lowered eyes, and the compressed, almost imperceptibly moving lips (the only register of emotion in an otherwise masklike face). His figure, once thin as a stamp, has thickened, and his hawklike profile has become a series of arcs and spheres. His famous style—a delicate and subtle tracery of single-note melodic lines framed by discreet chords—now comes in two grades: preset and largely predictable (a reflection of the boredom with their own skills that occasionally afflicts all perfectionists), and, when he is stirred by a good audience or an aggressive rhythm section, resplendent and exciting. Wilson's musical life had been unassailable and invaluable. His faultless taste has informed the music wherever he has gone. The very excellence of his style, though rarely directly imitated, has seemed to force his most gifted admirers (Billy Kyle, Nat Cole, Mel Powell, Hank Jones, Lenny Tristano, Jimmy Rowles) into shaping almost equally exceptional styles. He has helped give the music, long heedless and untutored, an awareness of its own elegance and brilliance.

Wilson was one of the first black jazz musicians to come from an educated, middle-class background. He was born in Austin, Texas, and raised in Tuskegee, Alabama. His mother was a librarian at Tuskegee Institute, and his father was head of the English Department. Wilson attended Talledega College for a year, but in 1929 he went North to try his wings as a jazz pianist. He joined Speed Webb (Roy Eldridge, Vic Dickenson) and then replaced Art Tatum in Milton Senior's band in Toledo, Ohio. He worked in local Chicago bands and filled in for Earl Hines at the Grand Terrace Ballroom. In 1933, he travelled with Lous Armstrong's indifferent big band, and before the year was out he had been summoned to New York by Benny Carter. The Carter Band (J. C. Higginbotham, Wayman Carver, Sidney Catlett) collapsed in 1934, and Wilson went on to Willie Bryant (Cozy Cole, Ben Webster, Carter). Then his sun rose. At the behest of John Hammond, he began making a series of all-star small-band recordings for Brunswick, many of them with Billie Holiday. (By the time the series ended, in 1941, he had recorded close to a hundred titles.) He also sat in with Benny Goodman at a party at

Red Norvo's house in Forest Hills; a few weeks later he was on the first of the Benny Goodman Trio records. He joined the Goodman band in 1936, and stayed three years. Jess Stacy was Goodman's regular pianist, so Goodman had Wilson appear only with the trio and, later, the quartet. It was a courageous time for Wilson. He was the first black musician to be attached to a big white jazz band—*the* big white jazz band, in fact. He was cheered on the bandstand but off the stand was relegated to "colored" hotels and boarding houses. In 1939, Wilson, encouraged by his sudden fame, put together his own big band. It was a clean, well-lighted group that included Shorty Baker, Doc Cheatham, Ben Webster, and J. C. Heard, but it lasted barely a year. It was done in by its sheer high-class professionalism and by the departure of Ben Webster, who went on to the Duke Ellington band. From 1940 to 1944, Wilson led a superb sextet at Café Society Downtown and Café Society Uptown. By 1950, bebop was entrenched, and swing was done. Wilson, only thirty-eight, had passed through the most productive period of his life. Since then, he has pieced together a brave career from teaching, radio work, recordings, and endless travelling as a solo act.

Wilson's style has changed little since 1935. At first, it was a mixture of what he admired in Earl Hines (the single-note melodic attack, the little right-hand tremolos, the restless left hand), the stride pianists (the rhythmic precision and the love of melody), and Art Tatum (the touch, speed, arpeggios, and fearless harmonic sense). But he quickly worked out his own style, and what we have come to be so delighted by is its calm, riffling runs, some of them the shortest distance between two points and some with a tricky sidewise motion; the short declarative single-note phrases, the first measure often repeated once or twice to give a pleasant stuttering effect; the dashing double-time single-note bursts; the peppery, sometimes quite dissonant right-hand chords; the way he tosses the melody back and forth between his hands like a juggler; the left hand constantly moving from tenth chords (on and off the beat) to single-note accents and patches of stride; the love of the middle and upper registers. It is easy to listen to a Wilson solo and hear very little of it. His solos are worked out so quietly and fastidiously that they give the impression that they would rather not be heard at all—that they would prefer to stay safely inside their originator's head. There isn't much for the listener to hold on to. The colors are light, the textures silken. There are almost no dynamics; each note is struck perfectly and with the same force as the one before it. Nor is there any rhythmic commotion. Wilson's solos move along one-two-three-four, one-two-three-four, and have none of the legato fooling-with-time experiments of Red Allen and Lester Young and Billie Holiday. (Part of the appeal of the Wilson-Holiday Brunswicks is the contrast—not to say struggle—between his rhythmic rectitude and her alarming and irresistible rhythmic liberties. She sometimes sang entire vocals just outside the beat while Wilson, in his accompanying and in his solo, effortlessly gave her a reading of her exact location.) What finally makes Wilson's solos difficult to get near is their melodic logic. (It has been said that his playing is cold. This is not true. The emotion is simply gloved.) They form landscapes of sound—ordered, serene (even the fast tempos), polite, beautiful.

King Again

It is hard now to understand why the Frank Sinatra who first appeared with Tommy Dorsey over forty years ago had such an electric effect. RCA has reissued, as "The Tommy Dorsey–Frank Sinatra Sessions," all eighty-three of the vocals that he did with Dorsey between February 1, 1940, and July 2, 1942, and they are, with a few celebrated exceptions, vapid and inert. Sinatra had broken with the bouncy, gingham style of Bing Crosby (although he seems to have listened to sleeker crooners, like Eddy Howard), and, by virtue of his simplicity and straightforwardness, he projected a kind of modernity. But his sense of phrasing was unfinished and his diction was unsteady—he tended to let his words drift away open-ended. There was a slight nasal quality to his singing, he was not always in tune, and he had little sense of dynamics. His vibrato sounded skinny. He has said that he modelled his singing on Dorsey's bland, stainless trombone playing, and his early singing does have the same creaminess, the same reluctance to rock the melodic boat. Of course, Dorsey, whose personality was the direct opposite of his playing, didn't make things easy for Sinatra. Fewer than a quarter of the songs Sinatra was asked to record are worth hearing more than once, and this was during the years when numbers such as "It Never Entered My Mind," "I Concentrate on You," "Blues in the Night," "The Nearness of You," "Bewitched," "How High the Moon," "It's So Peaceful in the Country," and "Soft as Spring" first came out. The tempos Dorsey chose were often so slow that the music sounded as if it might congeal, and the backgrounds, full of muted trumpets, high-pitched reeds, and dull rhythmic patterns, provided little support for the singer. The best things Sinatra recorded with Dorsey were done with the Pied Pipers. Four of these numbers— "I'll Never Smile Again," "Star Dust," "I Guess I'll Have to Dream the Rest," and "The One I Love"—still have a hymning, bas-relief quality.

It is equally difficult to connect the Sinatra of the Dorsey days with the Sinatra of "Trilogy," the surprising album he put out two years ago, and the Sinatra who recently gave ten concerts at Carnegie Hall. The vicissitudes of his career are well known: his being dumped by Columbia Records in the early fifties; his return to fame and fortune through Hollywood and Capitol Records in the fifties and sixties; his gradual vocal deterioration in the late sixties, and his retirement in 1971 (now referred to by Sinatra as a "vacation"); his often shaky comeback, begun in 1973; and the surpassing of his old strengths in "Trilogy," which contains several classic recordings—"It Had to Be You," "My Shining Hour," "More Than You Know," "Something," and "Love Me Tender." (The album also contains a section called "Reflections on the Future in Three Tenses." It is a fantasy, with words and music by Gordon Jenkins, in which Sinatra, narrating and singing and backed by a huge chorus and orchestra, takes a trip through space and prepares himself for old age and death. It's Sinatra with the sillies.)

Sinatra's new strengths were displayed in almost all the fourteen songs he did at his second Carnegie Hall concert. His voice, close to a tenor in his Dorsey days, has become a true baritone, and it has taken on timbre and resilience. He can growl and sound hoarse. He can shout. His vibrato is tight and controlled. He has a fine sense of dynamics. He has mentioned his admiration for Billie Holiday, and she seems at this late date to have subtly possessed him. He uses her exhilarating rhythmic devices and her sometimes staccato, rocking diction. Occasionally, his voice resembles the heavy, robed one she developed in the forties. Also evident are the definitive phrasing of Mabel Mercer and, in small pinches, the abandon of Ray Charles. The early Sinatra sang with veiled emotion; the present one was clearly moved by much of what he did at Carnegie Hall, and his transports were passed on to the audience. He did a slow, husky "Come Rain or Come Shine," using Billie Holiday's legato pacing, his face brimming with emotion. He did an ad-lib "When Your Lover Has Gone," backed by organ chords, and a rocking "The Lady Is a Tramp." He did another classic "It Had to Be You," a pushing "I Won't Dance," and an easy ad-lib "As Time Goes By." All his showmanship was in place. There were the searchlight blue eyes that give the impression they are looking into every pair of eyes in the hall; the ineffable cool and skill that make his singing appear effortless; the flashing smiles that dispel the emotion of the last song and prepare the way for the next one; the fluid stage motions, even including the seemingly ostentatious sipping of a glass of red wine.

Bunny Berigan _____

Louis Armstrong was the first sunburst in jazz—the light a thousand young trumpeters reflected. But two other trumpeters, both less imitable than Armstrong and both suffering from short, damaged careers, were also closely attended. One was Jabbo Smith, and the other was Bix Beiderbecke. These two had an equally evanescent admirer—Bunny Berigan. Out of fashion most of the forty years since his death, Berigan was once revered as a kind of Beiderbecke replacement. But he successfully absorbed both players (along with Armstrong, of course) and constructed his own passionate style.

Born in 1908 in Hilbert, Wisconsin, of a musical Irish-German family, Berigan took up the violin at six, switched to the trumpet at eleven, and had his first professional job when he was thirteen. He never finished high school, and was a full-time musician at eighteen. He moved to New York in 1928, got to know Rex Stewart and the Dorsey brothers, and in 1930 was hired by Hal Kemp. During the next four years, he did studio work, made a great many recordings, and worked for Paul Whiteman. He got married and had children and became a disastrous drinker. In 1935, he joined Benny Goodman. Jess Stacy was on piano, and he spoke recently of Berigan: "I worked with Berigan in the Goodman band in 1935—in fact, travelled across the country with him in Goodman's old Pontiac. He dressed conservatively, and, with his little mustache and his widow's peak and his glasses, he looked like a college professor. He was a wonderful man and an electrifying trumpet player, and he didn't have a conceited bone in his body. He was always kind of not satisfied with his playing. After he took a solo, he'd say, 'I started out great but I ended up in a cloud of shit.' His drinking was awful. We'd stop every hundred miles to get him another bottle of Old Quaker, or some such. Of course, business was so bad until we got to the Coast that it was a panic band, and that didn't help him. We played a dance in Michigan and thirty-five people came—all of them musicians. In Denver, we had to play dime-a-dance music, with a waltz every third number. Berigan used to complain about Goodman all the time. Berigan was playing lead trumpet and hot solos, and, finally, every night about eleven, after those difficult Fletcher Henderson arrangements and all the solos, he'd say, 'This is impossible,' and take the last drink—the law-of-diminishing-returns drink—and wipe himself out. We roomed together in Denver, and, what with his drinking and the altitude, he'd wake up at night, his throat dry, thinking he couldn't breathe. He'd tell me, 'I'm dying, I'm dying,' so I'd soak some towels in cold water and wrap them around his head, and that would ease him and he'd go back to sleep saying, 'You saved my life, Jess.' I don't know why, but Berigan left the Goodman band while we were at the Palomar in Los Angeles, just after we caught on, and came back to New York, where he had his own little group at the Famous Door, on Fifty-second Street. On the way back from the Coast, Goodman had a long, successful run in Chicago, and when we hit New York we were the top—the biggest thing in American music. I've always wondered if Berigan regretted leaving the band when he did. But he never let on."

Berigan was at his peak during the next couple of years. He recorded with Billie Holiday and Mildred Bailey, and with Tommy Dorsey, Artie Shaw, Johnny Hodges, Fats Waller, and Teddy Wilson. He sat in on a Louis Armstrong date, and one Sunday afternoon he backed Bessie Smith at the Famous Door. In 1937, he put together his own big band. It was spirited and swinging. (The likes of George Auld, George Wettling, Sonny Lee, Dave Tough, Buddy Rich, Joe Bushkin, and Allan Reuss passed through.) But Berigan was a poor businessman, and in 1939 he went bankrupt. His health had deteriorated. He worked briefly for Tommy Dorsey, and put a couple of temporary bands together. He died at the age of thirty-three, in 1942.

One side of Berigan's style was romantic, melodramatic, and garrulous. It had a kind of Irish cast. The other side was blue, emotional, down, funky. He would fool around in his lowest register, playing heavy, resonant notes—gravestone notes. He would play blue note after blue note. Both sides of his style would appear in a single solo. He might start two choruses of the blues in his down style. He would stay in his low register, growling and circling like a bear. (Only Ruby Braff and Charlie Shavers got the same sound down there.) He would use four or five notes, shaping them into short, reiterated phrases. At the start of his second chorus, he would suddenly jump to a high C or D, go into a flashy descending run, and wing through a couple of large intervals. His vibrato would become noticeable, and his tone would open up. He might dip into his low register at the end of the solo, but he'd finish with a ringing Irish high C. Berigan's execution was almost flawless. He was a daring and advanced improviser, who fooled with offbeat and behind-the-beat rhythms and with all sorts of tonal effects. Yet his melodic lines were logical and graceful. There was an outsize quality to all Berigan's playing; he was a three-man trumpet section pressed into one. He dominated every group he was in: on Benny Goodman's recordings of "Sometimes I'm Happy" and "King Porter Stomp" and on Tommy Dorsey's of "Marie" and "Song of India" his famous solos stand like oaks on a plain. Only Red Allen and Roy Eldridge achieved a similar majesty in their big-band work. (Louis Armstrong's big-band majesty was ready-made; he was often the only soloist.)

Berigan has been brought forward again by a Time-Life "Giants of Jazz" album and by Volume I of the RCA "The Complete Bunny Berigan," which will collect all eighty-nine of the recordings he made with his big band. The Time-Life album contains forty numbers made between 1930 and 1939. The first, a Hal Kemp "Them There Eyes," reveals Berigan as Louis Armstrong, and the last, an all-star "Blue Lou," as himself. Many of the finest numbers in the album were recorded in the mid-thirties with small pickup groups. (Omitted, though, are "Bughouse" and "Blues in E-Flat," done with Red Norvo and Chu Berry, and "Honeysuckle Rose" and "Blues," done with Fats Waller and Tommy Dorsey.) Of particular note are Berigan's long melodic lines on the two Gene Gifford numbers; the three Bud Freeman selections, especially "Keep Smiling at Trouble," where he moves readily back and forth between the two parts of his style; the growls and low, fat sorrowing notes on "Blues," made with his own group; and the rocking, irresistible way he plays the melody in the first chorus of Irving Berlin's "Let Yourself Go," backed by organ chords and a strong Dave Tough afterbeat. Tough and Berigan galvanized each other. In the Time-Life album, Tough also appears on Dorsey's "Marie" and "Song of India," set down on one January day in 1937. Berigan's solos in both those numbers possess the eternal resilience that all improvisation aims at but rarely reaches. This quality shines through Berigan's celebrated miniature trumpet concerto "I Can't Get Started." The number, lasting roughly five minutes, begins with a bravura twelve-bar trumpet cadenza played over sustained band chords. Berigan sings a chorus in his pleasant, piping voice. A second, nine-bar cadenza follows, and he launches triumphantly into the melody, ending with a celestial E-flat.

The RCA reissue has thirty-one numbers. The best are "I Can't Get Started," "The Prisoner's Song," "Caravan," "Study in Brown," "Frankie and Johnny," "Mahogany Hall Stomp," and "Swanee River." The rest of the album is given over to songs like "The Lady from Fifth Avenue" and "All Dark People Are Light on Their Feet." Whatever the material, Berigan is everywhere, playing lead trumpet, soloing, filling the air with his serene and muscular poetry.

Otis Ferguson

Jazz did not attract a steady group of commentators in America until the mid-thirties, when it was almost forty years old. This group, which included apologists, enthusiasts, hagiographers, and critics, grew steadily, and by the early forties it was made up of such as George Simon, Charles Edward Smith, John Hammond, Marshall Stearns, George Avakian, Wilder Hobson, Dave

Dexter, Jr., George Hoefer, Frederic Ramsey, Winthrop Sargeant, William Russell, Leonard Feather, Helen Oakley, Barry Ulanov, George Frazier, and Otis Ferguson. (For all his faulty exuberance, the father of these writers was the French critic Hugues Panassié, who in 1934 had published his *Le Jazz Hot,* the first book of unalloyed jazz criticism.) Ferguson stood out from the pack. He approached his subject with detachment and style and poetic overtones, granting it understanding and honor instead of zealotry and huzzahs. He was among the first to applaud the musicians' own musical intelligence and the first to write about the music with some regularity in a general-interest national magazine; nineteen of his jazz pieces appeared in *The New Republic* between 1936 and 1941. But in 1943 he was killed in action in Italy, and by the fifties he had become a cult, a kind of lesser James Agee—revered and out of print. So it is fine to have *The Otis Ferguson Reader,* which brings together all thirty-five of his jazz pieces, twelve of them previously unpublished. (It also includes some of his film criticism, pieces on the circus and on radio, autobiography, a poem that was printed in *The New Yorker,* and book reviews, one of them a surprisingly tough piece on Edmund Wilson's "The Boys in the Back Room," which had itself been published in *The New Republic* eight months before.) The book has been edited by Robert Wilson and Dorothy Chamberlain, Ferguson's former wife, and there is a helpful memoir by Malcolm Cowley, who worked with Ferguson at *The New Republic.*

Ferguson was born in 1907 in Worcester, Massachusetts. He spent four years in the Navy in his late teens, then finished high school, and was graduated from Clark University in 1933. He joined *The New Republic* the following year. Already an ambitious writer, he liked to think of himself as being on the side of the common man. His friend Jess Stacy has said of him, "The most I saw of Otis was when I was with Benny Goodman at the Pennsylvania Hotel in 1937. He was about five foot nine, and a down-to-earth guy. He liked me, I liked him, and we hung out together. We'd go to Kelly's Bar on Thirty-fourth Street between sets, and after work we'd go to the Hickory House and have a steak and listen to Joe Marsala. Then we'd walk over to my apartment, in Tudor City—it was on the twenty-second floor—and look at the boats on the river. We'd hoist a few and talk about music and listen to Walter Gieseking and Debussy and Ravel. He loved to hear those things. If we got loaded, we'd bad-mouth Benny and throw darts at a picture of him I had. Otis realized the importance of the piano in a big band, and when he came to hear us he'd sit practically under the piano on the bandstand, which annoyed the hell out of Benny, which pleased us."

The war between the poet and the Philistine permeated Ferguson's writing. He was influenced by Mencken and Hemingway, but he disguised his literary pretensions with slang and pseudo toughness. He speaks of Lionel Hampton as "this boy Lionel" (not intended as a racial slur) and of Benny Goodman's musicians as "hard-boiled, cynical bozos." He did not often bring the lyrical and the slangy sides of his style successfully together; his prose would lean precariously one way or the other. Sometimes he was silly, in the Carl Sandburg manner: "Jazz was the country where [Bix Beiderbecke] grew up, the fine high thing, the sun coming up to fill the world through the morning." Sometimes he slipped into a melodramatic gargle: "And, in the measure of his chorus, [Jack Teagarden] always uses the savage velvet of a good trombone, the beat of jazz and lilt of the phrases to arrive at something that is terrific on a leash or sad, or gorgeous, or enchanting with echoes of a better day." When the poet took over, he approached a mystical density: "I recommend for your pleasure and for posterity the 'Blues' . . . as being perfect in the collective feeling and very high and strange in the interludes of Norvo and Wilson, whose instruments come up through the pattern with the renewing sweetness of fresh-water springs." But once in a while everything worked, as in this passage from a previously unpublished piece on Bix Beiderbecke: "You will know him by the little ringing shout he can get into a struck note; by the way each note seems to draw the others after it like a string of cars, giving the positive effect of speed even in his artful lags and deliberation, a sort of reckless and gay roll; and by the way, starting on the ground, he will throw a phrase straight up like a rope in the air, where it seems to hang after he has passed along, shaking gently." And Ferguson could be sharp. On John Hammond: "He is to be respected and thanked, but not safely followed as a mentor." On jazz: "The best improvisation is a tune woven around the other tune, the original, an implied counterpoint but standing by itself." On the old rhythm sections: "The iron of the banjo chords."

The world of jazz was a different place in the mid-thirties. Despite the efforts of John Hammond and Benny Goodman, few jazz bands, of whatever size, were integrated. Black audiences were not welcome in downtown clubs, which were inhabited largely by white bands, and white audiences were no longer as free in the uptown clubs, which tended toward black bands. (Barney Josephson's Café Society, which opened in Greenwich Village in 1938, was the first night club to offer mixed bands to mixed audiences.) White jazz was easier for a white man to come by in the flesh, and this availability is reflected in Ferguson's output. His liberalism is clear, but he writes largely about white jazz musicians—his celebrated pieces on Beiderbecke, Jess Stacy, and Goodman, and his less well known ones on Ziggy Elman, Jack Teagarden, and Red Norvo. He sometimes seemed to have blinders on. In 1941, he wrote that Billy Butterfield was "the only really exciting new [trumpeter] to be heard in ten years"—a statement that eliminates Red Allen and Roy Eldridge and even Louis Armstrong. And what of Bunny Berigan? And where, in all these pieces, are Dicky Wells, Benny Morton, Art Tatum, Lester Young, Ben Webster, Harry Edison, Frankie Newton, Sidney Catlett, and Billie Holiday? He does have a thoughtful piece on Ellington, though, and a good one on Teddy Wilson (published here for the first time), and one of his last articles for *The New Republic* is an appreciation of the Spirits of Rhythm, which included the guitarist Teddy Bunn and the mad scat singer Leo Watson.

Making Do

FRIDAY: The Kool Jazz Festival New York has swallowed the Newport Jazz Festival-New York. Not only that, there will be twenty Kool Jazz Festivals in the United States this year, including the New York edition, which began late this afternoon with a solo recital by Art Hodes. It was held in the Forum Room of the New York Sheraton, a mirrored cave with raspberry trimmings and stalactite chandeliers. (Carnegie Recital Hall, the usual center for these events, is being renovated.) Hodes played seventeen numbers, and they included his mixture of stride pieces ("Grandpa's Spells," "Snowy Mornin' Blues"), blues, standards ("Am I Blue," "Sweet Georgia Brown," "Georgia"), and oddities ("Maryland! My Maryland!," "Battle Hymn of the Republic"). He used a lot of tremolo and two-handed staccato effects, but his playing lacked the elasticity and depth of his night-club performances. Concert-hall situations still make old speakeasy performers jumpy.

The evening came in two different parts. Max Roach brought his quartet (Odean Pope on tenor saxophone, Cecil Bridgewater on trumpet, Calvin Hill on bass), plus a string quartet, into Avery Fisher Hall, and they played three compositions that were a mixture of recycled bebop, bad Hindemith, and sheer Roachian pomp. The strings did little for Roach's drumming or for Pope and Bridgewater, neither of them a prepossessing soloist. The second half of the concert was given over to Freddie Hubbard, McCoy Tyner, Ron Carter, and Elvin Jones. Hubbard was lyrical in his overblown way, Tyner suggested ocean motion and Carter a royal palm, and Jones' multilayered, multicolored drumming was superb.

The second part of the evening was played at Carnegie Hall by the Stan Getz quartet (Jim McNeely on piano, Marc Johnson on bass, Victor Lewis on drums) and a Benny Goodman group (Teddy Wilson, Lionel Hampton, Phil Flanigan on bass, and Panama Francis on drums). Getz's seven selections (among them "The Night Has a Thousand Eyes," Bud Powell's "Tempus Fugit," and Billy Strayhorn's "Blood Count" and

"We'll Be Together Again") reaffirmed the fact that it was partly his reimagining of Lester Young, and not exclusively Young himself, that shook up so many young white tenor saxophonists forty years ago. Another reaffirmation: Getz, in the long ago, listened hard to Johnny Hodges and Don Byas. Goodman and friends did ten numbers, and the best were the medium-tempo "Someday Sweetheart," "It Had to Be You," and "Don't Be That Way." The flagwavers were short of breath. Goodman gave half a dozen instances of his old flair and brilliance. Hampton played percussively rather than melodically. Wilson was impeccable: each solo climbed and sank, sank and climbed; his touch was golden, his evenness justice itself.

SATURDAY: Good minions make good empires. In recent years, George Wein has hired others to produce his programs, and tonight at Avery Fisher Hall the American impresario George Schutz and the German critic Joachim-Ernst Berendt put together a three-hour concert called "Jazz and World Music." It was played by forty or so musicians from India, Brazil, Germany, Turkey, Senegal, England, Japan, and the United States. The American flutist Paul Horn, using taped flutes and electronic echo effects, played movie music with an Indian tinge—Deborah Kerr and Jean Simmons in the foothills of the Himalayas. Rainbow, made up of L. Subramaniam on violin, Ashish Kahn on sarod (a sitarlike instrument with twenty-five strings), Pranesh Kahn on tabla, and the American alto saxophonist John Handy, sounded like an Indian bebop group. The ensembles resembled unkempt unison bop figures, and there were solos based partly on Indian scales. Handy, a perfervid, big-toned descendant of Charlie Parker, was in good form, but it was too bad the group didn't allow itself more free collective interplay. Codona, the third group, consists of Don Cherry on pocket trumpet and doussn' gouni (a Malian guitar that looks like a giant tomato with a hoe stuck into it handle first), Collin Walcott on sitar and tabla, and Nana Vasconcelos on percussion. We heard Cherry on trumpet backed by sitar and conga drum; Walcott on sitar backed by maracas; Cherry on trumpet backed by tabla; Cherry on some sort of piccolo backed by maracas and cymbals. An American Indian tenor saxophonist named Jim Pepper did some chanting with Codona and played a John Coltrane saxophone solo. The final group of the evening, Karl Berger's Music Universe, was thirty strong, and on hand were the trumpeter Randy Brecker, the drummer Ed Blackwell, the violinist Leroy Jenkins, Collin Walcott, and the alto saxophonist Lee Konitz. Berger, a German-born composer and vibraphonist, conducted the two immense numbers, which, though melodically simple (the second was built around a four-note folk motif), were dressed up in constantly changing rhythms and instrumental combinations. There was also a parade of soloists, the best of whom was Konitz. He was accompanied at first by bass and drums; then he went on alone. He played a long, witty melody, a kind of very long song, that was beautiful. The rest of the two numbers had ensemble dissonances, singing and chanting, dancing, and the avant-garde big-band clutter that has become familiar during the past ten years in the works of Sam Rivers and Muhal Richard Abrams.

SUNDAY: Alec Wilder would not have been altogether displeased by the concert given in his honor at Carnegie Hall this afternoon: he always knew that beauty is rare, and that praise well given is even rarer. He would have threatened not to come but at the last would have appeared backstage or out front, dressed in his summer uniform—a rumpled linen jacket, gray trousers, moccasins. He would have roared in disbelief at the huge drawing of his head fastened to a baffle at one side of the stage, and the length of the concert would have made him restless. He would have been annoyed by some of the liberties taken with his music, and he might have disagreed with some of the selections. He might also have been mystified by the evening's refusal to swing—to get up off its somewhat sanctimonious rusty-dusty and go. But many things would have pleased him: the amount and variety of his music that was performed (about two dozen songs, including "Baggage Room Blues," "A Long Night," "Who Can I Turn To?," "Lovers and Losers," "Mimosa and Me," and "Blackberry Winter"; two woodwind-octet numbers; the third and fourth movements of

Suite No. 1 for Horn, Tuba, and Piano; all of the Jazz Suite for Four Horns; and all of the Suite for Baritone Sax, Horn, and Wind Quintet, written for Gerry Mulligan); the complex, tough chords that Marian McPartland used at the beginning of her solo on "Jazz Waltz for a Friend," written for her; the adept octet performances (by Walter Levinsky, Wally Kane, Raymond Beckenstein, Dennis Anderson, Don Stewart, Kenny Werner, Paul Meyers, and Edwin Schuller) of "Such a Tender Night" and "Kindergarten Flower Pageant"; the quality and strength of Mabel Mercer's voice on "Did You Ever Cross Over to Sneden's"; the snap that Gunther Schuller, conducting, got out of the horns in the Jazz Suite for Four Horns; Jackie Cain's straight, sad "Remember My Child"; Stan Getz's reverential, equally mournful "Where Do You Go (When It Starts to Rain)?"; and the stately readings, one muted and one open-horn, by the trumpeter Joe Wilder of "Trouble Is a Man" and "Blackberry Winter." Most of all, he would have relished the fact that the concert belonged as much to its performers as to him. He once said, "Players tend to like what I write; composers don't. Composers think of performers as necessary evils . . . But I consider the written music only a guide. The notes suggest, they tell only part of the story. I'll take half the credit, and all the rest goes to the performer. Performers! Those great, beautiful people are my saviors." Loonis McGlohon produced the program.

Praising the living is even harder work. Tonight, in Carnegie Hall, at "Buddy Rich: A Retrospective" (produced by the jazz writer Burt Korall), the drummer was lionized not so much for his drumming as for his show-business attributes. There were photographs of him as a child star, as a teen-age whiz in Joe Marsala's band, and as Tommy Dorsey's twenty-two-year-old wunderkind. He and Mel Tormé, who was the master of ceremonies, bantered, and there was a funny bit of slapstick between Rich and a Zildjian from the Zildjian cymbal factory, who was trying to give him an award. He did a short tap dance with Honi Coles, and he played number after mechanical number with the band. He also played one long solo, and it seemed— aside from brief passages near its end involving his cymbals and his drum rims—labored. What we did not hear was the tasty performer who surfaces in small-group situations—particularly in duos and trios and quartets. Once, at the old Newport festival, Rich opened a concert by sitting in with Teddy Wilson. On "Somebody Loves Me," he accompanied with great delicacy on wire brushes, then took a long-legged, spidery solo with his sticks which told more about his powers than anything tonight.

MONDAY: Including occasional non-jazz events in a jazz festival rubs the listeners' fur the wrong way, gives them valuable perspective. Early this evening, at Alice Tully Hall, Eileen Farrell and Mabel Mercer rendered thirty songs in such a way that words and music became a continuum: words were music, music words. Seated regally side by side, they seemed, in their ease and artlessness, to be at the very center of music—a pair of goddesses telling us what all songs should sound like. Ten numbers were done as duets, and each singer did about ten numbers alone—Eileen Farrell standing or seated, Mabel Mercer always seated. Eileen Farrell kept her voice within the bounds of her songs, allowing herself to soar only in "Over the Rainbow." Mabel Mercer sang two of her songs and did the rest parlando, and near the end of the concert she read A. A. Milne's "Vespers" and Edna St. Vincent Millay's "The Ballad of the Harp-Weaver," her voice both bleak and revelatory at the ballad's close:

> There sat my mother
> With the harp against her shoulder,
> Looking nineteen,
> And not a day older,
>
> A smile about her lips,
> And a light about her head,
> And her hands in the harp-strings
> Frozen dead.
>
> And piled up beside her
> And toppling to the skies,

Were the clothes of a king's son,
Just my size.

Eileen Farrell spoke at the beginning of the evening of how, as a
music student in the early forties, she first heard Mabel Mercer
sing, and of how Mabel Mercer had been a part of her life ever
since.

TUESDAY: We had the avant-garde at five and nine at Avery
Fisher this evening, but the old guard, brought in to restore law
and order at the end of the nine-o'clock concert, was routed. The
first concert had two groups—an octet led by the tenor saxophonist David Murray (commonly of the World Saxophone Quartet), and a septet led by the reedman Henry Threadgill (commonly of Air). Murray's group included Bobby Bradford on
cornet, John Purcell on alto saxophone, Craig Harris on trombone, John Hicks on piano, and Steven McCall (also of Air) on
drums. Its music was surprisingly conservative. The opening
and closing ensembles were played either freely or in a slightly
out-of-focus unison, the tempos were distinct, and the soloists
rested on organ chords or brief riffs. The soloists summoned up
Albert Ayler and Ornette Coleman and Roswell Rudd and Cecil
Taylor. It was good to hear Bradford, who worked with Coleman
almost thirty years ago in Los Angeles, and who plays with a
pleasant lyrical edge. Threadgill's group, made up of Harris, Olu
Dara on cornet, Brian Smith and Fred Hopkins (Air) on bass, and
Pheeroan Aklaff and John Betsch on drums, was more adventurous. After two brief ensemble numbers, it went into a half-
hour fanfare that sounded rougly like this: the drummers began
with smooth snare-drum rolls; the horns offered a martial
figure, and then parodied it; one bassist, playing arco, did a
unison figure with the trombonist, and the trumpeter played a
mournful figure backed by chords from the trombonist and the
alto saxophonist; the drummers rose up slowly behind a succession of brief solos, finally reaching a climax, which gave way to
short horn punctuations and a sudden, slamming end.
 The World Saxophone Quartet opened the second concert. In

addition to David Murray, it has Oliver Lake and Julius Hemphill on alto saxophones and Hamiet Bluiett on baritone saxophone. The group has grown more sedate since its first festival appearance, three years ago, when it indulged in funny Stepin Fetchit stage business and heavy parodying of such as Duke Ellington and Guy Lombardo. The parody remains, and so does the avant-garde fretwork of scrambled ensembles, animal-noise solos, and weak key centers, but the quartet has become hooked on rich reed sounds. It doubles constantly, and tonight we heard these combinations: bass clarinet, two soprano saxophones, and alto clarinet; two tenor saxophones, a soprano, and a baritone; three flutes and a bass clarinet; tenor, soprano, alto, and baritone saxophones; and three tenor saxophones and a baritone. The group delivers these instrumentations in a swashbuckling, aggressive way. Perhaps it is telling us how much it digs those old, statuesque sounds—those old sounds it also loves to parody—of Harry Carney and Ben Webster and Coleman Hawkins and Johnny Hodges.

The second half of the concert was taken up by four reedmen who, however slyly and glancingly, had been parodied by the World Saxophone Quartet. They were Stan Getz, Zoot Sims, Al Cohn, and Jimmy Giuffre, and they were meant to be a recreation of one of Woody Herman's late-forties Four Brothers saxophone sections. (Getz, Sims, Herbie Steward, and Serge Chaloff formed the first one.) But they seemed fatigued by the idea, and the only freshness came from ballad solos by Getz and Sims. The rhythm section consisted of Ben Aronov on piano, Frank Tate on bass, and Shelly Manne on drums. Manne was so busy tatting and sewing and knitting back there that sometimes the brothers couldn't get a sound in edgewise.

WEDNESDAY: There was a meandering, bucolic quality to "Salute to Pres," at Carnegie Hall tonight. It might even have pleased Lester Young, a reflective, poetic country man. (He died in 1959, at the age of forty-nine.) The evening began with a showing of Gjon Mili's 1944 short "Jammin' the Blues," in which Young, abetted by Harry Edison, Illinois Jacquet, Sid

Catlett, and Jo Jones, plays a couple of blues, his round, convex, Oriental face turned by Mili's closeups and moody lighting into a huge moon. Then Ira Gitlet, a producer of the concert and its master of ceremonies, read a tatterdemalion poem he had written about Young. The last stanza goes:

> He was a cat who was really laid-back
> His audience was always soulfully paid-back
> He floated like a butterfly and stung like a bee
> Long before the coming of Muhammad Ali.

Gitler went on to read a history of Young's life taken from some of his old liner notes and printed like a score in the festival program. Now and then, he paused and there was music—first by a big band that included Harry Edison, Jimmy Maxwell, Vic Dickenson, Eddie Bert, Allen Eager, Al Cohn, Budd Johnson, John Lewis, Bucky Pizzarelli, Milt Hinton, and Oliver Jackson. It played "Every Tub," "Jive at Five," "Jumpin' at the Woodside," and "Broadway," and was joined midway by Zoot Sims and Stan Getz. The band also did "Lester Leaps In," but it was sandwiched between two recordings—Count Basie"s 1936 "Evenin'," which was Young's first record date, and "Countless Blues," a 1938 small-band session on which Young plays clarinet. The big band departed for the evening, leaving its rhythm section, and Sims and Johnson did a soprano-saxophone duet on "I Want a Little Girl." A six-saxophone version of "Tickle-Toe" followed (Cohn, Sims, Eager, Getz, Johnson, Buddy Tate). The famous Holiday-Young sequence from the "Sound of Jazz" television show came next, and the concert wandered into a different pasture. A group made up of Edison, Tate, Dickenson, Pizzarelli, Hinton, Teddy Wilson, and Roy Haynes played three numbers that had nothing to do with Young, and Teddy Wilson did two piano solos, backed by Hinton and Jo Jones. (The rhythmic tussling in the three small-band numbers was fascinating. Wilson plays directly on the beat; Haynes scatters accents everywhere; and Edison, Dickenson, and Tate like to play behind the beat.) Young reappeared during the concert's last five numbers. These were an exceptional "These Foolish

Things" by Sims and an equally fine "Polka Dots and Moon-beams" by Getz; small-band versions of "D. B. Blues" and "Jumpin' with Symphony Sid"; and a 1943 Young recording of "I Got Rhythm," done on the Signature label with Bill Coleman, Dicky Wells, Ellis Larkins, and Jo Jones, and notable not for Young's uninspired solos but for Wells' two whooping, trium-phant choruses.

The celebration by themselves of sixteen supposedly young and unknown musicians at Carnegie Hall earlier in the evening was overcrowded and inconclusive. At least eight of the musi-cians are not unknown, and some are far from striplings. These were Chico Freeman on tenor saxophone, Wynton Marsalis on trumpet, James Newton on flute, John Purcell on alto sax-ophone, Craig Harris on trombone, Jay Hoggard on vibraphone, Anthony Davis on piano, and Hamiet Bluiett. It was difficult to judge most of the truly unknown players in their allotted time. These were Ronnie Burrage on drums, Kevin Eubanks on guitar, John Blake on violin, Daniel Ponce on percussion, Bobby McFer-rin on vocals, Paquito D'Rivera on alto saxophone, Abdul Wadud on cello, and Avery Sharpe on bass. But the fact that most of them are romantics came through clearly. Their compo-sitions dream, and their improvisations are lush and close. They have startling techniques, but they also seem to understand the emotional freight that the great jazz performers have carried forward from generation to generation. The bias of most of the sixteen is toward the recent avant-garde; absent from the pro-ceedings were such equally gifted but more conservative young players as the pianists Fred Hersch and Lee Ann Ledgerwood and the guitarists Emily Remler and Howard Alden. And where was Wynton Marsalis's brother Branford, a tenor saxophonist and possibly a more interesting player than the smooth, cool Wyn-ton?

FRIDAY: The Swiss pianist and composer George Gruntz and the American poet and playwright Amiri Baraka have written a jazz opera called *Money*, and about a third of it was given its world première tonight at the La Mama Annex. (The entire opera, in eleven scenes and using eighty performers, lasts four hours.) The music, played by a fourteen-piece onstage band that included Gruntz (conducting and playing piano), Chico Freeman, Frank Gordon (trumpet), Howard Johnson (tuba), Janice Robinson (trombone), Cecil McBee (bass), and Billy Hart (drums), is attractive and swinging, and Gruntz uses it imaginatively: the recitative and songs (none reach the level of arias) are backed with organ chords and by soloists, playing singly or together, and by various rhythmic combinations. The band is a constant and welcome presence. But Baraka's libretto is embarrassing. It deals with the romantic affairs and careers of a black singer (Vea Williams) and a black saxophonist (Chico Freeman), and a rich white American (Sheila Jordon) and a Russian diplomat (Kenneth Bell). Castro comes to power, Malcolm X is murdered, and there are bitter mentions of Ike and McCarthy and busing and freedom marches. There is too much recitative. Why not allow the singers to improvise their delivery, even improvise some of the lines? Why not allow the instrumentalists and singers to improvise together? Why not start again?

SATURDAY: Bob Wilber's new group, The Bechet Legacy, is an attempt to perpetuate the music of the New Orleans clarinettist and soprano saxophonist. Using Mike Camico on trumpet, Mark Shane on piano, Mike Peters on guitar and banjo, Reggie Johnson on bass, and Butch Miles on drums, Wilber plays loose adaptations of Sidney Bechet recordings, and, with his unique ability to get inside the musical skin of musicians like Bechet and Johnny Hodges and Johnny Dodds, he does them very well. He curbs Bechet's headlong vibrato and keeps his melodic trajectories closer to earth. He is more polite. Bechet the soprano saxophonist dominated every ensemble he played in, either forcing trumpet players to blow themselves purple or simply sweeping them aside. The Bechet Legacy gave a concert this afternoon in the Guggenheim auditorium, and, with Chuck Riggs sitting in for Miles, played "Cake Walking Babies from Home," "Kansas City Man Blues," "Roses of Picardy," "China Boy," "Blues in Thirds," "Love for Sale," "Summertime," and

"Oh, Lady Be Good!" Wilber also did half a dozen of Bechet's own songs, all of them inward and minor-sounding. Riggs' foot-pedal work was heavy, and so were his unimaginative snare-drum figures, both in his accompanying and in his solos. He should have remembered what Sid Catlett did two-thirds of the way through Bechet's recording of "Summertime"—shifted from wire brushes to a carpet of press rolls with his sticks. It lifted the recording from a good one to a magisterial one.

The singer Sylvia Sims suggested to George Wein last winter that he include in the festival a concert of songs by Americn women. Wein agreed, and we heard the ramshackle results at Avery Fisher tonight. Sylvia Syms, Carmen McRae, Carrie Smith, Bill Henderson, and Chris Connor sang the songs, Zoot Sims and Dizzy Gillespie improvised on them, and Mike Renzi (piano), Jay Leonhart (bass), and Shelly Manne accompanied. (Only about half of the women songwriters were identified, and we were never told whether they had done the music or the lyrics or both. Nearly all the songs are collaborations, but in the attributions below just the women involved are mentioned.) Carmen McRae remains locked within her mannerisms (the forced melismatics, the steplike phrasing, the dull, brassy voice). One of her five songs was unidentified, two were undistinguished, one was "Some Other Spring" (music by Irene Wilson Kitchings), and the last was Billie Holiday's "Billie's Blues." Zoot Sims played "Fine and Dandy" (music by Kay Swift), "I'm in the Mood for Love" (lyrics by Dorothy Fields), and an unidentified ballad. Carrie Smith's five numbers included "That Ole Devil Called Love" (music and lyrics by Doris Fisher) and Bessie Smith's "Back Water Blues." Bill Henderson, suffering from Avery Fisher nerves, didn't stop oversinging until his final number. "If They Could See Me Now" (lyrics by Dorothy Fields). Chris Connor is one of Anita O'Day's progeny, and she sang two songs by Peggy Lee, Ann Ronnell's "Willow Weep for Me," and songs by Bertha Scott and Dorothy Fields. Dizzy Gillespie did "Lullaby of the Leaves" (music by Bernice Petkere) and "The Way You Look Tonight" and "On the Sunny Side of the Street" (both with lyrics by Dorothy Fields). With the time almost gone, Sylvia Syms came on for "You Oughta Be in Pictures" (music by Dana Suesse) and "Them There Eyes" (music and lyrics by Doris Tauber), and everyone joined hands for a loose-wigged "How High the Moon" (lyrics by Nancy Hamilton).

SUNDAY: Mediocrity burns slowly, so it took a long time to get through the Lionel Hampton concert at Carnegie Hall tonight. Hampton's seventeen-piece big band did eight numbers, among them a semisymphonic "Moonglow" and a Japanese folk song. Then it was jam-session time. Hampton played some blues with Freddie Hubbard, Clark Terry, Al Grey, Phil Woods, Sonny Stitt, Arnett Cobb, Roland Hanna, Milt Hinton, and the drummer George Kawaguchi, and some ballads with Teddy Wilson, Dizzy Gillespie, and Stan Getz, plus the Hampton big-band rhythm section. The last number was an eight-cylinder "Flyin' Home."

1983

Old Wine, New Bottles _____

A new preservation movement, made up of young neo-swing musicians, came into being in the mid-seventies, and it is growing steadily. Already in its ranks are the guitarists Howard Alden and Chris Flory, the bassist Phil Flanigan, the saxophonists Scott Hamilton, Chuck Wilson, and Loren Schoenberg, the clarinettist Chuck Hedges, the drummers Butch Miles, Chuck Riggs, and Fred Stoll, the trombonist Dan Barrett, and the trumpeter Warren Vaché. These musicians have in a way moved beyond their predecessors; they contain the past and the present. They hold in balance the love of melody and tonal quality of the old swing musicians and an awareness of the harmonic expansions and rhythmic freedoms that have taken place in jazz in the past twenty years. Of all these players, one of the most impressive is Vaché.

He is a stocky, medium-sized man with brown hair, a brown mustache, and deep-brown eyes. He plays with intense concentration, but he is cool, and he has a sharp tongue. He lives in Rahway, New Jersey, not far from where he grew up, and he is married and has a baby boy. He recently talked about himself: "I was born in Rahway on February 21, 1951. My father is a bass player, and he still has a band that works around Rahway, but he made his living as a salesman when I was growing up. He was born in Brooklyn and was raised around Camden. My mother was born and raised in Brooklyn. I have one brother, Allan, who's two years younger. He plays very good clarinet with the Happy Jazz Band, in San Antonio, Texas. I started on the piano when I was seven, and switched to the trumpet at nine. I studied first with Jim Fitzpatrick, in Plainfield. He'd been with Hal Kemp. After that, I studied all through school and through Montclair State College. I even have a degree that will enable me to warp the musical minds of small children, should I ever wish to. It was the trumpeter Pee Wee Irwin who kept me in college. My dad discovered in the late sixties that Pee Wee and Chris Griffin had a music school not far from us, and he introduced me to Pee Wee, and it was love at first sight. He was one of the most underestimated musicians of all time. No one knows what a good trumpeter that man was. Anyway, I'd stop in and see him three or four times a week, and he'd teach me by example. He told me to get Charlier's 'Études,' and I did. I'd practice and get nowhere near where I was supposed to be. One time, I played an étude for him and he listened and said, 'Well, that's not quite right.' He didn't have his reading glasses with him, so he played the étude from memory—perfectly. My early jobs were with Dixieland bands, which were all over the place. I had a job with Billy Maxted, who fired me after a week, and with Dick Hyman's band—the one that accompanied Twyla Tharp in 1977. I was in the house band at Condon's for a while, and I had a trio at Crawdaddy. I travel with the Concord All Stars a couple of times a year, but most of the time I just gig around. I'd like to find work in New York with the trio, but a lot of the places that would be right—like Bradley's and the Knickerbocker and Zinno—have a no-horns zoning restrictions. I used to listen to Roy Eldridge at Ryans when I was at Condon's—he was awesome. And I'd drop in on Buck Clayton when he was at Crawdaddy. I liked to listen to the notes he *didn't* play. As far as I'm concerned, the best trumpeter walking now is Ruby Braff. The taste and intelligence! Ruby is inventing a new language. The hardest thing about any brass instrument is the sheer physical effort it takes to play softly and subtly. You can bull your way through the trumpet, and it will sound that way. But to play it right you have to lean all your muscle and emotion into it. Like Ruby. My dad had a large collection of swing-music records, and that was always in my ear. But I've never made a conscious decision about which way to go as a player. I was a Miles Davis freak in high school, and I listened to Fats Navarro and Clifford Brown. I think it came down to content. There is a lot of content—emotional and human—in the older music, in Bobby Hackett and Lester Young. If we're still being moved by Beethoven why shouldn't we still be moved by Bobby and Pres?"

There are ghosts of Clayton and Braff and Irwin in Vaché's playing, and, to a lesser extent, ghosts of Charlie Shavers and Roy Eldridge and Joe Wilder. But the heart of his work is his own. Many of the old swing trumpeters were laconic players. They didn't waste notes, because the fewer the notes used, the lighter the technical burdens. But Vaché is of the baroque persuasion. He is always looking for ways to stem the torrent of notes that besiege his imagination. In recent years, he has begun to succeed, and most of his solos are logical and ordered; there may still be extra phrases, but there are rarely extra notes. He has not, however, controlled his tendency to lark around in the upper register, where he sounds peaked and strained. He will start a solo by coming in just over the trees, using an oblique tone and a fragmentary opening phrase that sounds as if its first half were still lost in its native silence. His tone will slowly broaden, and he will go into an ascending phrase—a don't-mind-me phrase—repeat it an octave higher, and pause. Suddenly he will dart into a complex double-time figure, racing down his horn three steps at a time, come to rest on a trill, move into a rifflike four- or five-note figure, repeat it, and leap back up his horn and into the upper register, spraying eighth notes right and left. Vaché is one of the rare players who love the challenge of a song's bridge, of passing without injury through those eight-bar thickets. This time, he pauses, then lays back and delivers it in a studied, pulled-in rhythmic float. He will start the last eight bars of his solo in his upper register, go down into his middle register, pull his volume over his ears, and vanish whence he came. Vaché has picked up all the old tricks of his trade. He can play fine wa-wa plunger-muted trumpet, he can growl like Buck Clayton and half-valve like Rex Stewart, and he can make his tone swell on slow ballads. There is nothing academic or precious about his playing. He is, in a lesser way, as fresh and surprising as Red Allen and Roy Eldridge were in the thirties. Vaché is showing us that the sort of improvisation in which a player takes a melody and a set of chords and fashions from them a new, parallel melody that heightens the original and stands on its own is far from exhausted.

Earl Hines and Peck Kelley

Earl Hines, who died last spring, at the age of seventy-nine, was a bravura performer. Solidly built, with a big, square face and big, square hands, he moved constantly at the keyboard, swaying back and forth and feinting from side to side, his elbows pumping and his legs out like ski poles. He had a blacksmith's touch (he could untune a freshly tuned piano in twenty minutes), and he issued a steady, overlaying stream of grunts and exclamations. His face moved between joy and pain. He kept his eyes half shut, his gleaming teeth clenched, his lower lip in a permanent, breathing pout. No one knows exactly where his cornucopic style came from. For a long time, it was said that he had taken it from Louis Armstrong when the two first worked together in Chicago in the twenties—that he played "trumpet-style" piano. But Hines' playing seems to have been pretty much formed by the time he arrived in Chicago, in 1924. (He disavowed Armstrong's influence, and ordinarily this could be discounted, since many jazz musicians are devious about who their early models are. Hines, though, was not a devious man.) What took place between Hines and Armstrong takes place between any gifted young collaborators—intense mutual admiration. In his right hand he used single-note melodic passages, octave chords, winding arpeggios, and gentle, quick phrase-ending tremolos, which were like little vibratos. (Hines eventually discarded these tremolos, but they can still be heard in the playing of Jess Stacy, one of his earliest admirers.) His left hand was made up of tenths, offbeat chords, patches of oompah, and sudden single notes. Sometimes a single-note melodic line was carried from his right hand to his left and back. Hines liked to shake things up. He would break the tempo unexpectedly and fashion wild arrhythmic passages, in which he might scatter right-hand chords all over the upper keyboard, opposing them in the left hand with bucking, irregular single notes. The effect was more intense than counterpoint, because the two bodies of sound warred. These rhythmic squalls passed as abruptly as they came, leaving the water as unhurried and blue as before. Hines had other dramatic devices. He would fling clusters of notes out of his high register, filling the air with needles of sound. Or he would go into an octave tremolo in his right hand and keep it going for ten or twenty choruses, and then, the audience exhausted and waiting for his hand to fall off, he would stop, smile brilliantly, and retire the number with a modest sotto-voce coda. The pianist Dick Wellstood once wrote aptly of Hines:

For all the complexity in his playing, Hines exercises fairly simple harmonic vocabulary, and in any event his peculiar stuttering rhythmic sense gives his phrasing such force as to make harmonic analysis almost meaningless. The dissonances he uses are more the result of his fascination with the overtone of the piano than of any concern with elaborate harmonic substitutions. Accented single notes making the upper strings ring, or open fifths or octaves sounded a tone or semi-tone apart (either will do) at opposite ends of the keyboard are to him among the most beautiful of sounds. His is the music of change, based on the rhythms of the body in a graceful way unique to the older jazz players.

Hines invented a new way to play jazz piano. Before him, the music had been dominated by stride pianists (James P. Johnson,

Willie the Lion Smith, Luckey Roberts, Fats Waller) and by blues pianists (Pine Top Smith, Jimmy Yancey, Cripple Clarence Lofton, Charlie Spand). The stride pianists had taken ragtime piano and put a four-four engine in it, and the blues pianists had invented a deceptively simple, almost onomatopoeic music full of weather and trains and unrequited love. Hines moved into the uncharted territory between these attacks and became the first modern jazz pianist. His playing, framed by his hot big band, was broadcast almost nightly in the thirties from the Grand Terrace ballroom in Chicago, and it permeated the country—particularly the Midwest and the Southwest. Not many young pianists escaped his influence. Here are some who learned from him, directly or indirectly: Joe Sullivan, Teddy Wilson, Nat Cole, Mary Lou Williams, Count Basie, Jess Stacy, Mel Powell, Nellie Lutcher, Billy Kyle, Dave Bowman, Garnet Clark, Gene Schroeder, Clyde Hart, Countess Johnson, Eddie Heywood, Erroll Garner, Dick Wellstood, Art Tatum, and Lennie Tristano. And Hines' blood, thinning but unmistakable, can be followed down through Bud Powell and Bill Evans to Fred Hersch.

Few long careers ascend steadily, and Hines' was no exception. After the adventurous days of the twenties, he put together his big band, and it lasted twenty years. It was both a cushion for his playing and a school for exceptional young musicians and singers, among them Budd Johnson, Omer Simeon, Darnell Howard, Alvin Burroughs, Ray Nance, Trummy Young, Freddie Webster, Benny Harris, Bennie Green, Shadow Wilson, Charlie Parker, Dizzy Gillespie, Ivie Anderson, Billy Eckstine, and Sarah Vaughan. Hines had talent-scout ears. Then, in 1948, having been a general for almost as long as he could remember, he stepped back into the ranks and became a sideman with Louis Armstrong's All Stars, which included Barney Bigard, Jack Teagarden, and Sidney Catlett. He stayed four uneasy years, and settled on the West Coast, where he worked in assorted Dixieland bands. By the early sixties, he had fallen into despair and confusion, and he was ready to quit music and open a shop with his wife. But his old friend Stanley Dance, the English jazz critic, kept after him, and in the winter of 1964 Hines came East for the first time in ten years and gave two concerts at the Little Theatre, on West Forty-fourth Street. The reviews and the ensuing publicity got his wheels going again, and within a year or so he was working steadily, often as a soloist, and he went on working, from one end of the world to the other, almost to the day he died. Most jazz musicians find a style and stay within it, safe and unchanging. But after Hines' renaissance his playing gradually became more prolix, and his old one-chorus solos grew into Jamesian exercises. Each chorus became an elaboration of the previous chorus, and two or three notes did the work of one. Hines seemed to want to engulf his listeners. But he could still knock you out with an upper-register explosion or with three or four stuttering notes at the start of a bridge.

Hines' philosophy was rigorous and old-fashioned. He was one of the last of the great jazz showmen. He believed that a performer's primary task is to please his audience. He once said with satisfaction, "I never considered myself a piano soloist. I was happy just to take my little eight bars and get off. It's the public that's pushed me out and made me a soloist." (This was not strictly true, of course. He was an exceptional, even a radical, jazz soloist by the time he was twenty-two—long before he had any public to speak of.) He kept fit, dressed well, smiled a lot, spoke graciously to his audiences, and invariably played as hard as he knew how. (Flat-stomached and muscular his whole life, Hines used to throw a medicine ball with Joe Louis in the thirties, and he often did exercises to strengthen his fingers.) He didn't believe in taking his troubles onstage or in burdening others. "The greatest thing to draw wrinkles in a man's face is worry," he said in the sixties after his fortunes had changed. "Why should I be unhappy and pull down my face and drag my feet and make everybody around me feel that way, too? By being what you are, something always comes up. Sunshine always opens out."

Peck Kelley, the legendary Texas pianist, who died in his eighties in 1981, turns out to have been another Earl Hines admirer. Kelley became a legend because he was praised by the likes of John Hammond, Jack Teagarden, Pee Wee Russell, and

Harry James; because he refused all entreaties to leave Texas (he was born in Houston); and because he refused to make records. He was a Texas recluse who died, as far as we Yankees knew, preserved in silence. Not so. On two successive Sunday afternoons in June of 1957, Dick Shannon, a Benny Goodman clarinettist and a longtime Kelley admirer, persuaded the pianist to go down to the studios of radio station KPRC, in Houston, and play a little on what was said to be the best piano in town. He also persuaded Kelley to play with the tapes running. Kelley enjoyed the sessions, and he even enjoyed listening to the tapes in later years, but he refused to have them released. His playing at all into a tape recorder, though, set him going in the direction of the public arena, and Milt Gabler, of Commodore Records, has finished the trip for him. Gabler has released fourteen numbers from those two afternoons as "Peck Kelley Jam." (Also on hand were two guitarists, a bassist, and a drummer.) The album reveals Kelley as technically adroit, harmonically rich, inclined to rhapsody, and rather staid. He sounds as if he had listened to the old radio pianist Lee Sims in the twenties, to Earl Hines in the thirties, and to Art Tatum (who grew up on Sims and Hines) in the forties. Beyond that, he doesn't swing much, and when a number goes on too long he runs out of improvisational gas. But if Kelley sounded in the twenties and thirties the way he sounds here it would have been a surprise to run across him in some Houston or Galveston tonk. Discovering a professional in an unlikely place automatically makes him seem twice as large as life.

Whiz Kid

Jazz never lets up on its practitioners. It asks that they get up before an audience (perhaps a jaded one or an ignorant one) five or six nights a week and for several hours spin music out of their heads (perhaps in a noisy night club or in a half-filled concert hall with bad acoustics) which swings, is well played, and has never been heard before. And it asks that they do these things, as often as not, without adequate pay, without adequate rest or decent food (if they are on the road, as they are most of the time), without dressing rooms or tuned pianos, and without due praise. Some musicians meet these demands by constructing solos out of prefabricated patterns and figures. Some use the same solos over and over. Some plagiarize or parody themselves. Some grow obtuse and listless and uncaring. Some take drugs and alcohol. A few perform brilliantly as long as their strength lasts. As a result, the music is constantly searching for fine new players. When, every five or ten years, it finds one, he is often treated like a messiah, and this tends to strain his invention, turn his head, and subject him to the jealousy of his peers, and even of his elders. That is what happened to Ornette Coleman when he appeared in New York, in the fall of 1959. Still a raggedy Texas country boy, he arrived almost unknown from the West, and, laying his unorthodox, hellbent Charlie Parker style before enshrining hordes at the old Five Spot, he became the toast of the jazz world. (He was also ridiculed by such aging revolutionaries as Charles Mingus and Miles Davis; aging revolutionaries often become more inflexible than those they originally displaced.) Coleman took this adulatory roar to heart. By 1962, he had gone underground, because night-club owners and entrepreneurs and recording executives would not grant him the respect he felt he was owed, and would not pay him what he felt he was worth. And he has rarely come out since. So will success spoil Wynton Marsalis, the dazzling twenty-one-year-old trumpeter from New Orleans? For the past couple of years, Marsalis, a double enfant terrible, who plays jazz and classical trumpet with equal ease, has been bathed in acclaim. When he was seventeen, he was allowed into the Berkshire Music Center, at Tanglewood, a year early and won an award for being the outstanding brass player. A year later, he was wowing them at Juilliard, and CBS signed him to a recording contract as a jazz and classical player. Art Blakey hired him and Herbie Hancock hired him, and last year he was chosen best trumpet player in the *down beat* readers' poll, trouncing Miles Davis by almost five hundred votes. He also made a resounding début at the Kool Jazz Festival in New York. But all this tohubohu seems to have left him unmoved. The voice that comes through in the handful of interviews he has given to *down beat* and Columbia Records is steady, self-critical, and wry.

On classical music: "I studied classical music because so many black musicians were scared of this big monster on the other side of the mountain . . . I wanted to know what it was that scared everybody so bad. I went into it and found out it wasn't anything but some more music . . . I think—I *know*—it's harder to be a good jazz musician at an early age than a classical one. In jazz, to be a good performer means to be an individual, which you don't have to be in classical music."

On his own excellence: "It was funny being [at Tanglewood] because I could always tell how shocked they were that a black kid my age could play *their* music so well. In fact, because I was a kid and they didn't know until things progressed how good I was, I had to sit there on many a night listening to these other guys messing up parts I could have played correctly. But I remember how much I shocked Gunther Schuller . . . when he found out I could play jazz. You see, I knew they couldn't believe that a seventeen-year-old who could play the hell out of classical music also knew a lot about jazz."

On his image: "I do not entertain and I will not entertain. I'm a musician." "When you see me on the bandstand, I'm always going to look sharp. How can you get respect from an audience when you come on the bandstand looking like a bum? You're in the wrong before you play a note."

On his jazz playing: "So far as being a jazz musician, I have a lot to learn. My playing isn't spontaneous enough. I play too many eighth notes. It's not open enough."

On tradition: "The key is . . . to take what is already there and sound like an *extension* of that. . . . Music has a tradition that you have to understand before you can move to the next step."

Marsalis is dapper and of medium build; he has a round face

and wears round wire-framed spectacles. He was born October 18, 1961. His older brother, Branford, is a gifted post-Coltrane saxophonist, and his younger brother, Jason, is a trombonist who has not yet come out. Their father, Ellis Marsalis, is a late-bop pianist and teacher. Wynton Marsalis took up the trumpet when he was twelve and was playing first trumpet in the New Orleans Civic Orchestra by the time he was in high school. Marian McPartland heard him around then. "I heard Wynton five or six years ago when I had a trio at the Hyatt Regency in New Orleans," she said recently. "We did a concert in the ballroom for school kids, and Wynton and Branford brought their band and played. I was flabbergasted. I think they were about fifteen years old, and they were so together it was unbelievable. I give clinics for kids all over the country, and I hear a lot of people with great potential. But Wynton seemed fully grown from the first. His mother says he has always been a little man, that he was never a little boy. He's going from strength to strength. I don't know any kids who have the ambition he has. He has already listened a great deal and absorbed a great deal, and he obviously will continue to. Much of what he hears will be taken in, and what comes out in the next five or so years should be unlike anything we have heard before."

When Marsalis was at Juilliard, he played with the Brooklyn Philharmonia and in the pit band of "Sweeney Todd." His style was well defined three years ago. Unlike most of the new trumpeters of the past twenty-five years, it does not rest in the shade of Dizzy Gillespie. It belongs to the line established by Gillespie's peer Fats Navarro—a line that has been brought down to the present by Clifford Brown, Booker Little, and Woody Shaw. But Marsalis has big ears. By his own word and from the evidence of his playing, he has also listened to Louis Armstrong, Don Cherry, Miles Davis, Clark Terry, Freddie Hubbard, and Rex Stewart. All these trumpeters color his style, which is still inseparable from his formidable technique. Indeed, much of his energy goes into trying to control that technique, into trying to keep it from carrying him out of sight around the next corner. He has an acute sense of dynamics, and moves easily from murmurings to blares. His tone is round. He can play with or without a vibrato. He can growl, trill, half-valve, and use any sort of mute. He has complete possession of all his registers. And how he moves through them! His descending arpeggios are sometimes so crowded they almost flatten into glissandos. He loves yawning intervals, and will play a quick three-note phrase, drop an octave without missing a beat, and repeat the three-note phrase, producing an echo that suggests he is two trumpeters instead of one. He will start a downward run and suddenly break it, sound a single note an octave higher, resume the arpeggio exactly where he left off, break it for another upward octave leap, and finish the run. Despite the great number of notes he plays, he understands the value of silence, the dramatic effect of isolating single notes and meteoric passages with stillness. He also knows the value of surprise. He will cap several easy single notes with silence, then drop in a double-time phrase jammed with strange notes strangely placed. He will rocket in and out of his high register, leaving little stabs of sound behind. He will stroll unexpectedly through his low register, sounding big, dark, blank-faced notes. Marsalis is not yet complete. Technique, rather than melodic logic, still governs his improvising, and the emotional content of his playing remains hidden and skittish. (It is interesting to compare the work of Jimmy Blanton, Charlie Christian, and Clifford Brown when they were Marsalis's age. They had already balanced technique and emotion.) And ballads stump Marsalis. The old songs must be played from inside; the player has to breathe them. But Marsalis, overblowing, remains outside.

"The Sound of Jazz"

The confusion about the soundtrack of "The Sound of Jazz," the celebrated hour-long program broadcast live on CBS television on December 8, 1957, began a minute or so before the program ended, when an announcer said, "Columbia Records has cut a long-playing record of today's program, which will be called 'The Sound of Jazz.' It'll be released early next year." A Columbia recording by that name and bearing the CBS television logotype *was* issued early in 1958, but it was not the soundtrack of the show. It was a recording made on December 4th in Columbia's Thirtieth Street studio as a kind of rehearsal for the television production. It included many of the musicians who did appear on December 8th, and except for one number the materials were the same. Columbia probably made the recording as a precaution: a live jazz television program lasting a full hour (then, as it is now, the basic unit of television time was the minute) and built around thirty-odd (unpredictable) jazz musicians might easily turn into a shambles. It didn't. The soundtrack, which is at last available in its entirety—as "The Real Sound of Jazz," on Pumpkin Records—is superior to the Columbia record in almost every way, sound included.

"The Sound of Jazz" has long been an underground classic, and a lot of cotton wool has accumulated around it. So here, allowing for vagaries of memory, is how the program came to be. In the spring of 1957, Robert Goldman asked me if I would be interested in helping put together a show on jazz for John Houseman's new "Seven Lively Arts" series, scheduled to be broadcast on CBS in the winter of 1957–58. I submitted an outline, and it was accepted. I invited Nat Hentoff to join me as co-advisor, and we began discussing personnel and what should be played. Our wish was to offer the best jazz there was in the simplest and most direct way—no history, no apologetics, no furbelows. But John Crosby, the television columnist of the *Herald Tribune,* had been hired as master of ceremonies for the "Seven Lively Arts," and we feared that he would do just what we wanted to avoid—talk about the music. We suggested listing the musicians and the tunes on tel-ops (now common practice), but Crosby was under contract for the whole series, and that was that. Crosby, it turned out, pretty much agreed with us, and what he did say was to the point. For the brilliant visual side of the show, CBS chose the late Robert Herridge as the producer and Jack Smight as the director. The excitement of the camerawork and of Smight's picture selection—he had five cameramen—has never been equalled on any program of this kind.

Here is the form the program finally took: A big band, built around the nucleus of the old Count Basie band, was the first group to be heard, and it included Roy Eldridge, Doc Cheatham, Joe Newman, Joe Wilder, and Emmett Berry on trumpets; Earle Warren, Ben Webster, Coleman Hawkins, and Gerry Mulligan on reeds; Vic Dickenson, Benny Morton, and Dicky Wells on trombones; and a rhythm section of Basie, Freddie Green, Eddie Jones, and Jo Jones. This utopian band, which Basie seemed immensely pleased to front, played a fast blues, "Open All Night," written and arranged by Nat Pierce, who did all the arranging on the show. Then a smaller band, made up of Red Allen and Rex Stewart on trumpet and cornet, Pee Wee Russell on clarinet, Hawkins, Dickenson, Pierce, Danny Barker on guitar, Milt Hinton on bass, and Jo Jones, did the old Jelly Roll Morton–Louis Armstrong "Wild Man Blues" and Earl Hines' "Rosetta." The group was a distillation of the various historic associations, on recordings, of Allen and Russell, of Allen and Hawkins, and of Stewart and Hawkins, with Dickenson's adaptability holding everything together. The rhythm section was all-purpose and somewhat in the Basie mode. Thelonious Monk, accompanied by Ahmed Abdul-Malik on bass and Osie Johnson on drums, did his "Blue Monk." The big band returned for a slow blues, "I Left My Baby," with Jimmy Rushing on the vocal, and for a fast thirty-two-bar number by Lester Young called "Dickie's Dream." Billie Holiday sang her blues "Fine and Mellow," accompanied by Mal Waldron on piano and by Eldridge, Cheatham, Young, Hawkins, Webster, Mulligan, Dickenson, Barker, Hinton, and Osie Johnson. The Jimmy Giuffre Three, with Giuffre on reeds, Jim Hall on guitar, and Jim Atlas on bass, did Giuffre's "The Train and the River," and the show was closed by a slow blues, in which Giuffre and Pee Wee Russell played a duet, accompanied by Barker, Hinton, and Jo Jones. Crosby introduced each group, and there were prerecorded statements about the blues from Red Allen, Rushing, Billie Holiday, and Guiffre. (I found these intrusive, but Hentoff and Herridge liked them.) The show was held in a big, bare two-story studio at Ninth Avenue and Fifty-sixth Street, and the musicians were told to wear what they wanted. Many wore hats, as jazz musicians are wont to do at recording sessions. Some had on suits and ties, some were in sports shirts and tweed jackets. Monk wore a cap and dark glasses with bamboo side pieces. Billie Holiday arrived with an evening gown she had got specially for the show, and was upset when she found that we wanted her in what she was wearing—a pony tail, a short-sleeved white sweater, and plaid pants. There was cigarette smoke in the air, and there were cables on the floor. A ladder leaned against a wall. Television cameras moved like skaters, sometimes photographing each other. The musicians were allowed to move around: Basie ended up watching Monk, and later Billie Holiday went over and stood beside Basie.

The atmosphere at the Columbia recording session was similar. Many of the musicians had not been together in a long time, and a rare early-December blizzard, which began just before the session and left as much as a foot of snow on the ground, intensified everything. It also caused problems. Our plan had been to reunite the All-American rhythm section of Basie, Freddie Green, Walter Page on bass, and Jo Jones, but Page called and said that he was sick and that, anyway, he couldn't find a cab. (He didn't make the television show, either, and he died two weeks later.) Eddie Jones, Basie's current bassist, replaced him. Thelonious Monk didn't turn up, and that is why Mal Waldron recorded a four-minute piano solo, aptly titled "Nervous." There were various other differences between the recording and the show. Frank Rehak took Benny Morton's place on the recording, because Morton was busy. Harry Carney, a man of infinite graciousness, filled in for Gerry Mulligan, a man of infinite ego, because Mulligan insisted he be paid double scale, and was refused. Doc Cheatham solos on the Columbia session but only plays obbligatos behind Billie Holiday on the television show; he had asked to be excused from all soloing, claiming that it would ruin his lip for his regular gig with a Latin band. Lester Young provides obbligatos behind Jimmy Rushing on "I Left My Baby" on the Columbia record, and he also solos twice. He was particularly ethereal that day, walking on his toes and talking incomprehensibly, and most of the musicians avoided him. But he was intractable on Sunday during the first of the two run-throughs that preceded the television show. He refused to read his parts, and he soloed poorly. He was removed from the big-band reed section and was replaced by Ben Webster, and his only solo is his famous twelve bars on "Fine and Mellow"—famous because this sequence had been used so many times on other television shows and because of Billie Holiday's expression as she listens to her old friend, an expression somewhere between laughter and tears. Billie Holiday came close to not being on the show. A week or so before, word of her difficulties with drugs and the law had reached the upper levels at CBS, and it was suggested that she be replaced by someone wholesome, like Ella Fitzgerald. We refused, and were backed by Herridge, and she stayed.

It is astonishing how good the music is on "The Real Sound of Jazz." Billie Holiday and Red Allen and Jimmy Rushing are in fine voice. The big-band ensembles are generally dazzling. The solos are almost always first-rate. (Giuffre is dull, and Roy Eldridge is overexcited.) Listen to Dickenson's boiling, shouting statement on "Dickie's Dream," wisely taken at a slightly slower tempo than on the Columbia record, and to his easy, rocking solo on "Wild Man Blues." And listen to Rex Stewart, sly and cool, on "Wild Man" (he had recently emerged from a long semi-retirement) and to the way Jo Jones frames its breaks—suspending time, shaping melody, italicizing emotion. Some of the music on the show has not weathered well. Monk, surprisingly, sounds hurried and the Giuffre trio, which was extremely popular at the time, is thin and synthetic. And Pee Wee Russell swallows Giuffre in their duet. CBS never ran the program again, but it was shown at the Museum of Modern Art in the sixties, and there is now a copy at the Museum of Broadcasting.

Fauntleroy
and the Brute

Ben Webster was born in Kansas City, Missouri, on March 27, 1909. He was an only child, and, like many black musicians of his time, was raised by women—his mother, whom he called Mame, and a grandmother or great-aunt, whom he called Mom. Both were schoolteachers, and they created a genteel home, in which Webster, according to the bassist Milt Hinton, invariably "behaved like a Little Lord Fauntleroy." That was the angelic Webster. The other Webster, called the Brute by musicians in later years, hung out on the streets of Kansas City and became a womanizer, an expert pool player, and a dangerous drinker. His old friend Jimmy Rowles has said of Webster, "When Ben was sober, he was the sweetest, gentlest, nicest man in the world. When he was juiced, he was out of his head. Very few people could handle him. He was about four feet across in the shoulders, and he'd start throwing that left hand and he'd break things. I think he was eighty-sixed in every bar in Los Angeles. And he would not allow anyone to take the Lord's name in vain. He once threw Don Byas the length of a White Rose bar in New York because Byas was at a table saying Lord this and God that. Ben lived with his mother and grandmother in Los Angeles in the fifties, and when I'd pick him up for some golf or a record date his grandmother would say, 'Now, Benjamin, you fix up that back yard before you go, please, and, Jimmy, you sit down on that davenport and wait until he's finished.' Ben became a revered figure in Europe, but he was always lonesome there. He'd call on the phone from Copenhagen, where he lived, and play stride piano and talk, and he'd stay on for a couple of hours."

Webster played piano and violin before the tenor saxophone, and the piano was the unrequited love of his life. His mother encouraged him, and he learned from the blues pianist Pete Johnson, who lived across the street. In the late twenties,

Webster worked as a pianist in small territory bands; then Budd Johnson persuaded him to take up the saxophone, and gave him his first lessons. He spent three months in the Young family band, and had more lessons from Lester Young's father. (He also helped pull Lester out of the Rio Grande, and many years later he pulled someone out of the Hudson.) He joined Eugene Coy's Black Aces as a saxophonist, and during the thirties he passed through the big bands of Blanche Calloway, Bennie Moten, Andy Kirk, Fletcher Henderson, Benny Carter, Willie Bryant, Duke Ellington, Cab Calloway, and Teddy Wilson. Early in 1940, he rejoined Ellington, and he stayed three triumphant years. (He married in 1942, but it didn't stick.) Except for a brief return visit with Ellington in 1948, Webster scuffled the rest of his life. He played with countless pickup groups. (He turned up at the Metropole in 1964 with Buck Clayton, Max Kaminsky, Pee Wee Russell, J. C. Higginbotham, and Bud Freeman.) He made occasional records with Jimmy Rowles and Harry Edison. He appeared with Coleman Hawkins and Lester Young on the "Sound of Jazz" and was the strongest of the three. He drank more and more, and grew huge. He settled in Europe in 1964, and he died there in 1973.

Two of Webster's friends talk about his last years. The first is Milt Hinton: "By the early sixties, Ben's mother and grandmother were dead, and he had moved back East and was just floating around hotels in New York, so I had him come out and stay at my house in Queens. I'd buy a case of beer, and we'd go down in my basement and play, just the two of us. Or else, if I was at work, he'd just sit and drink beer and listen to tapes. At the time, Barry Galbraith, Hank Jones, and Osie Johnson and I were known as 'the New York rhythm section,' and we'd make as many as three recording sessions a day, at forty-one dollars and twenty-five cents per—which wasn't bad, because a hundred dollars went a long way then. Ben would get calls to make some of these sessions, but he'd ask for triple scale, and the producers always turned him down. But he had been with Duke Ellington, you see—he was a star, and that was it. Finally, my wife, Mona, told Ben that he had a God-given talent and it was a shame he wasn't using it. That surprised him, I think, and when he got an offer to go and play in Europe he took it, and, of course, he never came back. I saw him a few times over there, but his behavior had deteriorated, and after a while I avoided him."

The other friend is the trumpeter Doc Cheatham: "There was something Ben always wanted, but I never figured out what it was. It kept him unhappy all the time. He could be so nice on some people and so rough on others. I don't think any of that affected his playing, except I used to hear a sense of worry in his ballads. The last time I saw him was in England in 1967. He came to see me, and he had these great big bottles of stout, one in each pocket. All that drinking and something always on his mind. I don't think Ben wanted to live. He wanted to destroy himself, and he did."

Webster had two different styles. The first—a thin, angry-sounding extension of Coleman Hawkins—lasted from the early thirties until he joined Duke Ellington. His second style began to emerge during his first year with the band, and had become fully grown by the time he left. It grew in Johnny Hodges' hothouse—an influence that Webster was quick to acknowledge. (He once told a Danish radio interviewer, "That's what I tried to do—play Johnny on tenor.") And it must also have been shaped by Harry Carney's sound. Webster's tone grew bigger and bigger, he became a master of dynamics, and he developed an attack that took something from the heavily ornamented melodies of Coleman Hawkins and from Hodges' monosyllabic blues preaching. He became a supreme blues player and a supreme ballad player. He would start a medium-slow blues solo very softly with a weaving five-note phrase, pause, play a high, barely audible blue note, and duck back to his opening phrase, still as soft as first sunlight. He would harden his tone slightly at the start of his next chorus, issue an annunciatory phrase, repeat it, insert a defiant tremolo, and end the chorus with a dizzying, three-steps-at-a-time descending figure. He would increase his volume even more in his final chorus, and sometimes he would revert to his old style. His tone would grow hard, he would growl and crowd his notes, he would shake his phrases as if he had them clamped in his teeth. These blues solos were jazz improvisation as autobiography. Webster's ballads were very different. They were romantic and yearning. They were majestic but never pompous, passionate but never sentimental. A Webster ballad came in three parts. First, a heavy, robed statement of the melody, in which he moved along behind the beat, shifting a note here, adding a note there—a kind of combing and patting into place of the composer's song. Then an intense one-chorus improvisation, which converted the melody into a grand new Webster song. And then a half-chorus restatement of the original. As the years went by, Webster's ballads became more and more fervent, and in the late fifties and early sixties he would close certain phrase endings by allowing his vibrato to melt into pure undulating breath—dramatically offering, before the breath expired, the ghost of his sound. Webster's appearance matched his playing. He was of medium height, and had wide wooden-soldier shoulders and a barrel chest. He had an eagle nose and prominent eyes and a strong chin, which he raised slightly when he played. His saxophone was kept shieldlike in front of him, and he rarely moved. His badge was a small fedora, worn on the back of his head, its brim up. Seen in silhouette, it looked like a halo.

1984

Danger Dancing
All Around _____

Five years ago, the writer and trombonist James Lincoln Collier published *The Making of Jazz*, a cool, sturdy, nicely opinionated history of the music. Now, deepening his gaze, he has attempted a biography of Louis Armstrong. Called *Louis Armstrong: An American Genius* (Oxford), it is, despite its length—three hundred and fifty-one large, closely printed pages—and its authoritative voice, not nearly as conclusive or fresh or *biographical* as we might have wished.

Collier makes it clear that Armstrong, such a seemingly simple presence, was a complex group of people. One was the tough, primitive, poor, uneducated New Orleans black man (born not on July 4, 1900, apparently, but on an undetermined day a couple of years earlier) who could not, in Collier's words, "aspire to a meaningful education, a career or profession, even a white-collar job. He was condemned from birth to live out his life as a menial laborer, always poor, never sure that a job would last beyond the day, or that he would not be cheated of his wages, but certain that in old age he would be dependent upon the charity of friends and family." Armstrong nonetheless soon learned the value of a "white captain." Here, according to Collier, is what he told Larry L. King in 1967 in *Harper's:*

If you didn't have a white captain to back you in the old days—to put his hand on your shoulder—you was just a damn sad nigger. If a Negro had the proper white man to-

*reach the law and say, "What the hell you mean locking up
MY nigger!" then—quite naturally—the law would walk him
free. Get in that jail without your white boss, and yonder
comes the chain gang! Oh, danger was dancing all around
you back then.*

Armstrong's white captains were his managers: Tommy Rockwell, Johnny Collins, and Joe Glaser—all rough-and-ready men,
skilled in varying degrees in navigating the shoals and shadows
of show business. Another Armstrong was the gleaming show-
biz personality his captains eventually turned him into. This
Armstrong grew up in the minstrel-vaudeville tradition that
jazz had been a part of in its early days and that is still visible in
the posturings of such older musicians as Lionel Hampton and
Dorothy Donegan. This Armstrong—his marble eyes popping,
his coal voice rumbling, his teeth flashing—became addicted to
applause. Even in his last years, when he could sing but no
longer play, he could not resist performing. He also became,
because of his State Department tours and such enormously
popular vocal recordings as "Mack the Knife" and "Hello,
Dolly," a world figure—a nodding, happy-go-lucky universal
clown, whose onstage antics charmed millions and upset civil-
rights leaders. The most important and least known Armstrong
was the revolutionary trumpet player who, in the late twenties
and early thirties, changed the course of American music. He
did this largely through such recordings as "Knockin' a Jug" (the
wonderful low-register dancing in his first chorus), "Tight Like
This," "West End Blues" (the Bach-like introductory cadenza),
"Weather Bird," "Sweethearts on Parade" (the rhythmic dis-
placements in the opening muted solo), "Basin Street Blues"
(1933 version), "I Gotta Right to Sing the Blues" (the sorrowing,
long-held opening note of his solo, and the half-time legato
turnings), "I've Got the World on a String," "Hustlin' and
Bustlin' for Baby" (the dark bridge in his solo), "That's My
Home," and "Hobo, You Can't Ride This Train" (the rhythmic
momentum in his vocal and in his jiving behind the soloists).
These recordings are full of a majesty and melancholy that were

new to American music. Not only that—Armstrong's solos were improvised: black people, adept at spiritual and moral improvising, were stunned and grateful; white people couldn't believe that a black man could make such beautiful music. Its influence, Collier rightly points out, was incalculable. Not only did a couple of generations of jazz musicians feast on it but it has filtered down through the Beatles and the Stones and Linda Ronstadt. Collier puts a lot of musicological muscle into parsing Armstrong's playing and singing, and he is most valuable on the years from 1923 to 1928 and from 1945 to Armstrong's death, in 1971. But he stints on the thirty-three sides Armstrong made between 1932 and 1933 for RCA Victor, and he does not pay enough attention to the 1935–45 Deccas. Of the Victor trove, he completely ignores "I've Got the World on a String," "That's My Home," and "Basin Street Blues." Armstrong's second solo on "Basin Street," played an octave higher than usual and full of agitated swoops and blue notes, is celestial grandstanding.

Collier occasionally misleads us. He says that Armstrong was Joe Oliver's only protégé. (Red Allen became Oliver's protégé in New York in 1927, and even lived with Oliver and his sister.) He says that Oliver's Creole Jazz Band, of which Armstrong was a member from 1922 to 1924, was largely an ensemble band. (Musicians who heard the band in person speak of the long solos Oliver and the other musicians took. When the band recorded, however, it became an ensemble group because, in the three minutes allotted each number, collective playing was less likely to go awry than soloing.) He says that Sidney Catlett worked in Armstrong's big band for nearly a decade. (Catlett helped propel that ragtag band for less than four years.) He says the reason Armstrong never used his old friend Zutty Singleton for any of his working groups after 1930 was that he regarded him as a potential competitor. (Singleton stopped developing as a drummer around 1930, and in his later years often had unsteady time. Armstrong simply outgrew Singleton, and turned to the great Catlett, who, of course, had come out of Singleton.) Collier's haste with facts spills over into his writing:

There come at moments in history people who gather into themselves threads around them and weave from them a new pattern.

Among other things, [Joe] Smith had the good fortune to become tragically ill when he was in his prime.

By 1949, through a variety of happenstances, many serendipitous, others the result of shrewd management, Louis Armstrong had become a genuine star.

When he slows down, things improve:

But, as we always discover in attempting to analyze Armstrong's musical qualities, there was something beyond the analyzable—an openness, a directness, that allowed listeners to look through the flesh to the light inside. You could warm your hands in front of Louis Armstrong.

Collier dutifully logs Armstrong's four marriages, and he does a lot of psychoanalytic waltzing. He speculates that Armstrong was always insecure because of his severe childhood deprivations; that these deprivations made him a famous soft touch; that they made him prefer throughout his life the company of blue-collar people; that he was attracted to his rough managers because he had grown up fatherless. These conclusions explain some of Armstrong's behavior, but they don't bring us any closer to him than we were at the start of the book. It would have helped if Collier had used more reminiscences by musicians who knew Armstrong well—musicians like Bobby Hackett and Ruby Braff, who have set down in interviews descriptions of Armstrong that make him breathe.

For whatever reason, none of Armstrong's famous and frequent letters are in the book. He picked them out with one finger on a portable typewriter, often signing them "Red beans and ricely yours."

Michel Petrucciani
and Paul Whiteman

Jazz was once a spare, monosyllabic music. Improvisers thought in terms of individual notes, of bar lines, and of the twelve-bar (blues) or thirty-two-bar (standard) chorus. They grew up within the three-minute limitations of the ten-inch 78-r.p.m. recording, and they appreciated being given an eight- or sixteen- or twenty-four-bar solo. (Sometimes a slow number lasted only two choruses.) Such compression often resulted in beauty and high emotion. King Oliver and his protégé Louis Armstrong were wasteless players (Armstrong passed through a rococo period in his late twenties and early thirties), and so was Bix Beiderbecke, who hung his notes in the air like moons. They were joined in the thirties by Red Allen and Benny Carter and J. C. Higginbotham, by Lester Young and Ben Webster and Sidney Catlett and Jimmy Blanton. Some improvisers developed telegraphic styles—what they didn't play meant as much as what they did play. These included Count Basie, Joe Thomas, Emmett Berry, Bobby Hackett, Johnny Hodges, and Pete Brown. Then Art Tatum took hold. His travelling arpeggios, harmonic towers, virtuoso technique, and tireless desire to dazzle suggested that jazz could be a baroque music. Charlie Parker studied Tatum, Dizzy Gillespie studied Parker, Bud Powell studied all three, and by the time their countless students come forward jazz had become baroque. Improvisers filled their solos with runs and with sixteenth and thirty-second notes. New multi-noted chords bloomed like orchids. Soloists, encouraged by the twenty-five minutes to a side of the new L.P. recording, became garrulous. Few ever knew what they wanted to say, because they had so much time to decide. By the sixties, soloists were going on for forty-five minutes, for an hour, for an hour and a quarter. Listening to John Coltrane and Cecil Taylor became an unselfish act: you gave up an hour of your life each time one of them soloed. During recent years, this floridity has struck pianists particularly hard. In the manner of the great nine-teenth-century rhapsodists, they envision their pianos as the-atres. Consider their forefather, Dave Brubeck, carrying his immense Wagnerian solos from campus to campus in the fifties. Also Oscar Peterson, Chick Corea, Herbie Hancock, McCoy Tyner, Roger Kellaway, and Keith Jarrett. At first, the tiny, twenty-one-year-old French pianist Michel Petrucciani seemed the newest member of this group. He likes to show off his technique. He likes to rhapsodize and to wander through ad-lib meadows. He likes the loud pedal. But much of this is adoles-cent fat, for the more one hears Petrucciani the clearer it becomes that the improvisational horses he is driven by are tough and original.

He was born in Orange, and grew up in Montélimar, not far from Avignon. His father is Sicilian and his mother French, and he has two brothers. All the men are musicians. He settled in Big Sur a couple of years ago, and did his American apprenticeship with the tenor saxophonist Charles Lloyd. Petrucciani first appeared in New York at the Kool Jazz Festival in 1983, and he made his New York night-club début recently at the Village Vanguard. The girdling presence of a bassist (the Swede Palle Danielsson) and a drummer (Eliot Zigmund) helped bring his passionate style into focus. He has listened widely. He says that Bill Evans was "a god on earth," and he admires Debussy, Ravel, Bach, and Bartók—the idols of most big-eared jazz musicians. Evans is at the heart of his work, and there are passing allusions to Lennie Tristano, Erroll Garner, Thelonius Monk, Tatum, and Tyner. He has a strong touch. His hands are not large (he suffers from a bone ailment, and is just three feet tall), but they are steel. Petrucciani is a complete improviser, in the manner of Lester Young and Charlie Parker. He often plays his own com-positions, and he rarely states their melodies. This can be confusing, since American listeners love the pleasant game of ferreting out an improviser's sources. Even when he does a standard, he disguises it, keeping his melodic flags in the far distance. Like most young improvisers, he has a great deal to say, and sometimes he tries to say it all at once. Chords are piled on chords, arpeggios surge and vanish and surge again, complex single-note figures collide in the middle registers. He is an avid new reader telling you the entire plot of his first Dickens. But the next number will be open and uncrowded and breathing. He will play well-spaced single notes, placing them carefully around the beat and shaping them into beautiful new melodies. He will construct a ladder of octave chords, cap it with a two-handed tremolo, go into a short, double-time run, and return to his single notes, three or four of which he will repeat over and over, changing them slightly each time. He may use an ascending staccato pattern, his hand rocking rapidly up the keyboard, or he may rumble around in the cellar the way Eddie Costa used to. The piano has no vibrato, its timbres are limited, blue notes can be only hinted at, there is no way to play a Johnny Hodges dying glissando. But the sheer vivacity of Petrucciani's attack carries him through these obstacles, as does his use of certain emotion-producing devices: dynamics, placement of notes behind the beat on fast tempos or ahead of the beat on slow ones, large intervals, tremolos, and sudden forays into the highest register.

Paul Whiteman gave his first and most famous "Experiment in Modern Music" concert at Aeolian Hall on February 12, 1924. This past February, sixty years to the day, the conductor Maurice Peress and a twenty-one-piece orchestra offered a polished and imaginative re-creation of much of the original. (Praise should go to the percussionist Herbert Harris, who managed to find a way between swinging too hard and sounding stuffy; to the pianist Dick Hyman; and to Peress himself.) Whiteman gave the concert to enhance the reputation of his already celebrated orchestra, then ensconced at the Palais Royal, a night club at Broadway and Forty-eighth Street. He wanted the orchestra to be thought of not as a dance band but as the classiest, most accomplished musical ensemble in the world. Which is why at Aeolian Hall it played everything from a tongue-in-cheek Original Dixieland Jazz Band number to Irving Berlin and Zez Confrey to Victor Herbert and Edward Elgar, and why Whiteman invited Galli-Curci, Mary Garden, Leopold Godowsky, Fritz Kreisler, Rachmaninoff, and every New York journalist from Gilbert Seldes to Heywood Broun. But the actual reasons Whiteman offered for holding the concert are mystifying. His manager Hugh C. Ernst wrote in the original program, reproduced for the Peress concert:

The experiment is to be purely educational. Mr. Whiteman intends to point out, with the assistance of his orchestra and associates, the tremendous strides which have been made in popular music from the day of the discordant Jazz, which sprang into existence about ten years ago from nowhere in particular, to the really melodious music of today, which— for no good reason—is still called Jazz.

Whiteman had probably heard little jazz beyond the stylized, imitative galloping of the Original Dixieland Jazz Band. Few jazz recordings had been made, and the best of them—by Clarence Williams, Kid Ory, the Creole Jazz Band, and James P. Johnson—were not well known. And almost no jazz was available in the flesh in New York—Fletcher Henderson, with Louis Armstrong in his trumpet section, would not arrive at the Roseland Ballroom on Broadway until the fall of 1924. (Whiteman, his fadometer always working, soon learned about the music. Three years later, his orchestra was filled with jazz musicians.) We remember the Aeolian Hall concert because it included the première of George Gershwin's "Rhapsody in Blue," a piece commissioned by Whiteman, who liked to hand out such largesse. (Later on, he favored Aaron Copland, Duke Ellington, and David Diamond.) Peress dug up the original score, arranged for only a dozen or so instruments, and the piece—unwittingly such a stunning evocation of New York— sounded bony and exciting and newborn.

Like a Lilt

It has been almost fifty years since Count Basie, who died this spring, at the age of seventy-nine, brought his unknown band east from Kansas City and changed the course of jazz. (Basie was not by nature an innovator; most of the inventions embodied by the Kansas City band were accidental or necessary.) Although Basie's musical changes were not always imitable, they were freely offered. One was his rhythm section, which included him on piano, Freddie Green on guitar, Walter Page on bass, and Jo Jones on drums. Jazz rhythm sections had long been insistent, metallic, and inflexible; Basie's was double-jointed and oblique. It swung with one hand behind its back. Page played an easy four-four beat (and the right notes), Green clocked the chords and made butterfly sounds in the background, Jones connected Page and Green with his swimming high-hat, and Basie added metaphor, impetus, humor, brevity, and direction. No one has explained how the Basie rhythm section evolved, and probably no one will. Even Jo Jones, a man of many words, was stumped when he talked about it with the critic Stanley Dance: "It became a wedding. Instead of one and three [the beats sounded] and two and four, it became one, two, three, four, and then it was like a lilt." Another Basie gift was Lester Young. He had a light tone, a legato, horizontal attack, and a way of improvising that extracted and distilled whatever poetic content the original song had—and if it had none he supplied it. Young was unearthly. He floated just above the Basie band, never touching it yet never losing touch with it. His playing primed the young Charlie Parker and brought into being a teeming school of alto and tenor saxophonists, many of whom are still at large. Basie's last gift was his piano playing, which, in a sense, he never offered at all. For fifty years, he pooh-poohed it, all the while slowly emptying it of standard pianistic content, as if he hoped to make it vanish altogether. By the seventies, a Basie solo chorus might consist of only ten notes. But his playing— epigrammatic, swinging, flawless, witty—became cherished and famous. More often than he imagined, while the band played, the soloists soloed, and the singers sang his listeners waited for his next two or three choruses of blues, his next four-bar introduction, his next eight-bar bridge, and they were rarely disappointed. Despite his outward cool, Basie had unmistakable inner fires. He always got off in his solos a legato phrase or a cluster of blue notes that quickened the heart. And he was a supreme accompanist, with an alert, highly skilled harmonic sense. He'd place several perfect single notes behind a trumpet soloist, or a stairway of descending, marching chords under an ensemble passage, and his band flew.

The first part of Basie's long, commanding career ended in the early forties, when the Kansas City band began to harden, presaging the monolithic Basie machines of the fifties, sixties, and seventies. (What a bench that first band had—Buck Clayton, Harry Edison, Dicky Wells, Benny Morton, Vic Dickenson, Lester Young, Herschel Evans, Buddy Tate, Don Byas, Jack Washington, and the All-American Rhythm Section). By 1950, the days of the big dance bands were over, and Basie broke up his band. He put together a leaping small group that included Clark Terry, Buddy De Franco, Wardell Grey, Charlie Rouse, Serge Chaloff, Gus Johnson, and Buddy Rich. But no leader of a big band, accustomed to being wrapped in sound, can sit still long in a small band. It's like going back to the Matterhorn after Everest. In 1951, Basie assembled a big show band, a concert band. He hired the best arrangers and good but rarely distinguished soloists (arrangers had been necessary evils in the Kansas City band), and within a year or so he had a Jaguar of a band that could roar, whisper, and turn on a dime. The personnel changed slowly during the next thirty years (Basie always paid well), but the band never changed. When it did play for dancing, particularly in a confined space, it rippled and glistened with reserve power.

Basie was born an only child in Red Bank, New Jersey. He was intensely private, and parried all personal questions. But he was what he seemed to be—a shy, funny, monosyllabic man who liked to eat, laugh, and lead a big, swinging band. Short and well padded, he sat at the keyboard slightly ajar, directing the band with a succession of nods, pointed fingers, smiles, and stares. Once, when he was asked where his celebrated pianistic style came from, he said, in his deep, easy voice, "Honest truth, I don't know. If my playing is different, I didn't try for it or anything like that. I stumbled on it. I do know that in the earlier years I always loved Fats Waller's playing, and that Fats and the other guys had such fast right hands there was no use for me to try and compete with them. Another thing that helped was my rhythm section with Jo Jones and Walter Page and Freddie Green. They gave me so much freedom. I could run in between what Page and Freddie were doing. I didn't think a lot of execution on my part meant anything with them there. It would have just cluttered it up." So, no hyperbole, no sham, no put-on—just as in his music, which was always honest, even when it began, in later years, to resemble limousines and skyscrapers.

Morton Monologue

Jelly Roll Morton (1890?–1941) never quite got a handle on his life. Born in New Orleans, he was by trade a pianist, a singer, a composer, an arranger, and a bandleader, but he spent many of his first thirty-five years as a pool shark, a pimp, a minstrel, a promoter, and a nomad. When he did turn to music full time, in the mid-twenties in Chicago, it was too late. The sixteen classic small-band sides he recorded for Victor celebrated an ensemble jazz that had been in its prime ten years before. And when he moved to New York, in the late twenties, the big swing bands were at the ready, and jazz had become a music of soloists. The young New York musicians who hung out at the Rhythm Club, at 132nd Street, baited Morton, calling him corny and out of date. Like many gifted people, Morton was restless and inse-cure, and he hid behind a big mouth. He countered by claiming that everything New York musicians were doing he'd done first, that he was the greatest jazz pianist in the world. But in 1930 his Victor recording contract ran out. Morton, a practiced scuffler, tried the cosmetics business and played when he could. In the mid-thirties, he took a band on the road, coming to rest in Washington, D.C., at a seedy second-floor night club on U Street called the Jungle Inn. A record collector named Kenneth Hulsizer visited the Jungle Inn often in 1936, and he reported in the English magazine *Jazz Music* that neither Morton's playing nor his mouth had weakened. Hulsizer said he had "never heard Morton say a good word for another piano player." Morton put down Fats Waller ("All that singing and hollerin' he does. I originated that. . . . He just copied me"), Duke Ellington ("He ain't no piano player. . . . He's got [Barney] Bigard, a good New Orleans boy, sitting right beside him all the time, telling him what to do. Take Bigard away and Ellington ain't nowhere"), and Earl Hines ("He was flashy. Flashy but not solid. He tried to play more piano than he knew how"). Morton's boasting was part hyperbole, part conviction. It also had truth in it: Morton did record the first comic jazz vocal, and Bigard did help shape the Ellington band. Morton seemed more overbearing than he was, because he never stopped talking. Using this loquacity as a framework, Samuel Charters, a poet, novelist, translator, and jazz and blues historian, has written a funny and moving novella, *Jelly Roll Morton's Last Night at the Jungle Inn* (Marion Boyars). In it Morton sits down with a fan like Hulsizer after his last night of work at the Washington club (by the time he went back to New York, in 1938, Morton, out of fashion a decade, had begun to attract a coterie) and delivers an uninterrupted monologue on his life and work. It is a free improvisation on the musical autobiography Morton tape-recorded for the folklorist Alan Lomax at the Library of Congress in the spring of 1938. (Parts of this trove of Americana have been available from time to time on commercial recordings, and parts are transcribed in Lomax's biography of Morton, *Mister Jelly Roll*.) Charters has soaked himself in the Library of Congress material, and his Morton seems very close to the Master himself. Here are the humor, the bombast, and the intelligence. And here, just beneath the skin of the book, are the weariness and disappointment and bewilderment. The tone of Morton's voice is right, and so are his languorous speech rhythms. (He stammered when agitated, though.) The book begins:

I certainly want to thank you for coming around to the club here to listen to my music. An artist always appreciates it when folks come around and it's very, very nice when they want to sit down like this and talk and have a little drink. This is very lovely whiskey and I certainly appreciate you leaving the bottle on the table here. Of course there have been a lot of parties, people coming to hear me play and bringing their friends and booking agents and managers and so forth and so on. It always is that way when you have something to offer the people and I always have had something to offer which they couldn't get from nobody else. If it's jazz music you're thinking about, when you come to see Jelly Roll Morton you don't need to go no further because I'm the one that invented it. I am the one that started it all. Of course you know that. When you come here the first time and we sat talking I told you all about that and I know you were listening because you got a pair of ears and you don't use them just to keep your hat off the end of your nose.

Compare these passages from Charters' novel and Lomax's biography. First, Charters:

Of course the music was right there, in us. Negroes had been making up music for so long we had everything there inside us. We just didn't know how to get it out, and it never was any kind of music that you could write down all of it on paper. You could get some of it, and I myself was considered one of the best when it came to getting down the true sound of jazz on paper, but if you took a blues or one of those type of number there was no way you could put it down in notes.

And Morton speaking to Lomax:

*When you have your plenty rhythm with your plenty swing,
it becomes beautiful. To start with, you can't make crescendos and diminuendos when one is playing triple forte.
You got to be able to come down in order to go up. If a glass
of water is full, you can't fill it any more; but if you have a
half a glass, you have the opportunity to put more water in it.
Jazz music is based on the same principles.*

The novel drifts from episode to episode. Morton tells us of a
dive outside Pensacola named Boodie's Place and of its huge
bouncer, Skinny Walter; of country honky-tonks divided down
the middle, with whites on one side and blacks on the other; of
the bloody Robert Charles riots in New Orleans in 1900, set off
when a black man shot two white policemen; of New Orleans
whorehouses, where he played as a young man; of a love affair in
Tijuana with a beautiful girl named Rose; of his meteoric
passage through New York before the First World War; of his
time in Chicago and his hilarious affair with his landlady, a
country woman named Mildred; and, briefly, of his sad days in
New York in the thirties.

Several of the best comic passages have to do with racial
matters. In one, Morton explains that many blacks were convinced that the white man had brought on the Depression just to
put the black man, who was on the rise, back down again. Here
is another: "When you got onto the train you'd meet up with
your old friend Jim Crow again and he'd say to you, no, you don't
want to sit down in the car here that's nice and clean and has a
washroom at the end of it. I have a special car just for you. Now
it's not so clean, maybe, and some of the people in it are kind of
rough, but that's where you and me are going to sit. Now you
could say, no Mister Crow, I don't like the looks of this place,
but he'd just shake his head and take you by the arm and you'd
go sit down where Jim Crow put you." And here is Morton
attempting to finagle his way into Mildred's room in the middle
of the night:

*So I said in a low voice, you don't know what kind of money
a guy like me makes on a job when there's plenty people lis-*

*tening and giving you tips for their request numbers. Of
course she got very interested when I said money, but she
came back at me, what you talking about, what kind of
money. It's just one kind of money that I ever heard of. What
is this special kind that you got?*

*That kind of stumped me on account of I had just came in
from the street, but I said back at her after a minute had
gone by, sweetheart, I got dollar bills here that go so high up
in their numbers that they don't just print the President's
head on it. They got his whole body standing there in a new
suit of clothes.*

Morton scuffled when he got back to New York; then it
looked as if his fortunes had turned. He recorded over thirty
numbers—his first of consequence in nine years. He appeared at
Nick's, in Greenwich Village, with an all-star band, he was
offered a job on Fifty-second Street, he was on the radio. But,
attracted by rumors that his late godmother may have had some
diamonds, he hooked together his two big old cars and drove to
California, where he died six months later. This time, he was
too early. The New Orleans revival was under way, and by the
mid-forties such compatriots as Bunk Johnson and Kid Ory and
Zutty Singleton were becoming famous. Morton, working his
mouth, would probably have been the most famous of all.

The Blue Notes

Alfred Lion and Francis Wolff, the visionary German immi-
grants and ardent jazz-record collectors who founded Blue Note
Records in New York in 1939, created a classic catalogue of
recordings during the first five or so years of the company's
existence. The two men worked exclusively and unfashionably
with black musicians, and they mixed them up in unique and

joyous ways. They put the New Orleans clarinettist Edmond Hall with the Chicago boogie-woogie pianist Meade Lux Lewis (on celeste) and added the fleet young avant-garde Oklahoma City guitarist Charlie Christian (on acoustic guitar) and the bassist Israel Crosby. The four numbers they made are airy and spacious and delicate. Lion and Wolff combined the trumpeter Frankie Newton with the trombonist J. C. Higginbotham, and on one date they added Sidney Bechet. The rhythm sections included either Lewis or his Chicago peer Albert Ammons, the bassist Johnny Williams, and Sidney Catlett. Lion and Wolff put Bechet with Lewis, the guitarist Teddy Bunn, Williams, and Catlett, and Bechet made a surpassing four-minute "Summertime," which became something of a best-seller. They let Ammons and Lewis loose on twelve-inch 78-r.p.m.s for the first time, giving them the room to find their imaginative limits. They even allowed Lewis to record a slow blues, "The Blues," which lasted twenty-five minutes and filled five 78-r.p.m. sides. (They also let him do four twelve-inch sides on harpsichord. It was not a fortunate meeting: both Lewis and the instrument sounded put upon and helpless.) Blue Note's last great early outpouring took place between 1943 and 1945 and included the likes of Sidney De Paris, Hall, Vic Dickenson, Benny Morton, Harry Carney, James P. Johnson, and Catlett.

Some of these recordings were reissued thirty years ago on ten-inch L.P.s. After Blue Note was sold to Liberty Records, in 1965, some were released chaotically on twelve-inch L.P.s. All have long been out of print, and it has seemed in recent years as if Lion and Wolff's early records might vanish. But a record producer and jazz writer named Michael Cuscuna and a former recording executive named Charlie Lourie have started Mosaic Records, and they intend to reissue most of the early Blue Note recordings (as well as material from other labels) by leasing them from whoever owns the labels, packaging them in limited editions, and selling them by mail. Their first reissue of the early Blue Notes collects all the solo work the boogie-woogie pianists Meade Lux Lewis and Albert Ammons did for the label between 1939 and 1944. Called "The Complete Blue Note Recordings of Albert Ammons and Meade Lux Lewis," the set contains thirty-four sides, only twelve of which have been reissued before and eight of which have never come out at all.

Boogie-woogie is blues piano music. The left hand plays a variety of basses—two- and three-note four-four basses, complex four-note eight-to-the-bar basses, octave "walking" basses, and basses that are a mixture. Most are ostinato, but some are interrupted by odd climbing or descending single-note figures. The main function of the left hand is to provide an insistent rhythmic impetus that sets off the right hand. The right hand uses a lot of dotted eighth or sixteenth notes, heavy, often hammering chords, riffs, floating offbeat chords (sometimes placed just behind the offbeat), tremolos, and single notes spaced out four or five to a chorus. The result is a sort of counterpoint, in which there is a lot of dissonance—and a lot of consonant poetry. At its best, boogie-woogie was a powerful, primitive blues music—a strange outpouring of the black South and Southwest around the time of the First World War. The oddest thing about this music was that it became a fad in this country between 1938 and the early forties. But the music was too limited, too ingrown to withstand such exposure, and the craze almost destroyed it. The craze also destroyed its chief practitioners, all of them worn musically threadbare long before they died.

By the time they made their first Blue Note recordings, Ammons and Lewis, nurtured by Pinetop Smith and Jimmy Yancey, were quite different from one another. (In 1928, Smith, Ammons, and Lewis lived in the same rooming house in Chicago.) Ammons was a loose, swinging pianist. His left hand rocked ("Boogie Woogie Blues"), and his right hand was a constantly revolving array of tremolos, glinting upper-register figures, and brief single-note melodic lines. "Suitcase Blues" (after Hersal Thomas's recording) and "Bass Goin' Crazy" are jumping. They are full of billows and wind. Lewis was probably the better pianist, but he had a hard, narrow quality. (None of the boogie-woogie pianists were highly accomplished; their techniques generally allowed them to play what was in their heads, and missed notes and uneven chorus lengths were ignored in the hustle.) Ammons worked in oils; Lewis did etchings. Lewis's onomatopoeic train pieces ("Honky Tonk Train Blues," "Chicago Flyer," "Six Wheel Chaser," "Bass on Top") are thundering wonders, but they have a mechanical quality— they *are* machines. This quality comes through in the celebrated twenty-five-minute "The Blues." Done in a medium-slow tempo, it is a meditation on the blues spelled out in offbeat chords, low-register single notes, and occasional tremolos, accompanied by a gentle four-four single-note left hand. It is absorbing to compare Lewis's long blues with any of the slow blues that Art Hodes has been setting down in recent years. Lewis's work does not have the "down" feeling, the blue intensity, the deep melancholy of Hodes, who grew up in the same place and time as Lewis and Ammons and is probably—though he is rarely given his due—the greatest of blues pianists. (Lion and Wolff recorded Hodes in the mid-forties.)

Mosaic Records' second and third batch of reissues of the early Blue Notes is made up of "The Complete Recordings of the Port of Harlem Jazzmen" and "The Complete Blue Note Forties Recordings of Ike Quebec and John Hardee." The first album has just one L.P. and consists of ten numbers—five set down on April 7, 1939, by Frankie Newton, J. C. Higginbotham, Albert Ammons, Teddy Bunn, Johnny Williams, and Sidney Catlett, and five set down two months later by the same group plus Sidney Bechet and with Meade Lux Lewis replacing Ammons. The Quebec and Hardee album, on four L.P.s, has forty-nine tracks, fourteen of them previously unreleased. They were done with eight different small groups between 1944 and 1946, and among those on hand are Tiny Grimes, Catlett, John Simmons, Marlowe Morris, the late Trummy Young, Milt Hinton, Oscar Pettiford, Buck Clayton, Keg Johnson, John Collins, and J. C. Heard.

An extraordinary number of good jazz recordings were made in 1939. These include Count Basie's "Dickie's Dreams," Duke Ellington's "Tootin' Through the Roof," the Benny Goodman Sextet's "Soft Winds," Lionel Hampton's "Haven't Named It Yet," Erskine Hawkins' "Tuxedo Junction," John Kirby's

"Royal Garden Blues," Jack Jenney's "Star Dust," Woody Herman's "Woodchopper's Ball," Andy Kirk's "Big Jim Blues," Glenn Miller's "In the Mood," Jelly Roll Morton's "Mamie's Blues," Jimmie Lunceford's "Uptown Blues," Muggsy Spanier's "Relaxin' at the Touro," Coleman Hawkins' "Body and Soul," Billie Holiday's "Fine and Mellow," and Rex Stewart's "Solid Old Man." But none of these dim the Port of Harlem recordings. Made at the height of the big bands, which depended largely on monochromatic ensembles interrupted by brief solos, the Port of Harlem recordings were given over almost completely to improvised solos. They also concentrated on the blues, slow and medium. They were not designed for the giddy, the loose-wigged, the jitterbug. Lion wanted his musicians to go *down* into the instrumental blues further than anyone had gone before, and that's pretty much what they did.

The personnel on both dates was drawn from the new Café Society Downtown (Ammons, Lewis, Newton, Williams), from Louis Armstrong's big band (Higginbotham, Catlett), and from the Spirits of Rhythm (Bunn). Bechet, of course, had his own groups. It was a daring combination. Newton was a gentle, lyrical trumpeter, a legato performer who liked to drift down his solos, and Higginbotham was an eloquent trombonist who liked to shout and exult. Bechet took his own musical world with him wherever he went, and it didn't matter to him if it fitted or not. The pianists were solo boogie-woogie players, not much used to working with ensembles, and the rhythm section was modern but adaptable. (Catlett purposely plays old-fashioned, down-home drums, using press rolls and on-the-beat rim shots as well as beautiful tongue-in-cheek Baby Dodds ricky-ticky on his bass-drum rim; compare his dashing, driving ultra-modern work just six months later with Hampton on "Haven't Named It Yet.") "Daybreak Blues," from the first session, is built around Newton, who, instead of playing blue notes and smears, constructs a lovely melody in his first solo. (He does this again in the opening of "Port of Harlem Blues.") Higginbotham is equally melodic in "Wearyland Blues," which is built around him, and in "Port of Harlem Blues" the two men commune, establishing a musing quietness that carries through the ensemble at the end. The tempo goes up slightly in "Mighty Blues," which has two clarion Higginbotham choruses. (The Blue Notes are among the best and most consistent records Higginbotham made.) "Rockin' the Blues," the last number of the session, is a stomping boogie-woogie band number that Catlett carries in the palm of his hand.

The second session, with Bechet, has a different feeling. The first two numbers are again set around Newton ("After Hours Blues") and Higginbotham ("Basin Street Blues"), and are notable for Higginbotham's four-bar breaks—especially the next to the last. Newton and Higginbotham rest on "Summertime," which is a Bechet extravaganza. The remaining two sides are by the whole band, and they are soaring slow blues that come to a fiery conclusion in the jammed closing ensemble of "Pounding Heart Blues." The original Port of Harlem 78-r.p.m.s sounded as if they had been recorded in a closet, and the first three numbers on the Mosaic reissue still do; the rest have been opened up, although there is a disturbing cavern effect here and there. (Eight of the ten numbers were done on twelve-inch discs—a rarity for the time, and certainly a contribution to their looseness and sense of space.) But the sound doesn't matter. The dignity and beauty and simplicity of the music pass directly from the players into the listener.

The tenor saxophonist Ike Quebec was born in 1918 and died in 1963. He became known in the mid-forties through his Blue Note records and as a member of Cab Calloway's band, and he had a brief return to favor in the late fifties when he again recorded for Blue Note. A member of the Coleman Hawkins–Ben Webster school, he had a big, rough tone and a big vibrato, and he took up a lot of room when he played. He tended to dominate his recordings, both because of his sound and because of his attack, which was direct and emotional. He dominated his listeners, too: whole solos stay in the mind forty years later, as do various short passages, such as the devastating three-note phrase with which he opens his solo on "Mad About You." Unlike Hawkins, who was not particularly comfortable with the blues and preferred the harmonic ladders of the thirty-two-bar song, Quebec was at ease with both the blues and standard songs. He grafted blues emotions onto his slow ballads, and he brought the lyrical urgency of ballad playing to his blues. There are five different Quebec sessions on the Mosaic reissue, and they range from quintets to septets. There are good numbers in each session: "She's Funny That Way" and the great "Blue Harlem" from the first; "If I Had You" and "Mad About You" from the second; "Dolores" and "The Day You Came Along" from the third ("The Day You Came Along" has never been released before); the master of "I Found a New Baby" and both takes of "I Surrender Dear" from the fourth; and "Basically Blue" and the first take of "Someone to Watch Over Me" from the last. Listen to Buck Clayton on "I Found a New Baby" (he is uncertain on the alternate take) and to Keg Johnson on the master of "I Surrender Dear." He was the tenor saxophonist Budd Johnson's older brother, and he was a complex and original soloist who never got his due.

John Hardee was a Texas tenor saxophonist who was born in the same year as Quebec and died last spring. He enjoyed a small success in New York in the late forties, then went back to Texas for good. He did three dates for Blue Note, and they reveal his big Southwestern tone and his sure sense of swing, but they also show that he was an uncertain improviser, whose melodic lines lacked logic and continuity. Sid Catlett is on drums on the first two sessions, and he makes Hardee work.

With the release of "The Complete Edmond Hall/James P. Johnson/Sidney De Paris/Vic Dickenson Blue Note Sessions" and "The Complete Blue Note Recordings of Sidney Bechet," Mosaic Records has nearly finished its rescue and restoration of the best of the early Blue Notes. The first of the two new reissues has sixty-six selections, on six L.P.s, many of which are by a kind of repertory company consisting of De Paris, Hall, Ben Webster, Dickenson, Johnson, Jimmy Shirley, and Sidney Catlett. Hall leads one of the repertory-company sessions, and he also leads three other, very different sessions, which include

Charlie Christian, Red Norvo, Teddy Wilson, Benny Morton, Harry Carney, Carl Kress, and Catlett. There are also eight James P. Johnson solos and a Vic Dickenson date. The Bechet set has seventy-four selections, on six L.P.s, recorded by Bechet with the Port of Harlem Seven, a trio with Josh White, his own quartet, and assorted bands made up of De Paris, Dickenson, Max Kaminsky, Art Hodes, Sandy Williams, Wild Bill Davison, Albert Nicholas, and Jonah Jones.

Four of the eleven groupings on the first album are by the repertory company, and the first three are as fresh as they were forty years ago. (The fourth suffers from the absence of Catlett, who is replaced by the plodding Arthur Trappier—not "Al," as he is called in the personnel listings.) The versions set down of "High Society," "Royal Garden Blues," "After You've Gone," "Everybody Loves My Baby," and "Ballin' the Jack" have never been surpassed, and "After You've Gone" is one of the great jazz recordings. There are also five lilting medium-slow blues. The music on these recordings is not classifiable. It may have been designed by Alfred Lion to mesh with the New Orleans revival then under way, but it has little to do with New Orleans music. Edmond Hall was born not far from New Orleans, but he came up in big and small swing bands, as did Webster, De Paris, Dickenson, and Catlett. James P. Johnson, of course, was one of the pioneer stride pianists, and he helped build the bridge from ragtime to jazz. (He doesn't actually fit very well here. Someone a little sleeker—a Joe Bushkin or Eddie Heywood or Kenny Kersey—would have been better.) The ensembles are loosely arranged or jammed, but they are not in the New Orleans or Chicago mold. The voices do not strive or jar or jostle; they coast and converse, they cast no shadows. The solos they enclose are often exceptional, and they are often supported by riffs or organ chords. It is an amiable, cool New York music of a kind now gone—and it should be studied by such modern archeologists as David Murray and Henry Threadgill. The brilliant "After You've Gone" is, like the soaring "Sweet Sue" done eleven years earlier by Red Allen, Dicky Wells, Benny Carter, and Coleman Hawkins, simply a string of solos. But they are so good and fit so tightly that the number gives the impression it is going faster and faster when it is actually moving easily and steadily and with grand momentum toward its triumphant final chorus: Sidney De Paris paraphrasing the melody over organ chords and Catlett's lifting half-open high-hat. (Listen all through these numbers for the rhythmic hide-and-seek Catlett plays with De Paris and Dickenson, who rarely played as well with other drummers, and to his tongue-in-cheek Dixieland drumming on "Ballin' the Jack.")

One of Edmond Hall's four sessions is quite famous. It includes Hall, Charlie Christian on acoustical guitar (the only recordings he made with an unamplified instrument), Israel Crosby on bass, and Meade Lux Lewis on celeste, a chichi forerunner of the electric piano. Hall, with his cordovan Albert-system clarinet sound and his growls and stilted rhythmic sense, represented the old school, as did Lewis; Christian, then with Benny Goodman, belonged with early modernists like Lester Young and Thelonious Monk; and Crosby, reading the future, often played melodic rather than rhythmic bass. Despite Crosby's big low register, it was a treble group, full of piping and tintinnabulation. It also never quite swung, and it is still not clear why. Perhaps Hall was ill at ease. (He liked a strong Catlett-style flow under him.) Perhaps Crosby's melodic ruminations got in the way. Perhaps Lewis, a tractor-trailer driver, felt he had been put at the wheel of a Morris Minor. Perhaps Christian did find Hall and Lewis archaic. The remaining Hall dates swing and are free of pretension. One has no drummer and includes Red Norvo, Teddy Wilson, Carl Kress, and Johnny Williams, and the other has a rhythm section made up of Don Frye, Everett Barksdale, Junior Raglin, and Catlett, and a horn section of Hall, Benny Morton, and Harry Carney. The first session is cheerful and cool (Norvo and Wilson, true style-mates, are in excellent form), and the second has great melodic beauty—attend to both takes of "It's Been So Long" and "I Can't Believe That You're in Love with Me." The album has one other blessing—a 1951 Vic Dickenson date on which the trombonist plays four numbers backed by Bill Doggett on organ, John

Collins on guitar, and Jo Jones on drums. Dickenson does two good medium-tempo numbers and two classic slow numbers—sly, satiric readings of "Tenderly" and "I'm Gettin' Sentimental Over You." Tommy Dorsey made this last famous as his theme song, but, never able to improvise, he always played it smooth and straight. Dickenson performs it with a cunning smoothness, then steps off into an improvisation full of smears and asides and whispers that gently twit Dorsey's silkiness and the tune itself. And there are three choice solos by Collins, a fine guitarist who worked for Art Tatum and Nat Cole.

Although Sidney Bechet's New Orleans style never changed, he regarded himself as a modern musician who liked to travel in fast musical company—thus the sides made for Victor in 1940 and 1941 with the likes of Red Allen, De Paris, Rex Stewart, Charlie Shavers, Higginbotham, Dickenson, Sandy Williams, Earl Hines, Kenny Clarke, and Catlett. But, for whatever reasons, many of the seventy-odd numbers he recorded for Blue Note during the next fourteen years were made with inferior musicians. There were exceptions. The De Paris–Vic Dickenson session of 1944 contains the Bechet slow blues "Blue Horizon," played on clarinet and full of antediluvian melancholy, and it also has a lovely "Muskrat Ramble." A date done a month later with Max Kaminsky has some high-spirited ensembles—particularly those in which Bechet, again playing clarinet, moves through his own hollowed-out space between the trumpet and the trombone ("High Society" and "Salty Dog"). A 1945 session with Wild Bill Davison swings (despite the ponderous rhythm section), and there is a serene series of duets done the next year with the New Orleans clarinettist Albert Nicholas. The final session on the album, done in 1953, during Bechet's last visit to this country (he had settled in France), is with fast company. Jonah Jones is on trumpet, and there is a streamlined rhythm section built around the fine, little-known pianist Buddy Weed. Jones is majestic throughout and Weed sparkles, and Bechet responds to them both.

♪

Mosaic has reissued the last of the early Blue Notes under the title "The Benny Morton and Jimmy Hamilton Blue Note Swingtets." Included are four numbers apiece by Benny Morton's All-Stars (Morton, Barney Bigard, Ben Webster, Sammy Benskin on piano, Israel Crosby, and Eddie Dougherty on drums), Jimmy Hamilton and the Duke's Men (Hamilton, Ray Nance, Henderson Chambers on trombone, Otto Hardwicke on alto saxophone, Jimmy Jones on piano, Oscar Pettiford on bass, and Sidney Catlett), and the Sammy Benskin Trio (Benskin, Billy Taylor on bass, and Specs Powell on drums). Although none of the three sessions are first-rate, there is fine work throughout. These include Morton's rare bravura open-horn blues chorus on the slow "Conversing in Blue," and the closing ensemble, in which the horns nod and whisper and consult; the same group's flying, lissome "Limehouse Blues"; Catlett's ringing, relentless let's-get-this-going accompaniment all through Hamilton's boppish "Slapstick"; and Benskin's light, pleasant Marlowe Morris solos on his trio numbers. Despite its weaknesses (overarranging on the Hamilton date, Bigard's clichés), the album nicely closes Mosaic's invaluable early Blue Note reissues.

Vic

André Hodeir, the French critic and composer, once wrote that a jazz musician's musical life ends at forty—that thereafter he becomes repetitious and increasingly weary, whether for psychological or physical reasons. But Hodeir laid down his infamous dictum thirty years ago, when jazz was barely sixty years old and the first generation of truly accomplished jazzmen had only begun passing into middle age. Since then, the list of aging

musicians who have defied Hodeir's Law by playing with fresh-
ness and invention, by even playing with deepening inspiration,
has steadily increased. A partial accounting: Milt Jackson,
Jimmy Knepper, Count Basie, Bobby Hackett, Benny Carter,
Marian McPartland, Jim Hall, Johnny Hodges, Charlie Rouse,
Buck Clayton, Buddy Rich, Doc Cheatham, Teddy Wilson,
Ornette Coleman, Red Allen, Warne Marsh, Zoot Sims, Buddy
De Franco, Art Farmer, Red Norvo, John Lewis, Edmond Hall,
Cecil Taylor, Art Tatum, Charles Mingus, Ben Webster,
Thelonious Monk, Lee Konitz, Jo Jones, Joe Venuti, Dizzy
Gillespie, Art Hodes, Erroll Garner, and Vic Dickenson. Of all
these marvels, Dickenson, who died a month ago, at the age of
seventy-eight, was the most ageless. As the years went by, he
never seemed to look any older, and his playing never diminished. Keeping his cool was essential to him—it was a matter of
pride—and perhaps that insulated him. The only thing that
visibly gave out was his feet, and their failure left him in his last
decade with a slow, leaning-tower gait. He had a tall, narrow
frame and a tall, narrow head. His arms and hands and legs were
long and thin. The expression in his eyes flickered between
humor and hurt, and his smile went to one side. He was a
laconic man who said he had become a musician because "I
know I wouldn't have been a good doctor, and I wouldn't have
been a good cook. I know I wouldn't have been a good janitor,
and I don't have the patience to be a good teacher. I'd slap them
on the finger all the time, and the last thing I ever want to do is
mess up my cool." He always liked a drink, and he made his
drinks evenly spaced signposts that ran through his days and
nights; before he took his first one of the day, he'd say, "Ding
ding," a placative phrase borrowed from his friend Lester Young.
Dickenson enhanced every group he played with, in the way
that the expert and unassuming hold life together. You knew
that his solos would be witty and inventive. You knew that each
one would give you—in a laughing smear, in the way he sidled
up to a melody, in a tight, swinging *speaking* phrase—some
music to take home with you. You knew that he did not merely
play the trombone but used it, with his soft tone and gloved

attack, to appraise what went on around him, to express his bemused, amused view of the world.

Dickenson's life was his music. He had come up, as was customary in his time, through the big bands (Blanche Calloway, Claude Hopkins, Benny Carter, Count Basie), and he did not find them congenial. He did not like the drudgery of section work, and he was put off by the generally skimpy solo space. He first made his mark in the early forties in Eddie Heywood's smooth sextet. Heywood had the sense to let Dickenson stretch out, and he would do lazy-daddy parodies of songs like "You Made Me Love You," pulling their lachrymose melodies out of shape and advancing the notion that music could be funny without being clownish. Dickenson worked with Doc Cheatham in Heywood's band, and Cheatham recently said of his friend, "Vic was always helping people, getting them jobs, looking out for them. He helped me correct several things—little melodies I was doing wrong. There wasn't anything he didn't know about music. Sometimes I'd call him on the telephone just to stick him. I'd sing him some obscure tune I'd found, and he'd name it right off. You had to work with him a long time to appreciate him, because he didn't talk much. That was the only thing wrong with him. He'd answer your question, that's all. He could do anything—make biscuits, things like that. Once, when we were working for George Wein in Boston, my wife and I lived with him in this tenement, wood, on the third floor, a terrible firetrap, and one morning just after Vic had finished making biscuits and we were sitting down to eat, the firemen came running up the stairs and said the building next door was on fire and we'd better get out. Well, Vic told the firemen, 'We'll get out after we eat our ham and eggs and biscuits,' and we did. My first child was born while we lived there, and Vic never charged us any rent or anything." From the late forties on, Dickenson was usually in New York, playing in this or that small band, occasionally leading his own group, and filling his nights and ours with countless solos, each newborn and affecting. He wrote songs, too, and he gave them melodies that sounded like his improvisations. He also gave them special titles—"What Have You Done with the Key to Your Heart?," "Constantly," "I'll Try." He was chagrined that none of them ever caught on.

Bobby Hackett became the centerpiece of Dickenson's musical life in the fifties. The tall and the short of it, they complemented each other perfectly, and worked together every chance they got. (Hackett died in 1976.) Hackett was the logician and Dickenson the humanist. Hackett had bells in his sound and Dickenson voices. Hackett rhymed and Dickenson was in free verse. Dickenson, who was nine years older, laughed a lot with Hackett, who was on a constant, funny low boil, and he revered Hackett's "beautiful, perfect playing." When they were on the road together, they would retire to their hotel room after work, and Hackett would play his guitar (Glenn Miller had hired him as a guitarist), and Dickenson would sing in his nasal, upturned voice. In 1969, Dickenson and Hackett were invited to play at one of Dick Gibson's September jazz parties in Aspen, Colorado, and Hackett, who was a diabetic and was not supposed to drink, fell off the wagon the night before. He and Dickenson sat together the next morning on the bus to Aspen, and Hackett looked ashen and transparent. He slept most of the way, his head back, his mouth open. He did not move when the bus stopped for lunch in Vail, but Dickenson got off and came back with some soup and a sandwich and made Hackett sit up and eat. By the time the bus reached Aspen that afternoon, Hackett was restored and ready. Dickenson said he never got over missing Hackett after his death. Nor would Hackett have got over missing Dickenson, had things worked that way. Nor will we.

1985

Classic Jazz Quartet;
David Murray's Octet;
and Zoot Sims
and Al Cohn

Dick Wellstood, Joe Muranyi, Marty Grosz, and Dick Sudhalter have formed a group, and it had its first full run in the middle of January at Hanratty's. Muranyi, a gusty, ongoing man who held down the clarinet chair in the Louis Armstrong All-Stars for five years, talked about the origins of the group: "We first played together at a party Hayes Kavanagh gave at his place in Westchester in the summer of 1983. He's a lawyer and a jazz fan, and he gave the party to raise money for an East Berlin Dixieland band that was on its way to a festival on the Coast. It was an eating-hot-dogs-in-the-sun kind of affair, and we played one set and liked each other very much. We talked about doing it again sometime, but nothing happened for six or eight months. Then we did some one-nighters, and a New Orleans promotion at Lord & Taylor—making gumbo on the third floor, that sort of thing—and Grosz and I went out for coffee and a hamburger and we both said 'Hey!' and that established it. We realized we had a bird in hand. We started writing material and rehearsing, and we made a record for George Buck's Audiophile label. We did Garrison Keillor's radio show. The group's a true coöperative. Everybody can yell at everybody else, and everybody writes for it. Grosz and Sud are fast, and Wellstood and I are slow. The band gives us a venue for our music, and as a musical entity it can do anything—it has sweep. Sud is involved with the twenties, with Bix and Whiteman, and Grosz is into the thirties and swing, and Wellstood can be quite moderne. Nothing in our repertory suffers from a lack of attention. If anything, we an-

127

alyze everything too much. Grosz came up with a name—the Bourgeois Scum—but we settled on the Classic Jazz Quartet. The group has no one personality, because it is made up of all of our personalities, which are very different. I think of Wellstood as gruff and tough, which is both genuine and a front. Sud is Mr. Prissy, and Grosz is an out-and-out comedian. Sud is the most compelled of all of us. Wellstood and Grosz and I have been around longer and are sluggards by comparison. I think we want to get on the concert and festival circuit, and we should be able to handle everything in New York from Condon's to the Carlyle."

The group is what one expected—fresh, tight, swinging, and witty. It's a summation and a reworking of the best small-band jazz from the twenties to the early fifties. (Bebop is still beyond its ken, if not altogether beyond its powers.) On opening night, the group recalled the Bechet-Spanier Big Four, the John Kirby Sextet, the Spirits of Rhythm, the Delta Four, Woody Herman's Woodchoppers (mid-forties version), the Gerry Mulligan Quartet, Joe Marsala's Delta Four, and Joe Venuti's Blue Four. The ensembles are in unison or in harmony, and sometimes they are jammed. Wellstood and Grosz occasionally mix in harmonically, and Muranyi moves between clarinet and soprano saxophone, and Sudhalter between open horn and a variety of mutes. Solos are backed by piano and guitar, by just piano or guitar, by riffs and Ellington chords, by group singing (as in the Gerry Mulligan Quartet), and by nothing—a-cappella soloists are let loose over the abyss whole choruses at a time. These devices change constantly, and sometimes a little nervously, mockingbird fashion. Grosz is a good Fats Waller singer, and the quartet sings Paul Whiteman's "Mississippi Mud" in German. (Muranyi, who is of Hungarian descent, says he has little German but is boning up on it. He has also begun writing an account of his years with Louis Armstrong. The opening sentence goes, "I first met Louis Armstrong in the Bronx.") The repertory, so far, tends to be precious, and even campy. Sudhalter and Grosz like to resurrect songs of the twenties and thirties, so we get Harry Warren's "Cryin' for the Carolines"; James P. Johnson's

"Porter's Love Song to a Chambermaid"; DeSylva and Brown's "Turn On the Heat"; "My Gal Sal"; Jimmy Durante's "Inka Dinka Do"; "A Cabin in the Pines"; and McHugh and Fields' "Freeze and Melt." (Refurbishings of such excellent ancients as "That's a Plenty" and "Sweet Substitute" would not be amiss, and neither would reworkings of such contemporary pieces as John Lewis's "2 Degrees East, 3 Degrees West," Thelonious Monk's "Blue Monk," and Benny Golson's "Whisper Not.") Wellstood's accompanying opening night rocked the group and gave it the bottom its generally treble sound needs. Grosz is a strong rhythm guitarist and a good chordal soloist. The horns set each other off well. Sudhalter is an elegant, if sometimes brittle, Beiderbecke admirer, and Muranyi soars and shouts in his Jimmy Noone–Sidney Bechet way.

David Murray's Octet, now five years old, more or less takes up where Wellstood and company stop. It is investigating and redefining the jazz of the fifties and sixties and seventies, with occasional trips back into the forties, and even the thirties. It is part of the avant-garde, if the avant-garde in jazz is avant anymore, having reached the great age of twenty-five. Like Air and the World Saxophone Quartet, of which Murray is also a member, the octet has been examining its roots. One hears John Coltrane and Albert Ayler and Archie Shepp and Ornette Coleman, but one also hears Ellington and Charles Mingus and Paul Gonsalves and Sonny Rollins and J. C. Higginbotham and Cootie Williams. Indeed, the octet rests largely on Mingus and Ellington; its chief differences are a fondness for playing outside the key system, a tendency to overblow (a prevalent sin among musical pioneers trying to prove themselves), and avoidance of a four-four beat. In its semitonal way, Murray's music has a cacophonous edge—a grating quality that is close to the sound of some of the earliest jazz performers, who sounded that way because they couldn't sound any other way. It is an uphill sound, but once the ear gets used to it, it becomes less rebellious; the ear likes to balance opposing sounds, just as the mind likes to hold opposing thoughts. Murray writes and arranges all his materials. He often keeps two or more themes going at once, he uses Ellington backgrounds, and he finishes pieces with what appear to be free-for-all ensembles. He admires Mingus's tempo changes, his textural variety, and his tumultuous approach to music. Very little daylight filters through Murray's arrangements, and sometimes the music is impenetrable. Murray is a good, and even eloquent, melodic composer ("Home" and "Lovers"), and he is a player who moves from Gonsalves runs to Ayler animal noises to Coltrane squeals to fat Buddy Tate notes. The octet was at Sweet Basil in January, and on hand were John Purcell on reeds, the trumpeters Hugh Regan and Olu Dara, the trombonist Craig Harris, the pianist Adegoke Steve Colson, the bassist Wilbur Morris, and the drummer Steve McCall. (The hand of the Association for the Advancement of Creative Musicians still lies heavy on the avant-garde.) Dara has an imposing tone, and Harris likes J. C. Higginbotham. It would be enlightening to hear the octet and the Classic Jazz Quartet on the same bill—the octet moving and bruising, the quartet laughing and scratching.

Zoot Sims and Al Cohn have been working as a duo and in countless other combinations for nearly thirty years. Both admired Lester Young when they were starting out and have since become adjoining branches on Young's mighty tree. Both are emotional players, with Sims being the less heated. They have larger tones than Young; sometimes they match the big-house sounds of Coleman Hawkins and Ben Webster. They also like high, bent notes—alto-saxophone notes—that suggest Stan Getz, who came up with them and may have influenced them, or been influenced by them, or been influenced by still another Young student, Herbie Steward, who may have influenced all three of them: such matters are now lost in the fogs of jazz time. Sims and Cohn breathe each other's air, and could probably, if the need arose, take each other's solos. They did a week at the Blue Note early in January, and they also gave a concert at the Church of the Heavenly Rest, using as accompanist Dave McKenna, a pianist whose left hand encompasses guitar, bass, and drums. McKenna began the concert with a loping "I Can't

Believe That You're in Love with Me," following it with a fast, cleansing "Please Don't Talk About Me When I'm Gone," and an "Alice Blue Gown" in which he doubled and halved the tempo and skidded into a little accelerando. Sims joined McKenna and reached his customary high lyricism on a slow "My Old Flame," then surpassed himself on a very slow "Willow Weep for Me." He went backstage, and Cohn did four voluptuous selections—a fast "Them There Eyes," a slow "Embraceable You," a fast blues, and a slow "When your Lover Has Gone." By this time, McKenna—almost fossilized by a steady job as a solo pianist at the Copley Plaza, in Boston—had caught fire and, his great hawk face loose with emotion, played an exhilarating solo on "Them There Eyes" and chomping, tilting guitar accompaniment on "When Your Lover Has Gone." It was time for Sims to join Cohn, but Gerry Mulligan, who loves to sit in, came on with his baritone saxophone, and played a beguiling "Georgia." Sims and Cohn reappeared, and the three horns sailed through "Broadway" and "It's a Wonderful World," using riffs in their ensembles and unwittingly making one long for Mulligan's mid-fifties sextet, in which the four horms developed an improvised collective music that hadn't been heard before and hasn't been heard since.

The Mulligan Sextet and Paul Gonsalves

Gerry Mulligan's sextet lasted only from the middle of 1955 until the end of 1956, and it filled a lacuna in Mulligan's career between his pianoless quartets of the early fifties and the big band he put together in 1960. The sextet included Jon Eardley or Don Ferrara on trumpet, Zoot Sims on tenor saxophone, Bob Brookmeyer on piano and valve trombone, Mulligan on piano and baritone saxophone, Peck Morrison or Bill Crow on bass, and Dave Bailey on drums. Brookmeyer and Eardley had worked in Mulligan quartets, and Sims and Mulligan had played together off and on in New York and on the Coast. Morrison and Bailey sat in at a Mulligan rehearsal, were admired, and became part of the sextet. It is not clear where the idea of the sextet came from. Certainly Mulligan's quartet, which was formed in 1952 and was dependent on the mannerly, counterpoint of Mulligan and the trumpeter Chet Baker, contributed to it. And Mulligan must have listened to the serpentine melodic lines that Lee Konitz and Warne Marsh were working out with Lennie Tristano, and to the early contrapuntal investigations of the Modern Jazz Quartet and Dave Brubeck. He may also have had in mind the old Adrian Rollini groups, which he relished. The result was a partly written, partly jammed music built on unison or free-flowing ensembles, solos backed by organ chords or Ellington melodic fragments, and a clear, uncluttered rhythmic pulse, not unlike Tristano's metronomic timekeeping. It was a dense, swinging music, and when the four horns took off at the end of a number for several chorures of collective soloing (far less staccato and far more melodic than the soloing of the ordinary Dixieland or New Orleans ensemble) audiences found themselves shouting and jumping. But Mulligan was heady and restless at the time, and because the public response was limited, or there weren't enough jobs, or he wanted to get on with other things, he dissolved the group.

Fortunately, the sextet went into the Mercury recording studios five times, and the results give a loose idea of what it sounded like. Three L.P.s, made from thirty-four numbers set down (including alternate takes), were released in the fifties, and have long been out of print. PolyGram has reissued the best of them, "Mainstream of Jazz: Gerry Mulligan and His Sextet," and it has also issued, on "Mainstream of Jazz: Gerry Mulligan and His Sextet," Volumes II and III, fourteen numbers never released before. The original "Mainstream of Jazz" remains a superior album. On "Ain't It the Truth," "Igloo," "Lollypop," and "Blue at the Roots," there are good jammed ensembles, and on the first number Mulligan and Sims play a long and successful duet—a fresh approach that doesn't turn up anywhere else on the records. The two "Blues" in Volume II have some ensemble jamming, and so does "Demanton," which is based on "Sweet Georgia Brown." There are more glimpses of the group's collective work on "Broadway," in Volume III. The ardor and ease of Brookmeyer and Sims held the sextet together, and countered Eardley's stiffness and weak lip and Mulligan's tendency to keep trying to make indelible emotional statements. (Don Ferrara appears only on four numbers, all done at the group's last recording session and included in the original "Mainstream of Jazz" album.) The longer the sextet went on, the hotter and more inventive it became. It's too bad Mulligan let it go.

The tenor saxophonist Paul Gonsalves joined Duke Ellington in 1950, at the age of thirty, and stayed until his death, in May of 1974, nine days before Ellington himself died. Gonsalves became famous in 1956, when Ellington, closing the third Newport Jazz Festival, let him loose in his "Diminuendo in Blue" and "Crescendo in Blue," and Gonsalves, driven by a rocking, hypnotic Sam Woodyard beat, played twenty-seven choruses, which lifted the crowd to near-pandemonium and gave Ellington, who had been somewhat sluggish for several years, a boost that helped carry him through the rest of his career. It was a bravura performance that Gonsalves was forced to ape again and again (he once played sixty-six choruses), even though such flag-waving was contrary to everything he and Ellington stood for. Gonsalves, who was a flowing distillation of Coleman Hawkins, Ben Webster, Don Byas, and Charlie Parker, was most comfortable at medium and slow tempos. This is clear on a new and strange Ellington record, "Duke Ellington and His Orchestra: Featuring Paul Gonsalves" (Fantasy). It was made in New York on the afternoon of May 1, 1962, and all eight numbers are given over to Gonsalves. The session had apparently long been in Ellington's mind, and that is odd, because he had never allotted so much space to one of his soloists, and he never would again. So here is Gonsalves playing all the way through "C Jam Blues," with its many breaks, through "Take the A Train," through "Happy-Go-Lucky Local," and through "Caravan." Four of the eight tunes are fast or have fast sections, three are medium, and one is slow—a languorous reading of Ben Webster's famous vehicle "Just A-Sittin' and A-Rockin'," in which Gonsalves plays a chorus of embellishments and a chorus of improvisation. "Caravan," in medium tempo, has a passage of the sort that jazz fans wait for in the way baseball fans wait for inside-the-park home runs, triple plays, and umpires reversing themselves. Gonsalves plays around the melody for the first sixteen bars, and at the bridge he shifts into another dimension. He goes into a kind of half time, and invents a beautiful, full-blown song that has nothing to do with "Caravan" but floats serenely over it, a complete composition. It lasts just eight bars, and has the ethereal air of Jess Stacy's famous 1938 solo on Benny Goodman's "Sing, Sing, Sing." The Ellington band eventually had the same effect on Gonsalves that it had on most of its star soloists; few broke away, and those who did generally came back, cowed by the outside world. Ellington should have urged his stars to continue doing small-band sessions under their own leadership, as they had done so frequently in the thirties and forties. These recordings at least made them feel they owned their own skins. They also produced some imperishable music. Ellington's nod toward Gonsalves' gifts on that May afternoon twenty-three years ago was gracious but double-edged: it benefitted the master as well as the servant.

Cootie Williams
and Jo Jones _____

Within two weeks, near the end of the summer, Cootie Williams and Jo Jones died. Williams was seventy-five and Jo Jones seventy-three.

134

Cootie Williams spent twenty-three years with Duke Ellington. His first stint lasted from 1929 until 1940 and his second
from 1962 until Ellington's death. He became the first Ellington
star. When Benny Goodman hired him away from Ellington in
1940 (with Ellington's blessings), the bandleader Raymond
Scott recorded a number called "When Cootie Left the Duke."
Williams was celebrated for his use of the plunger mute, and no
one ever equalled him, despite the beauties of such Ellington
colleagues as Rex Stewart and Ray Nance. Bubber Miley, Williams' predecessor in the Ellington band, had picked up the
technique from King Oliver, who pioneered it, and had passed it
on to the trombonist Tricky Sam Nanton, who taught Williams.
It is a curious technique—as specialized and delicate and ar-
duous as lacemaking or truffle hunting. The trumpeter places a
small metal mute in the bell of his horn and, with his free hand,
manipulates a plumber's rubber plunger over the bell to achieve
wa-was, trains-across-the-bayou moans, whinnyings, whoops,
and all manner of intricate quasi-human vowel sounds. Some of
these effects are done partly with the lip, and all depend on lung
power. Williams' open-horn playing was stately; he was an
ebullient Louis Armstrong admirer, and he had an enormous
tone. But when he took up his mutes he became shadowy and
keening, he spoke in unearthly tongues. Williams' plunger-
mute work was particularly effective on the blues. He would
start a chorus tightly muted, and play a three-note phrase made
up of a short note, a higher long note, and a short note that fell
between the first and second notes. It was a secret sound that
passed directly into the inner ear. He would repeat this phrase,
making it louder and holding the second note a fraction longer,
then go into a simple ascending phrase, opening and closing the
plunger to achieve wa-was, which would be soft and would fall
just behind the beat. He'd end the phrase with the plunger
slightly ajar, and deliver a dying blue note. Next, he would
start a growling sotto-voce note, gradually increase his volume,
and slowly open his plunger. When the growling became almost unendurable, he would abruptly cut it off. Using large
intervals, he would lapse into laughing sounds, moving the

mute rapidly from side to side, slip in a tricky double-time phrase, and close the chorus with another tightly muted note. The agility of these effects was startling, but Williams never lost track of what he was doing. The strange and beautiful sounds he made were always fastened to handsome underlying melodic statements.

Williams stayed with Goodman a year. Although he loved the band, it was not a profitable musical time for him. Ellington's backgrounds had supplied him with handsome melodies against which to shine, but he sounded naked and somewhat primitive with Goodman—perhaps because of Eddie Sauter's over-padded arrangements. During the next twenty years or so, he had a successful big band and a durable small band, which played at the Savoy Ballroom. He liked to hire young revolutionaries, and he helped bring along Bud Powell and Thelonious Monk. His plunger-mute work eventually fell into abeyance, and when he rejoined Ellington it had lost its swiftness and surprise. His open-horn work was still majestic; on a blues like "The Shepherd," he talked of wind and darkness. Williams was medium-sized and straight-backed and barrel-chested. He had a dark, granitic face, and he looked like an emperor up in the trumpet section. (The drummer Elvin Jones once said of his own brief stay with the Ellington band, "I guess I didn't connect with the anchormen, because they complained about my playing to Duke. I don't know whether Cootie, who kept giving me the fisheye, wanted me to call him Mr. Williams and shine his shoes or what.") But he became highly animated when he moved front and center to solo. His face twisted with effort, his eyes closed, he would slowly lift his shoulders, drop them, and lift them again, lean to the right or left, and, when he paused to let someone else take eight bars, execute little dances and talk to himself. At the end of his solo, he'd bring his horn down smartly to his side, do an about-face, and march back to his chair. Williams made little of his consummate skills. He once said, "I laughed out loud at first when I heard those weird wa-wa-wa jungle sounds. Then it seemed to me since I'd been hired to take Bubber Miley's place, I better learn to play the mute like him. I never heard Bubber in person, so I learned from Tricky Sam Nanton. Duke didn't tell me I had to learn, I just did, and it didn't take very long."

Jo Jones took the clutter out of jazz drumming. As part of the Count Basie rhythm section of the late thirties and early forties, he helped demilitarize jazz rhythms. He brought the high hat forward, using it to propel ensembles and soloists, and, by playing irregular figures on it, to give the impression he was sliding back and forth under the band, like a sheepdog rounding up his charges. He made the beat even more fluid by continually changing his ride-cymbal patterns and by dropping in offbeats on his bass drum. His snare-drum accents did not frame and tint what he heard—they exploded. Sidney Catlett used his snare accents to parse the solos he backed; Jones' accents were italics and exclamation points. Jones' wire-brush playing was clean and spare and ringing. His wire-brush solos danced and laughed and jubilated. But his solos with sticks tended to be agitated and abrupt. He disguised this by evolving a master solo based on one developed in the forties by Catlett. He was, like most of the older drummers, a great showman, an unabashed showoff. He twirled his sticks and crossed his arms and made windmill patterns. He was a handsome man, and he smiled continually when he played. When he wasn't playing, he talked. Primed by a single question, he would deliver several hours of uninterrupted stream-of-consciousness. He tended in these monologues to be arch and a bit of a blowhard. He called the musicians he mentioned Mr., and he made his listeners feel they were paying court. Toward the end of his life, his delicate style thickened, and occasionally he parodied himself or had unsteady time. But the next night everything would fall into place, and he would play with his old buoyancy, and, with a rimshot or an exhilarating high-hat fill, suddenly take your breath away.

Romantic Agony

Bill Evans, who died in 1980, at the age of fifty-one, became the most admired and influential pianist since Bud Powell. He continues to be celebrated. Elektra Musician has issued—in a two-L.P. set called "Bill Evans: The Paris Concerts"—selections from a pair of concerts Evans gave in one evening in Paris in November, 1979. And Fantasy has brought out "Bill Evans: The Complete Riverside Recordings," a blunderbuss album made up of a hundred and forty-six numbers (on eighteen L.P.s) set down between 1956 and 1963, when Evans moved from Riverside to another label. (The album is misnamed; Evans made a good many other Riverside records, as is made clear in the exhaustive album booklet.)

When he played, Evans sat back a couple of feet from the instrument, his back bent completely, his forehead almost touching the keyboard. He kept his hands flat, and during the last decade of his career they rarely strayed from the two middle registers, as if they were invisibly hobbled to middle C. This abject, prayerlike posture suggested several things: that Evans was paying homage to his instrument, to his music; that he was so enfeebled by drugs that he couldn't sit up straight (his addiction, reportedly conquered during much of the seventies, was an open secret); that he was overpowered by shyness. The last was probably true, and it had a strange effect on his playing, which was always, as I wrote in these pages when Evans first appeared, "a contest between his intense wish to practice a wholly private music and an equally intense wish to express his joy at having found such a music within himself." His music seemed to be withdrawing, to be bowing out, slipping away. His diffidence was such that he had to be persuaded to make his first solo recording, and he then waited two years before making another. By his own admission, Evans was a slow learner with medium gifts who had to work very hard for everything he achieved. He was pleased by facility in young players, but he most admired those who made their way inch by inch. He gave as an example Miles Davis's slow but spectacular progress from imitative bumbler in the mid-forties to lyrical innovator in the late fifties, when Evans briefly worked for (and influenced) him. Evans' constant inner struggle made him difficult to listen to, whether on records or in the flesh. His playing demanded concentration of a sort not usually found among jazz audiences, who like to take easy emotional gifts away with them. His music was lucid and orderly, but it had a contemplative, rarefied, almost abstract quality, which kept its emotional content at various removes from the listener. This was particularly true during the last ten or so years of his career, when his playing became so pallid and secretive that it seemed to have lost its emotional center. All of which makes his famous, sparkling "All About Rosie" solo that much more startling. Delivered in the midst of a George Russell piece at a 1957 Brandeis University concert, it seized you immediately, and remains one of the classic recorded jazz piano solos.

Evans' style was a distillation of Bud Powell and Lennie Tristano. He had been trained as a classical pianist, and his style also reflected his admiration for Chopin and Grieg, for Debussy and Ravel and Scriabin. His right-hand single-note melodic lines were short and rhythmic and beautifully shaped. They had a smooth, logical flow that needed no decorative devices. The first note in each phrase, generally struck a fraction ahead of the beat, pulled the notes that came afterward, and by themselves the lead notes formed one melody while the secondary notes formed another. Evans would often conclude a solo with a chordal passage, which suggested the "locked hands" parallel chords of Milt Buckner or the harmonic piles of Art Tatum. These chordal layings-on occupied Evans increasingly in his last years, and he would sink into them, his ad-lib flags unfurled, his loud pedal engaged. He worked hard at a Nat Cole kind of touch, but he was never a pianistic player. He rarely used either end of the keyboard, and one sometimes wondered if he wouldn't have been a brilliant guitarist. (Red Norvo once pointed out that many musicians end up on the wrong instrument.) He was a romantic who kept his edges firm, who attracted apologists, as

Martin Williams' notes to the Fantasy album attest. He had none of Bud Powell's tough, bitter edge and none of Lennie Tristano's mathematical directness. His slow solos bloomed, and his fast ones wheeled like terns.

The "Riverside Recordings" album chronicles in massive detail Evans' progress from flashy bebop pianist to his studied lyrical self. Twenty-five of the numbers are with three different small groups, which include Jim Hall, Zoot Sims, the young Freddy Hubbard, and Cannonball Adderley, and not a great deal happens. Seventeen selections are solo piano, thirteen of them previously unissued. These are often ad lib or done in implied rhythms, like "All the Things You Are," which is almost abstract, and "I Loves You, Porgy," which Evans played again and again. They are Evans at his most private. The remaining hundred or so numbers in the album were done by six different trios. Three were put together solely for recording, and three were working groups. The most famous trio had Scott LaFaro on bass and Paul Motian on drums, and it existed from late 1959 until the summer of 1961, when LaFaro was killed in an automobile accident. LaFaro, in his mid-twenties, was an admirer of Charles Mingus and a brilliant bassist, whose methods are best heard in the work of Michael Moore. Dancing, crowded, passionate melodic lines poured out of him, and he quickly and probably unwittingly became the dominant voice, forcing Evans in on himself and making the group his own. Evans, of course, wanted the trio to be three equal voices, not a piano with bass-and-drums accompaniment, but LaFaro's imaginativeness wrecked this idealistic notion. Evans, reportedly bereft when LaFaro was killed, apparently didn't fully realize LaFaro's strength. Or did he? Listen to the solo numbers Evans made not long after LaFaro's death and to the new trio, with Chuck Israels on bass. Evans holds forth, he sparkles, he swings ("Show-type Tune," "Ev'rything I Love," "Stairway to the Stars"), and much the same is true of the last quartet in the album. (Larry Bunker, a less assertive drummer than Motian, had come in.)

It has been said that the "Paris Concert" L.P.s mark a return to Evans' outgoing brilliance of the late fifties, that they are the

beginning of a new period in his playing. (His final trio had Marc
Johnson on bass and Joe LaBarbera on drums.) To be sure, he
moves around more on the keyboard, and he is adventurous
harmonically ("Gary's Theme," "Laurie"), but what seems new
is a long-windedness ("Nardis"), an absorption with *sound*
("Noelle's Theme"), a kind of pianistic pomposity. Perhaps the
struggle within him was at last over, and the extrovert had come
forth.

Peakèd

FRIDAY: The avant-garde concerts that Verna Gillis has produced during the past five years for the Kool Jazz Festival, which
began today, have been moved from Irving Plaza to St. Peter's
Church. The first of four concerts was opened tonight by Walt
Dickerson, a fifty-four-year-old vibraphonist from Philadelphia.
Dickerson, who hasn't played much in New York in recent
years, arrived here in 1960, was heralded as the most important
vibraphonist since Milt Jackson, and moved on to Europe. He
plays softly, using small rubber mallets instead of felt ones, and
he covers the instrument with sixteenth notes, delivered at the
speed of a sandpiper's legs and isolated by silences or pools of
reverberating Milt Jackson notes. He did what appeared to be
one forty-five-minute piece, divided into short sections. The
cumulative effect was miniaturist and skittery. He was accompanied by the bassist Doug Christner, who played unison and
harmonic lines or laid out and watched the notes swarm.

The singer Carmen Lundy, accompanied by Harry Whittaker
on piano, Curtis Lundy on bass, and Victor Lewis on drums,
took up the second half of the concert. She sang a dozen or so
numbers by Jobim, Stevie Wonder, Cole Porter, George Benson,
and Jerome Kern, and she was hindered throughout by poor
acoustics. (That man's beseeching sounds tend to evaporate as

they rise in His churches is one of God's meanest jokes.) The drummer and bassist overpowered her, and even when they rested she blared or echoed. It was nonetheless clear that she is a good singer. She has a strong contralto and sure pitch, and her distortions of melody and lyrics (she falls somewhere between Betty Carter and Sarah Vaughan) seemed to be exactly what she wanted them to be.

Marian McPartland gave the first of the Festival's one-hour solo piano concerts in Carnegie Recital Hall late this afternoon. Her program included Duke Ellington's tricky, funny "The Clothèd Woman," a blues, a John Coltrane number, Johnny Mandel's fine "Emily," her own "Ambience," Alec Wilder's "I'll Be Around," "I Hear a Rhapsody," Ahmad Jamal's pretty, steplike "Without You," Bob Haggart's elegant blues "My Inspiration," Cole Porter's "From This Moment On," and "Royal Garden Blues." But almost every selection was submerged in thick chords and deep bass figures—these last resembling Dave McKenna's left-hand drone. Whenever a single-note melodic line came into view, it would be caught from behind by a chordal wave. Presenting jazz pianists alone, as pure and elevated as it may seem, rarely works. Without rhythmic support and guidance, they tend to turn into rhapsodists.

SATURDAY: The principal difference between Carla Bley's and Archie Shepp's avant-garde ensembles of twenty years ago and David Murray's big band (his octet plus three) is that Murray has replaced the satiric pokes Bley and Shepp took at earlier jazz with admiration, and even with reverence. Time and again, one hears in his compositions and arrangements his respect for Sidney Bechet and Duke Ellington and Charles Mingus, and hears in his own playing his respect for Ben Webster and Paul Gonsalves. Murray, who is just thirty (he looks like Ben Webster at the same age), grew up on Cecil Taylor and Ornette Coleman and Albert Ayler, and their harmonic and rhythmic and improvisational investigations overlay his music. They tint his vision of what Bechet and Ellington and Mingus were. He loves Ellington's harmony and odd instrumental combinations— particularly as they evolved in his last versions of, say, "Caravan," which became more and more acidulous harmonically. (Hear Murray's "Terror.") He uses Mingus's accelerando and decelerando, and his "free" ensembles, in which the instrumental voices sound as if they were arguing amiably. (Hear Murray's "Train Whistle.") He borrows the stampeding quality at the heart of much of Bechet's music in the thirties and forties. (Hear Murray's "Bechet's Stomps," in which, however, he mistakenly uses two-beat rhythms; Bechet was a four-to-the-bar man.) All this was on view tonight at Town Hall, where Murray's big band gave its first concert. In the band were Murray on tenor saxophone and bass clarinet, Baikida Carroll and Olu Dara on trumpet and cornet, Steve Coleman and John Purcell on alto saxophone, flute, and clarinet, Craig Harris on trombone, Bob Stewart on tuba, Vincent Chancy on horn, John Hicks on piano, Fred Hopkins on bass, and Marvin (Smitty) Smith on drums. Six of the eight numbers were by Murray and the rest by Lawrence (Butch) Morris, who conducted. Morris has great freedom. He decides when to bring in the background figures, what combinations they will play in and for how long, and what the background dynamics will be. This fluid "arranging" makes each version of a Murray piece different from the last, and is akin to the old "head" arrangements used by the big bands of the thirties and forties. The most impressive soloists were Murray, who plays passionately but has not yet successfully bridged the gap between his Albert Ayler squeals and his Paul Gonsalves hymns, Harris, and Olu Dara, who has a singing tone. Purcell, Chancy, and Stewart were not far behind. Some of the soloists— Murray included—went on too long, and strained the group's collective fabric.

George Wallington, one of the early bebop pianists, came out of a long Florida retirement to appear in Carnegie Recital Hall this afternoon. Bop pianists especially need rhythmic undergirding; one of the first things they did in the forties was to turn over the rhythmic duties of the left hand to their bassists and drummers. To compensate, Wallington used thunderous left-hand chords, which obliterated his lively right-hand Bud Powell figures. Worse, he played only his own original songs and didn't tell us what he was doing. Jazz fans relish the shock of melodic recognition, and when it doesn't come they grow disoriented and gloomy.

SUNDAY: Dave Frishberg the skinny, promising house pianist at the old Half Note twenty years ago has long since become Dave Frishberg the successful pianist-songwriter-singer. This Frishberg writes funny lyrics, usually with a topical or autobiographical bent, which descend from Gilbert, Porter, Hart, Mercer, and Burrows and are clothed in modest melodies, themselves often funny. Frishberg's most famous songs are probably "I'm Hip" (done with Bob Dorough), "Peel Me a Grape," "Van Lingle Mungo," "Sweet Kentucky Ham," "The Wheelers and Dealers," and "My Attorney Bernie," and they deal with life as it once was and life as it is among the pacesetters. Frishberg has a vibratoless voice, and no one sings him better. This afternoon at Carnegie Recital Hall he did more than a dozen numbers, including "I'm Hip" ("I'm too much. I'm a gas! I am anything but middle-class") and "My Attorney Bernie," and also "Zanzibar," "Blizzard of Lies" (a list of the endless deceptions we practice on each other every day: "We'll send someone right out. Now this won't hurt a bit. He's in a meeting now. The coat's a perfect fit"), "The Dear Departed Past" ("Tomorrow wasn't built to last"), and "Do You Miss New York?" ("And do you ever run into that guy who used to be you?"). Frishberg is a fine two-handed pianist who has a way of making everything he plays fresh and valuable. Witness this afternoon his affecting medium-tempo version of Ellington's "The Mooche."

MONDAY: George Wein likes to build amorphous concerts around departed jazz musicians, and tonight he gave us the dazzling, disordered Bud Powell, who died, aged forty-one, almost twenty years ago. Powell distilled his style from Art Tatum and Billy Kyle and from Charlie Parker and Dizzy Gillespie. It consisted of abrupt single-note melodic lines in the right hand and insistent, often monotonous offbeat chords and single notes in the left hand. His playing was deceptive. At fast tempos, which he loved, his galvanizing melodic lines gave the impression of great heat, even though they concealed a cold-ness, an inertness. At slow tempos, he sometimes verged on the lackadaisical. But Powell influenced nearly every jazz pianist who grew up in the forties and early fifties, and, filtered through Bill Evans, he can still be heard everywhere. The concert to-night, held at Town Hall and arranged by Ira Gitler, was built around the pianists Walter Davis, Jr., Tommy Flanagan, George Wallington, Barry Harris, and Walter Bishop, Jr., all followers of the Master. Davis appeared with the tenor saxophonist Jimmy Heath, Ron Carter, and the drummer Art Taylor; Flanagan with George Mraz and Taylor; Wallington (amazingly) again by him-self; Harris with the bassist Marc Johnson and the drummer Leroy Williams; and Bishop with Jon Faddis, Heath, the alto saxophonist Jackie McLean, the baritone saxophonist Cecil Payne, Johnson, and Roy Haynes. Davis aped Powell in a color-less, insistent way. Wallington muddied him. Bishop was matter-of-fact. Flanagan, who also listened to Nat Cole and Hank Jones when he was coming up, was seraphic. And Harris, a sometimes stolid pianist, celebrated Powell with a laid-back lyricism. (Bebop pianists stayed on top of the beat.) Harris, in fact, took the evening. He did an easy, clear-eyed version of Powell's "Celia," a medley of Powell tunes (Powell had a distinct gift for composing), and a lovely "Tea for Two," done just as Powell might have but couldn't have, because he lacked Harris's warmth and reverential hindsight. In the middle of the evening, we were shown forty minutes from an unedited docu-mentary film about Powell which was shot in France and Denmark in the fifties by Francis Paudras. We saw Powell playing in night clubs in Copenhagen and Paris, often with Kenny Clarke and the bassist Pierre Michelot; Powell endlessly walking in a city and near a waterfront; Powell playing with Charles Mingus; and Powell and Thelonious Monk, their arms around each other. The occasional glimpses of Powell in repose, his eyes hooded and empty, his face stone, were chilling.

WEDNESDAY: Most jazz musicians don't put it all together until they are around thirty. Then their technique catches up with their inspiration or their inspiration catches up with their technique, they digest early models and influences and find their own voices, and they learn to swing. This axiom has been repeatedly tested by the young wizards, most of them in their early twenties, who have poured into New York in the past ten years, including George Lewis, Anthony Braxton, Scott Hamilton, Howard Alden, the Marsalis brothers, Michel Petrucciani, Terence Blanchard, Donald Harrison, Fred Hersch, and David Murray. These musicians already have more technique, musical awareness, and historical sense than their predecessors ever had. This is true of the spectacular New Orleans contingent, many of whom appeared in Carnegie Hall tonight for a concert called "Young New Orleans." The trumpeter Terence Blanchard and the alto saxophonist Donald Harrison came on first, with Mulgrew Miller on piano, Phil Bowler on bass, and Ralph Peterson, Jr., on drums. They played five long hard-bop numbers. Blanchard, who looks about fourteen, has a sweet tone and is out of Miles Davis and Art Farmer, and Harrison has listened to Coltrane and Ornette Coleman and Charlie Parker. Miller plays long, ropy single-note lines, and Peterson did not leave an accent unturned. The group's emotional level is low, and it never quite swung. It was followed by Kent Jordon, a flutist, who got off one smooth up-tempo number. He gave way to the Dirty Dozen Brass Band, a kind of marching band made up of two trumpets, a trombone, a tenor saxophone, a baritone saxophone, a snare drum, and a bass drum. It plays Monk and Ellington and Herbie Hancock and also old numbers like "Lil'l Liza Jane" and "St. James Infirmary." It uses a lot of riffs, and its soloists tend to be edgy and staccato. The snare drummer, Jenell Marshall, who also serves as leader, is not as strong as he should be (a deeper snare drum and rimshots would help), and the group's refusal to jam any of its ensembles repeatedly leaves it at the edge of high merriment.

The second half of the evening was given over to the twenty-three-year-old grand master Wynton Marsalis, accompanied by Marcus Roberts on piano, Charnett Moffett on bass, and Jeffrey Watts on drums. He played two unidentified fast numbers, two ballads ("Lazy Afternoon" and "Dear Old Southland"), and "St.

James Infirmary," and the glassy brilliance so evident when he first appeared a couple of years ago had softened. Miles Davis is still clear in his playing, but tonight there was a lot of Rex Stewart, and even some Harry James. Marsalis played six or seven choruses of medium-tempo blues in his last number, and they made it clear that he has begun to let his emotions mingle with his technique.

THURSDAY: Microscopic Septet and Curlew occupied the second of Verna Gillis's avant-garde concerts at St. Peter's Church tonight. The Septet, which opened the evening, is made up of Joel Forrester on piano and Phillip Johnston on soprano saxophone (they are co-leaders, and write and arrange most of their material), Don Davis on alto saxophone, Paul Shapiro on tenor saxophone, Dave Sewelson on baritone saxophone, David Hofstra on bass, and Richard Dworkin on drums. The Septet has been together, jobs allowing, for seven years, and reflects the *nouvelle cuisine* that flavors so much modern jazz. The Septet has been affected by Duke Ellington (in its voicings and in the work of Johnston and Davis, who suggest various sides of Johnny Hodges) and by the satiric doings of Carla Bley and Archie Shepp. It likes old blues riffs, free Ornette Coleman jamming, Charles Mingus tempo changes, and a steady four-four beat. It makes whinnying sounds and Queen Mary roars—devices that go back at least to the Original Dixieland Jazz Band. The group smiles a lot. This is distracting, for it is not clear whether its members are laughing at themselves, at their materials, or at us. Or at all three.

Curlew is composed of George Cartwright on tenor saxophone, Fred Frith on electric bass and violin, Tom Cora on cello, and Pippin Barnett on drums. It is a fast-walking, lightweight version of the Art Ensemble of Chicago and of various Ornette Coleman groups. It plays dissonant bird-sound ensembles, has Milford Graves drumming, some of it electronic, and is as solemn as the Microscopic Septet is jokey.

FRIDAY: It must be difficult for Ray Charles to maintain the emotional level demanded by his way of singing. But he almost always does, and when he doesn't the façade stays in place, the sounds are right, the mood is at least approximate. Tonight, at Avery Fisher Hall, he sang ten songs, backed by his big band and by the Raelettes, and was resplendent. He did his anthems ("Busted," "I Can't Stop Loving You," "Georgia," and "What'd I Say"), and he did "Oh, What a Beautiful Mornin'," "Some Enchanted Evening," and "How Long Has This Been Going On?," the last of which he converted into a cuckold's lament. He talk-sang through most of "Busted," and he did "Georgia" so slowly you could count its spokes. He also suspended a beautiful falsetto over it. He made his renditions of "Oh, What a Beautiful Mornin'" and "Some Enchanted Evening" instances of funk ennobling bunk. And in "I Can't Help Loving You" he sang a jumble of melismatic notes in the first chorus which were so crowded and rich they gave off heat.

When Roland Hanna, that small, regal, expert pianist, appeared in Carnegie Recital Hall at the 1979 Festival, he leaned on his rhapsodic side. He also played a lot of his own compositions. He did both again there this afternoon. Five of the eight songs were his, and notable were the stately "After Paris," dedicated to Coleman Hawkins, and the larking "Century Rag," dedicated to Eubie Blake. Hanna sits straight and stock-still for some moments before each number, as if he were marshalling the notes he is about to play.

SATURDAY: In recent years, the Festival has broadened its scope to include certain downtown jazz clubs. Fat Tuesday's is one, and Phil Woods' quintet was there tonight. Woods, one of the best of Charlie Parker's descendants, has long had a quartet, with Hal Galper on piano, Steve Gilmore on bass, and Bill Goodwin on drums, but he has now added the trumpeter Tom Harrell, an exceptional player who suggests Fats Navarro. Tall and thin, Harrell stands onstage absolutely motionless, his head bowed and his eyes closed, his shoulders bent, and his trumpet hanging at his knees from crossed hands. When he plays, he raises his head, holds his trumpet straight in front of him, bends his knees slightly, and undulates slowly. He has a good tone, and uses almost no vibrato, giving his slow ballads a flat, ribbonlike quality. At medium and fast tempos, he shapes silvery melodic lines that move along just below his upper register and are interrupted by rests and by nice staccato single notes. His agile Dizzy Gillespie runs are connective rather than for show. He never lets up, and he never loses his improvisational thread. His solos think. He was superior tonight, particularly on his own "Gratitude" and on a number called "Round About." Woods, who is primarily an alto saxophonist, played clarinet on a couple of numbers. He should play it more often; he sounds like Benny Carter.

Bradley's is not officially part of the Festival, but it is only a little south of Fat Tuesday's, and Tommy Flanagan and George Mraz were there tonight. Bradley Cunningham has instituted a policy of silence while the music is playing—a revolutionary move in a temple of noise. It worked tonight, and it seemed to have a sensational effect on Flanagan. He played with a knock-about invention and passion. He slammed into the beginning of each improvisation and into his reprises after the bass solo. His single-note lines surged, his chords gleamed, the wind was constantly at his back. Flanagan's first two sets were reminiscent of the exhilarating night at Bradley's when Zoot Sims, armed only with Sidney, his soprano saxophone, took on Stan Getz for half a dozen numbers (they were accompanied by Jimmy Rowles and Horace Silver), and won.

Mingus at Work _____

Late in the afternoon of September 18, 1965, at the Monterey Jazz Festival, after three hours of music by Gil Fuller's big band, by the pianist Denny Zeitlin, and by the alto saxophonist John Handy, Charles Mingus brought onstage a new octet, made up of three trumpets (Lonnie Hillyer, Hobart Dotson, Jimmy Owens), a French horn (Julius Watkins), a tuba (Howard Johnson), an alto saxophone (Charles McPherson), drums (Dannie Richmond), and himself on bass and piano, and in the next half hour or so played four numbers, the last of them a parody of "When the Saints Go Marching In," and left the stage. It was a puzzling performance. The music was spiritless and unevenly played, and the set had an abortive air. It looked at the time as if Mingus was out of sorts because the preceding band, a quintet led by John Handy, a former Mingus sideman, had given a fiery, perhaps untoppable set. It turns out, with the release of "Charles Mingus: Music Written for Monterey, 1965: Not Heard . . . Played in Its Entirety at U.C.L.A." (East Coasting Records), that Mingus's lacklustre behavior had nothing to do with Handy. The album, recorded at a U.C.L.A. concert a week later, includes the eight numbers Mingus had planned for Monterey. It also offers two solutions to the Mingus Monterey mystery. One is given in the liner notes, in a paraphrase of something written by Jimmy Lyons, the festival's producer and founder, in a kind of history of the festival published five or six years ago as "Dizzy, Duke, the Count and Me." The passage in the book goes like this:

The following year we brought [Mingus] back. But there was a screw-up with some records he recorded himself and wanted to sell at Monterey. You had to buy them through him. He said the records were never shipped out here. That's when I had to get on my knees.

He was wearing a bowler hat, dark suit. He got me on stage and said to his band, "I think I'll just take the money and pay you guys off and this ofay bastard is standing here and he's going to make me play when he hasn't done what he was supposed to be doing." He looked at me and said, "You want me to play?"

I said, "Of course, it's in your contract. I've given you half the money."

150

*"Okay, you get down on your hands and knees and beg
me."*
I got down on my knees.

Mingus offers the second solution. In his opening remarks in the
album, he says, "We're going to play the music we planned to
play [at Monterey]. But for some reason—this is not an
apology—we only had twenty minutes. No one knows who the
guy was with the red beard—Jesus, Buddha, Moses, Muham-
mad, somebody, but he say get off. They can't find him. Neither
can I." The truth may lie somewhere between. The concert was
already three hours old and people had started to leave, which
wouldn't have pleased Mingus much; Mingus, never patient,
was probably exasperated at having to wait so long; and maybe
some records that he wished to sell *hadn't* arrived. In any case,
we now know what we missed on that hot, blue afternoon, and
we also have, in the East Coasting album, an invaluable account
of Mingus at work. Mingus had the U.C.L.A. concert recorded,
and he released it on his label a year later. (Only two hundred
copies were pressed.) It included not only all the music (except
for an "I Can't Get Started") but also his introductions, his
admonishments to the band, an aside to the "New York jazz
critics," jokes, philosophy, and his recitation of one of his song-
poems. Mingus was a natural man. He never adjusted to a
situation; the situation adjusted to him. So here he is working
hard in front of a college audience—a musical magician, a
tireless agitator, a brilliant seer. This is how the album goes:

After his introduction, Mingus and his tubist, Howard Johnson, start an eighteen-minute number called "Meditation on
Inner Peace." It is one of Mingus's "conversation" pieces. That
is, at various points the soloists, instead of constructing abstract
musical improvisations, "talk" to one another through their
instruments, making sounds that resemble questions, exclamations, laughter, expressions of sympathy, and the like. Mingus
begins arco over Johnson's two-beat ground bass. Jimmy Owens
and Mingus play contrapuntally. Owens drops out, and Mingus

plays solo double-stops. McPherson enters, and he and Mingus "talk." Dannie Richmond reinforces Johnson's two-beat bass. Julius Watkins and Mingus talk. Mingus plays by himself, then talks with one of the trumpeters. The trumpeter starts playing high notes, the band comes in behind, and things become agitated. The ground bass gets faster and faster. The band goes into one of Mingus's semitonal collective scrambles, and falls away as the ground bass slows down to a walk. There are more trumpet shouts, Richmond sets off some round-the-set explosions, Mingus plays some piano chords, and the piece ends. Mingus introduces his sidemen, and announces "Once Upon a Time, There Was a Holding Corporation Called Old America." He talks to the band, and they go into a mournful melody and stop. Mingus plays the melody on the piano, and the band starts and stops again, and he sends half the band "to the back room to figure this thing out," keeping Hillyer, Richmond, and McPherson. These three plus Mingus begin "Ode to Bird and Dizzy," a fast mixture of solos and quotes from such famous bebop numbers as "Salt Peanuts," "A Night in Tunisia," and "Hot House." McPherson solos while Mingus and Richmond trade four- and two-bar breaks behind him (a unique accompanying device), and Hillyer solos. Mingus and Richmond move forward together in an exhilarating way, and Richmond solos. (Mingus loved Richmond. He had converted him from a tenor saxophonist into the best drummer he ever had, and one of the best of the post-bebop drummers.) The number ends at an unmanageable speed. The full band plays an ad-lib dirge that was done at Monterey—"They Trespass the Land of the Sacred Sioux." It lasts eight minutes, and is arranged around a lovely Mingus melody and solos by Owens and McPherson. "The Arts of Tatum and Freddy Webster" follows. What it has to do with Art Tatum and Webster is not clear; it is still another dirge, and it is taken up with some lush Hobart Dotson trumpet and by several tempo changes. More rich Mingus melody is offered in the second (and successful) attempt at "Once Upon a Time, There Was a Holding Corporation Called Old America"—a somewhat disjointed eleven-minute piece full of Mingus shouting, wild

French horn, and trumpet solos. Mingus offers some of his vest-pocket philosophizing before the number starts: "I feel pretty free here [in America]," he tells the audience. "I don't feel confined, or anything like that. . . . You're only confined by your own self and what you wanted to do and didn't do when you was a little boy or a big boy, and all of a sudden you find yourself trapped by yourself, but you blame it on other people. It's a pretty way of thinking." Then Mingus does a rough, not very convincing parody of "Twelfth Street Rag" (not "Muscrat Ramble," as it is called on the album), and breaks for an intermission, first taking care of business by summoning (presumably) the student in charge of the concert: "Peter James Thompson, I'd like to see you in the back. Peter, we have a little matter to work out financially." A pleasant, eight-minute medium-tempo number, with two strains, called "Don't Be Afraid, Because This Clown's Afraid, Too" opens the final section of the concert, and is followed by "Don't Let It Happen Here," a Mingus recitation-with-music that goes in part:

One day, they came and they took the Communists, and I
said nothing, because I was not a Communist.
  Then one day, they came and they took the people of the
Jewish faith, and I said nothing because I had no faith left.
  One day they came and they took the unionists, and I said
nothing, because I was not a unionist.
  One day they burned the Catholic churches, and I said
nothing, because I was born a Protestant.
  Then one day they came and they took me, and I couldn't
say nothing because I was as guilty as they were for not
speaking out and saying that all men have a right to freedom
on any land.

The liner notes of the album include reproductions of documents explaining how the master tapes of the U.C.L.A. concert, stored with Capitol Records in New York in the sixties, were destroyed in 1971 when the New York studio was closed. If Mingus wasn't bedevilling himself, someone else was bedevilling him.

1986

Basie Slips By ⸺

In the late thirties and early forties, the two greatest big bands in jazz were led by Count Basie and Duke Ellington. They remain without equal. They also remain antithetical. Basie and Ellington grew up in the shadow of ragtime and of such stride pianists as James P. Johnson, Willie the Lion Smith, and Fats Waller, but by the late thirties Basie had begun the self-editing that would result in his telegraphic style, and Ellington had turned to a harmonic attack rich enough to foster Thelonious Monk and Cecil Taylor. The Basie band had grown out of the Southwest bands of Walter Page and Bennie Moten. (When it was brought to New York from Kansas City by John Hammond in 1936, it was enlarged from nine to fourteen pieces by its booker, Willard Alexander.) The Ellington band was a New York band with a New Orleans bias and had grown organically out of the heart and mind of its leader. The musical pecking order within the Basie band was soloist, arranger, composer. In the Ellington band, it was the reverse. The Basie band swung from the beginning, but the Ellington band swung consistently only after the arrival, in 1939, of the bassist Jimmy Blanton. Basie was microphone-shy, and conducted from his piano bench. Ellington loved the microphone and was an outsized presence onstage, sometimes playing, sometimes conducting on his feet, sometimes shouting, always moving. Basie was short, genial, shy, and laconic. Ellington was tall, smooth, gracious, and outgoing. It is not surprising that Ellington himself wrote most of his life story, in *Music Is My Mistress*. (Stanley Dance helped him pull the book together.) Nor is it surprising that Basie decided to tell his story to the writer Albert Murray—a task that was completed before Basie's death. The book has now been published, by Random House, as *Good Morning Blues*.

What is surprising about Basie's book is its length and heft. His taciturnity was celebrated, and in *Good Morning Blues* he tells us, "I never did have a lot of words. Hell, I still don't have but so many right now." So the book's four hundred closely printed pages immediately raise expectations—maybe this secret little man, this wizard pianist and bandleader, is at last going to let us in on how he has done what he had done so well and for so long. The best and longest part of the book takes Basie to the age of thirty-seven. (He died at seventy-nine.) There are glimpses of growing up black and poor in fashionable Red Bank, New Jersey, in the years before the First World War. Basie's mother, who was from Virginia, took in washing and did some free-lance cooking. His father, also from Virginia, was a caretaker and a gardener. (Did either of them ever work for the family of Edmund Wilson, who was growing up safe and well-to-do on the other side of the tracks? Basie probably never read Wilson, and Wilson probably never heard Basie. They did, however, come to form the bookends of mid-twentieth-century American culture.) Music consumed Basie early, and he never got any farther than junior high. ("I used to stay in one grade so long it was shameful.") He wanted to be a drummer but changed his mind after he heard his friend Sonny Greer, who lived in nearby Long Branch. He took some piano lessons and listened to such stride pianists as Willie Gant and Donald Lambert. He gigged around the Jersey shore, and in 1924 he took off for New York. He ran into Greer, met Duke Ellington and Willie the Lion, and signed up with a vaudeville act called Katie Krippen and Her Kiddies. They travelled by train, and the experience produced one of the few lyrical patches in the book: "I have always been crazy about trains. I love the way they sound, whether they are close up or far away. I like the way the bell claps and also all the little ways they do things with the whistle.

And I also like the way they feel when you are riding them and hearing them from the inside." After a year on the road, Basie settled briefly in Harlem. Fats Waller gave him some pointers on the organ, and he worked with the trombonist Jimmy Harrison. He wanted to be an entertainer rather than a full-time pianist, and his uncertain pianistic skills lost him two jobs—to the stride pianist Joe Turner and to Claude Hopkins. He went back on the road in 1926 with a singer and dancer named Gonzelle White. "She must have been in her late twenties or early thirties," Basie told Murray. "She was very light-skinned, and she had curly red hair and was very well put together. She was not a large woman. She was the kind of small, nice-looking woman that you think of as being very cute. And, of course, she always wore fine, stylish clothes and costumes, and she also sported a diamond in one of her front teeth." He heard Earl Hines in Chicago, and he met Hot Lips Page and Jimmy Rushing in Tulsa. Page and Rushing were with Walter Page and His Blue Devils, who mesmerized Basie. The book has some funny passages in it. One night after Basie had joined the band, Lips Page lent Basie one of his three suits:

I didn't know what I was getting myself into. I couldn't get rid of him. Everywhere I went he was right there with me, saying, "Don't lean on that."

Or he'd say, "Hey man, that chair is kinda dirty."

"Hey, Basie, watch it sitting down." . . . That was one of the most uncomfortable evenings I've ever had in my life.

The Blue Devils ran out of work, and Basie went to Kansas City and played organ for the movies at the Eblon Theatre. He finally heard the famous Bennie Moten band, and was as taken with it as he had been with the Blue Devils. He knew that Moten was the band's pianist, but, he tells us, "I have always been a conniver and began saying to myself, I got to see how I can connive my way into that band." He did it—by collaborating on some arrangements with Eddie Durham, Moten's trombonist and guitarist. He became the group's leader briefly in the early thirties, and when it disbanded he took over a group at the Reno Club in Kansas City. He brought in former members of the Blue Devils and the Bennie Moten band, and in due course had the nine-piece group that John Hammond heard over station W9XBY and evenutally sent on its way.

By the mid-forties, the Basie band had begun to lose its heat, its easy, left-handed drive, its misterioso quality. The deep blueness of "Song of the Islands" and "Goin' to Chicago" and "Nobody Knows" gave way to such strident Art Deco numbers as "Avenue C" and "The Mad Boogie." The band was becoming the sleek leviathan that Basie would perfect in the fifties. The book itself becomes mechanical at this point. There are endless itineraries, lists of recording dates and personnel changes, show-business encomiums to left and right, and pleased accounts of playing for American Presidents and English royalty. (Murray has done a lot of legwork on the logistical details of Basie's bands—down to what forgotten movie was accompanying a Basie show—and he has put it all into Basie's mouth, not always comfortably.) It becomes clear that Basie has slipped genially by again without saying much of anything. He tells us at the outset that there will be no intimate revelations, but we learn that he liked to play the horses, that he liked to drink and womanize, that he could be scheming, that he was married twice and had a daughter, and that he spent a lot of time in the "doghouse." But we don't learn what we wanted to learn—where his exquisite, pearl-by-pearl piano style came from, how it felt to lead and to play with such extraordinary sidemen as Lester Young and Herschel Evans and Buck Clayton and Dicky Wells and Jo Jones, how such a fun-loving man happened to conceal the vein of melancholy that was so clear and poignant in his blues piano solos. The reader wants Murray to *make* Basie talk about his music. If he did try, maybe Basie, who had perfected the art of self-denigration, just laughed, winked, and shook his cool head.

American Jazz Orchestra
and the Leaders _____

A new repertory group, the American Jazz Orchestra, has been brought into being by the critic Gary Giddins. John Lewis is its musical director, and Cooper Union, where it recently gave its first concert, is its sponsor and base. The notion of trying to preserve and reproduce an improvised music was first sanctified during the winter of 1973–1974, when the National Jazz Ensemble, headed by the bassist and composer Chuck Israels, gave five concerts at Alice Tully Hall, and the New York Jazz Repertory Company, headed by Sy Oliver, Billy Taylor, Gil Evans, and Stanley Cowell, gave fifteen concerts at Carnegie Hall. (There were earlier repertory attempts: the neo-New Orleans music of the early forties; the re-creation of the Fletcher Henderson band, with many of its original members, at the Great South Bay Jazz Festival in 1957; the Red Allen, Count Basie, and Billie Holiday segments of "The Sound of Jazz," given later that year; and Duke Ellington's constant refurbishings of his own old beauties.) The National Jazz Ensemble, using sixteen pieces and imaginative arrangements, favored the small-band music of the forties, fifties, and sixties, but it took as its theme a near-showstopper from 1927—a unison transcription, played by the entire band, of Louis Armstrong's solo on his Hot Five version of "Struttin' with Some Barbecue." The New York Jazz Repertory Company, using a pool of a hundred or so musicians, did everyone from Bix Beiderbecke to John Coltrane, often with elephantine results. Both groups lasted several seasons and died from public apathy and a lack of funds. But jazz repertory has continued in one form or another. Dick Hyman and Bob Wilber have re-created the music of King Oliver, Jelly Roll Morton, Sidney Bechet, James P. Johnson, and Duke Ellington, and Vince Giordano has done various dance bands of the twenties, thirties, and forties. Harvey Estrin has brought the Sauter-Finegan band back to life in several concerts at the 92nd Street Y. Lee Konitz has assembled a nonet that bears a close resemblance to the Miles Davis group of 1949. Panama Francis has resurrected the Savoy Sultans, and Paul Whiteman has been done by Dick Sudhalter and Maurice Peress. The Classic Jazz Quartet is, in its way, a repertory group that gets inside the small-band music of the twenties and thirties. And Sphere and Dameronia have revived Thelonious Monk and Tadd Dameron. But Gary Giddins feels that the time has come to institutionalize such homegrown attempts. He recently wrote in the *Village Voice:*

The next step, it seemed to me, was to create permanently housed jazz ensembles under the auspices of arts centers. They would have to be every bit as stable, secure, and accomplished as the orchestras that conserve nineteenth-century European music in practically every major city in the United States. Under the batons of great conductors (a relatively new line of work in jazz), such orchestras would not only reclaim and refurbish seventy years of indigenous music, but provide a stream of commissions to contemporary composers.

But the problem of how to re-create an improvised music has never been completely solved. Many solutions have been put forward. Recordings have been transcribed note for note and played either note for note or with new solos. Old solos have been transcribed and scored for reed or brass sections, then incorporated into old arrangements. Old solos have been used as the basis of new improvisations. But what of these stubborn questions: Why reproduce, say, Jelly Roll Morton's 1926 "Doctor Jazz" when the original recording is available and clear? Is it more informative and enjoyable for an untutored audience to hear the number imitated in the flesh than to hear the original record on decent sound equipment—particularly since audiences tend to listen with their eyes instead of their ears? How do young musicians re-create music originally played in a combustible, semi-intuitive manner? How do they get inside the music rhythmically? (Tone and timbre can be matched with relative ease.) And what of the fact that many old recordings failed to capture their subjects faithfully, whether because of poor sound, misguided supervision, time limitations, or nervous musicians? These recordings may be fixed in our ears, but they are nonetheless false. A theatrical repertory company works from a true text; a jazz repertory company works from old, often unreliable recordings, improvisation frozen by time, and an array of unorthodox attacks and timbres. Poets, not copyists, are needed for such work.

The American Jazz Orchestra concert, given in the Great Hall at Cooper Union, didn't solve any problems, but it inadvertently advanced one that didn't exist in 1973. The National Jazz Ensemble and the New York Jazz Repertory Company had on tap many musicians who had played the original music or known it first hand. It was going home for Budd Johnson to do an Earl Hines concert, for Joe Venuti to do the Blue Four, for Cozy Cole to do Cab Calloway, for Taft Jordan to do Chick Webb, for Ray Nance to do Duke Ellington. Most of these musicians have died, and Giddins and Lewis have had to call in musicians who came up in bebop or hard-bop days (Hank Jones, Dick Katz, Jimmy Heath, Eddie Bert, Jack Jeffers, Jimmy Knepper, Ted Curson, Major Holley, Charli Persip), or even more recently (Jon Faddis, Randy Brecker, Marvin Stamm, Craig Harris, John Purcell, Hamiet Bluiett). The program included Fletcher Henderson ("Big John Special," "Wrappin' It Up," "King Porter Stomp"), Duke Ellington ("Cottontail," "Concerto for Cootie," "Jack the Bear," "Harlem"), Jimmie Lunceford ("For Dancers Only," "Lunceford Special," "Yard Dog Mazurka"), Count Basie ("Taxi War Dance," "Jive at Five," "Every Tub," "One O'Clock Jump"), and Dizzy Gillespie ("Confirmation" and Slide Hampton's "Fantasy on 'Shaw 'Nuff' and 'Anthropology'"). There was tentativeness everywhere. Charli Persip never took hold (there are few things more tonic than a big band in full shout, with a Sid Catlett or a Sonny Greer or a Jake Hanna in command), and John Lewis's tempos tended to be too slow. The ensemble passages didn't have much snap; there was very little *swinging*. The fresh solos were often better than the re-created ones (Loren Shoenberg's Lester Young on "Taxi War Dance" was an exception, and so was Virgil Jones' open-horn section of "Concerto for Cootie"), and notable among them were Jimmy Knepper's two triumphant choruses on Hampton's "Fantasy," Hamiet Bluiett's swaggering on "Jive at Five," and, on the Hampton, Dizzy Gillespie's soft, slippered exchanges with Jon Faddis, who, as in his wont, overblew. Probably the most successful piece of the evening was Ellington's "Harlem," a twelve-minute tone poem commissioned by the NBC Symphony in 1950. Maurice Peress conducted with verve, and the band responded. Gary Giddins made onstage comments about the music between sections, and, though to the point, they recalled the days when jazz was armored in apologetics. Let us hope that future concerts will enlist such magical reproducers of old music as Dick Hyman, Howard Alden, Vince Giordano, Dick Sudhalter, and Dick Wellstood, and also Bob Wilber and Scott Hamilton, both of whom would have added a great deal to the Ellington the other night. Let us hope, too, that newly commissioned pieces will be carefully weighed; many of the new pieces done in the past by repertory groups have turned out to be all wind and motion.

The Leaders is a six-piece all-star band formed a couple of years ago for the purpose of touring European jazz festivals, and it made its first New York appearance at Sweet Basil. It included Lester Bowie, replacing Don Cherry on trumpet; Arthur Blythe on alto saxophone; Chico Freeman on tenor saxophone; Kirk Lightsey on piano; Cecil McBee on bass; and Famoudou Don Moye on drums. The group falls somewhere between hard bop and the avant-garde of the sixties and seventies. (Most of its members are in their forties.) It has been marked by the rhythmic practices of Charlie Mingus and by the parodic and eclectic tendencies of the Association of the Advancement of Creative Musicians. Bowie and Moye are early members of the Art Ensemble of Chicago, which came out of the A.A.C.M., as did Chico Freeman; Lightsey has played for Dexter Gordon and been an accompanist to singers; McBee has worked with everyone from Miles Davis to Sam Rivers to Freeman; and Blythe is an adaptable and excitable post-Coltrane player. The group didn't do much at an early set late in the week. There were three long numbers, and the disappointingly brief ensembles were in vague unison or in free form. The rest of the time was occupied by solos. Freeman is the most impressive member of the group. He has something of Paul Gonsalves' inner-directed flow (but none of his sly subtlety), and he has a sure, rich sound. Bowie likes to anthologize other trumpeters' licks (Cootie Williams, Dizzy Gillespie, Miles Davis), and he is not above making neighing sounds. Blythe gives the impression that he is flying over his materials. Moye is a good melodic drummer, but he is overbearing, and that caused Lightsey and McBee to shout in order to be heard. The group's closing number, a short parody of "Blueberry Hill," had a thunderous afterbeat, and it swung harder than anything that had come before. The parodied strikes back!

The Big Bands ───────────────────────

Gunther Schuller and Martin Williams have put together for the Smithsonian Collection a recorded history of the big jazz bands, called "Big Band Jazz." Stretching from 1924 to 1955, it contains two Paul Whitemans, five Fletcher Hendersons, two McKinney's Cotton Pickers, one Luis Russell, one Jesse Stone, one The Missourians, one Casa Loma Orchestra, two Bennie Motens, four Earl Hineses, four Chick Webbs, five Jimmie Luncefords, five Benny Goodmans, one Andy Kirk, four Tommy Dorseys, six Count Basies, two Charlie Barnets, three Artie Shaws, three Glenn Millers, two Harry Jameses, one Benny Carter, two Erskine Hawkinses, seven Duke Ellingtons, one Louis Armstrong, two Lionel Hamptons, four Woody Hermans, one Billy Eckstine, two Boyd Raeburns, two Dizzy Gillespies, two Claude

Thornhills, one Elliot Lawrence, and one Stan Kenton. It does not contain anything by the Mills' Blue Rhythm Band, Bob Crosby, Les Brown, Gene Krupa, Jay McShann, Lucky Millinder, Teddy Wilson, Red Norvo, Teddy Powell, Bob Chester, Jimmy Dorsey, Sabby Lewis, Hal McIntyre, Jack Teagarden, Spike Hughes, the Metronome All-Star bands, Cootie Williams, Cab Calloway, the Sauter-Finegan band, Georgie Auld, or the Savoy Sultans. To judge simply by what has been left out and by the number of selections granted certain of the bands, it is clear that "Big Band Jazz" is an eccentric and even capricious anthology. Taken as a whole, though, it is a testament to a body of jazz music that was rarely as good as it should have been yet was often better than the mass-production standards that governed it.

Ragtime, early in the century, was the first nationwide popular-music fad in this country, and the big bands, which flourished from around 1930 to 1950, were the second. (Popular singers came next, then rock.) The big bands grew indirectly out of the New Orleans ensemble of trumpet, clarinet, trombone, piano, guitar, bass, and drums. (By big bands I mean big bands with a jazz inclination, and not such sweet, Mickey Mouse bands as Guy Lombardo, Wayne King, Russ Morgan, and Sammy Kaye.) They swelled from around ten pieces in the twenties to twenty and sometimes thirty in the forties, and eventually they included four or five trumpets, three or four trombones, five reeds, and a rhythm section of piano, guitar, bass, and drums. String sections of various sizes came and went. Because such a number of instruments could not play polyphonically in the New Orleans manner, arrangers came into being. They wrote figures for the various sections to play, leaving space here and there for improvised solos. These figures were riffs (short, repeated phrases); rhythmic punctuations, especially for the brass; organ chords played by any or all of the sections; and straight-out melodies or melodic fragments. In the early big-band days the sections worked in a kind of call-and-answer pattern: the reeds would play a riff and the trumpets would answer with a wa-wa phrase, the trombones would state a melody for eight bars and the reeds would answer with an eight-bar variation of that melody. There wasn't much harmonic adventurousness. Unison and octave-unison voicings were common, and the reed sections, generally made up until the late thirties of two alto saxophones and two tenor saxophones (with everybody doubling on clarinet), had a Goody Two Shoes sound. Fletcher Henderson perfected this foursquare mode of arranging, and it became prevalent and lasted into the forties. But in the late thirties such experimental arrangers and arranger-leaders as Duke Ellington, Benny Carter, Sy Oliver, and Mary Lou Williams began to be felt. They made the big bands they wrote for sound like small bands. They added new voicings and new harmonies, they pointed up the timbres of their soloists and made them an organic part of their surroundings, they eliminated blare and pomp, they put color and texture in their background figures, they loosened the staid nineteen-thirties rhythmic underpinnings. Each had his own voice. Mary Lou Williams was lean and poetic. She might use only three or four instruments in ensemble passages, and when she used her full resources the band resembled an octet. Like Carter and Ellington, she added the dimension of mood to many of her arrangements. Some were misterioso, some were melancholy, some were silken. Benny Carter's bands never sounded big, either. He wrote long, complex melodies for his reed section, and he pitted biting brass figures against them to keep them from cloying. He was a master of dynamics, and his own exemplary improvisations on alto saxophone, trumpet, and clarinet lifted his arrangements. Sy Oliver had a gift for catchy melodies. He also had a sure sense of dynamics and a love of rhythmic excitement. It took iron drummers like Jimmy Crawford and Buddy Rich to weather the rhythmic jolts in his arrangements. He had, like Ellington and Williams, a gift for mood. Ellington turned the big jazz band into a work of art. He collected idiosyncratic soloists and wrote miniature concertos around them. These were notable for their voicings (he often combined instruments from the different sections), for the stream of beautiful submelodies that floated through the background of every arrangement, for the band's soaring sound when he pressed all his instruments into one voice. Ellington moved from the big-band medium into his own sphere. One more gifted experimental arranger appeared in the forties—Gil Evans. He learned from Ellington, and he favored an instrumental palette that included horns and tubas. He was a romantic, and his sounds were rich and stately. The leaves were always turning in Evans' music. There were hundreds of big bands in the thirties and early forties, but there were also many small groups. Some were contained within the big bands, and would come forth once or twice an evening to show off the big group's star soloists. Some were working groups, and were generally found in night clubs. If the big bands were novels, the small bands were short stories.

The big bands were inescapable. Not only did they endlessly crisscross the country but many were heard every night on network radio between eleven and one. They were, of course, dance bands, and hearing them in the flesh could be an exhilarating experience—the intensity of the sound, the timbres of both the sections and the soloists, the rhythmic momentum, the excitement of never knowing what a musician would play when he stood up to solo. (Some bandleaders ordered their stars to repeat note for note the solos they had recorded, particularly if the records were hits.) In turn, people packed twenty deep in front of a bandstand could make a soloist do exultant things. There were three kinds of big bands: the young, heedless, swinging ones (Erskine Hawkins, Bennie Moten, the 1945 Woody Herman); the great commercial bands (Tommy Dorsey, Artie Shaw, Benny Goodman, Glenn Miller, Lionel Hampton, Jimmie Lunceford); and the iconoclastic bands (Duke Ellington, Count Basie, Andy Kirk, Benny Carter, Claude Thornhill). The Smithsonian album is a mixture of all three.

Here is what happens on two numbers in the album. The first is Jimmie Lunceford's 1936 recording of Sy Oliver's "Organ Grinder's Swing." It is a subtle and ingenious set of variations, taken at a medium-slow tempo, on the old eight-bar children's refrain "I like coffee, I like tea, I like the girls, and the girls like me." The melody is played in unison the first time through by muted trumpet, muted trombone, and clarinet (Ellington's "Mood Indigo" trio), accompanied only by temple blocks. There is an eight-bar bridge, in which a baritone saxophone states a variation of the melody while Sy Oliver growls on muted trumpet. The theme is restated by a celeste, accompanied again by the temple blocks. A four-bar clarinet interlude gives way to an eight-bar open-horn trumpet solo by Paul Webster, with saxophone chords behind. Then Oliver, again muted and growl-ing, solos against pushing, off-beat saxophone chords, and the eight-bar theme reappears, played this time by the baritone saxophone, the growling Oliver rampant behind.

The second number is Duke Ellington's 1941 version of Billy Strayhorn's "Just A-Sittin' and A-Rockin'." It consists largely of an eloquent dialogue between Ben Webster and the band, with afterthoughts by Tricky Sam Nanton and Barney Bigard. Ellington and Jimmy Blanton share the four-bar introduction, and Webster states the four-note, two-bar melody and is an-swered by the band. Over the course of two thirty-two-bar choruses, he plays this theme twenty-four times, each time slightly differently, and is immediately answered by the band. He is a Lewis Carroll figure trying again and again to get his way, and being told with every nuance authority can think of, "We shall see." Ray Nance takes the bridge in the first chorus and Webster in the second. Webster finishes his queries, and Nanton and Bigard divide the last chorus. Nanton solos while the band plays Webster's theme, and Bigard picks the melody up and finishes. Ellington and Blanton close with a four-bar coda. A simple, daring, elegant piece of work.

The other choice numbers in the album include Jimmie Lunceford's "Uptown Blues," with Snooky Young's lordly trumpet solo; Ellington's "Take the 'A' Train," "A Gypsy Without a Song," "The 'C' Jam Blues," "Perdido," and the charging "Main Stem"; Mary Lou Williams' bony, sad "Big Jim Blues," played by Andy Kirk; Count Basie's "Sent for You Yesterday" and "9:20 Special," the last chorus of which is graced by a visiting Coleman Hawkins, who is backed by Jo Jones rimshots and those stepping-into-the-cellar Basie left-hand chords; Erskine Hawkins' "Tuxedo Junction" and "Mid night Stroll," both full of light, cool motion; Woody Herman's soaring "Apple Honey"; and Claude Thornhill's humming "Donna Lee" and "Robbins Nest." There are also a generous and welcome number of selections by the big commercial bands, among them Glenn Miller's "In the Mood" and "A String of Pearls," which rests on Bobby Hackett's indestructible one-chorus cornet solo; Tommy Dorsey's "Well, Git It!," "On the Sunny Side of the Street," and "Opus No. One"; Artie Shaw's "Star Dust" and "Begin the Beguine"; and Charlie Barnet's "Skyliner."

There would have been room in the Smithsonian album for a good many of the omitted bands if the selections by Ellington, Basie, Lunceford, Herman, Goodman, Hines, Henderson, and Webb had been pared down—excellence makes its point quickly. Leaving out such mediocre—even poor—material as Louis Armstrong's "Leap Frog," Lionel Hampton's "Till Tom Special," Harry James' "The Mole" and "Friar Rock," Luis Russell's "Ol' Man River," and Glenn Miller's "I Got Rhythm" would have made even more room. And do we need to wade through all of "Sing, Sing, Sing" *again*, particularly when Andy Kirk and Benny Carter are given just one number apiece? The text of the handsome album booklet is by Schuller and Williams, and it is a good primer on big-band jazz. The photographs are plentiful and excellent. Some of the solo credits are incomplete, and we are not told, among other things, that Sy Oliver's "Well, Git It!" is a reworking of the old "Bugle Call Rag."

B.G.—
and Big Sid

Benny Goodman sometimes gave the impression that he would live forever. Like most prolific virtuosos, he was difficult to keep in focus. He made a pass at retiring when he was forty, but he kept reappearing with a new group or a new recording. He was the first important jazz musician to play classical music—a seeming trespass that caused bewilderment and concern among the faithful of both persuasions. His image gradually changed from severity (rimless glasses, patent-leather hair, business suits) to geniality (horn-rims, tousled hair, tweed jackets). He disappeared into his own legend, which decreed that he was a monster—a penny-pinching, thoughtless martinet, who bullied his sidemen and hogged the solo space. It was often said after he reached fifty that his abilities had declined. Yet, however uneven he may occasionally have sounded (he was plagued by depressions and back problems), he played almost as well at the end of his career as he had at the beginning.

But Benny died in June, at the age of seventy-seven, and perhaps it is time to tally the results. There were a lot of Benny Goodmans: the pioneer jazz virtuoso who made the clarinet as important a solo instrument as the trumpet was in the thirties; the unwitting and perhaps unwilling musical evangelist who, in 1935, introduced the young of this country to their own great native music, aerating their Depression lives and making them dance like Shakers; the tough Chicago boy who married a Vanderbilt; and the second-generation Russian Jew who became one of the most famous of the many Russian Jews who have graced American music for the greater part of this century.

Goodman was the ninth of twelve children. His father worked in the stockyards, and his mother was illiterate. He studied with the classical clarinettist Franz Schoepp, who also taught Jimmy Noone and Buster Bailey. He joined the musicians' union when he was thirteen and Ben Pollack's band when he was sixteen. He worked for Pollack on and off from 1925 to 1929, in company with Glenn Miller, Jack Teagarden, Bud Freeman, and Jimmy McPartland. From 1929 to 1934, when he formed his first big band, he scuffled in New York, playing in Broadway pit bands and doing radio shows, and recording with everyone from Bessie Smith to Enrique Madriguera and Ruth Etting. In 1934, his band became one of three bands chosen to play on a weekly three-hour NBC program called "Let's Dance." "If anyone were to ask what was the biggest thing that has ever happened to me," Goodman once told this writer, "landing a place on that show was it." A year later, at the behest of his booker, Willard Alexander, he took his band on the road. They played Pittsburgh, Milwaukee, Denver, Salt Lake City, and San Francisco without much success. But when they got to Sweet's Ballroom, in Oakland, the NBC show had begun to take effect, and there were lines around the block, and it was eventually the same at the Palomar, in Los Angeles, where they were held over for a month. They stopped at the Congress Hotel, in Chicago, on their way east, and stayed six months. They had the country jumping. Back in New York, they had a long engagement at the Hotel Pennsylvania, then went west again to do the Palomar and make a movie. They were at the Pennsylvania in the fall of 1936, and during the winter they made their uproarious appearance at the Paramount Theatre; the audiences, thoroughly worked over by Goodman's recordings and almost daily radio broadcasts, danced in the aisles, stood on their seats, and sometimes stayed through all five shows. In January of 1938, Goodman reached an apogee when, still the unwitting groundbreaker, he gave his famous Carnegie Hall concert. (It was a press agent's idea.) With the exception of Jess Stacy's "Sing, Sing, Sing" solo, the evening was not musically prepossessing, but the concert gave jazz a stature it had not had before.

By this time, the band included the trumpeters Ziggy Elman and Harry James, the pianist Jess Stacy, the drummer Gene Krupa, and the small-group specialists—the pianist Teddy Wilson and the vibraphonist, drummer, and singer Lionel Hampton. The personnel of Goodman's bands rarely remained fixed for more than a week. He constantly fired musicians, or they quit, offended by his capricious behavior. He had a particularly hard time with drummers. Here is an incomplete list of the drummers, stars and journeymen, who passed through his bands between the mid-thirties and the mid-forties: Sammy Weiss, Gene Krupa, Lionel Hampton, Dave Tough, Buddy Schutz, Nick Fatool, Harry Jaeger, Jo Jones, J. C. Heard, Sidney

Catlett, Ralph Collier, Alvin Stoller, Howard Davis, Morey Feld, Buddy Rich, Louis Bellson, Lou Fromm, Tom Romersa, Don Lamond, and Cozy Cole. Duke Ellington used Sonny Greer from the mid-twenties to 1951.

For whatever reasons—perhaps it was an unconscious wish to keep the competition down within his band—Goodman never hired any first-rate trombonists or tenor saxophonists in the thirties. (Goodman could be inscrutable. In 1938, he borrowed Lester Young from Count Basie for a recording date, and in the course of six numbers allowed Young just one eight-bar solo.) This most famous of the Goodman bands was sandwiched between the frenetic trumpet playing of Elman and James and the heavy, here-we-go-down-the-pike drumming of Gene Krupa, with Goodman as its main soloist. The band never had the subtlety of Basie and Ellington and Andy Kirk. It was a very white band, and relied on bravado and muscle. It tended to shout when it played "Bugle Call Rag" and "King Porter Stomp," and to breathe heavily in slow ballads.

Goodman's next and most important band was altogether different. It began to take shape in the late thirties, after James and Krupa departed and Goodman switched from Victor to Columbia. He hired the lead trumpeter Jimmy Maxwell and, in the next year or two, the trumpeters Cootie Williams (from Ellington) and Billy Butterfield (from Artie Shaw), the guitarist Charlie Christian, the trombonist Lou McGarity, the pianist Mel Powell, and, in 1941, the bassist John Simmons and the drummer Sid Catlett. And the satiny arranger Eddie Sauter took over. But this graceful band didn't last long. Christian fell ill and died, Simmons and Williams left, Catlett was fired, Billy Butterfield went with Les Brown, and Mel Powell was drafted. The musicians'-union recording ban, which went into effect in the summer of 1942 and lasted almost two years, was the final stroke. Toying occasionally with bebop, which he never liked much, Goodman had a series of middling bands in the late forties. He had, by then, made close to a hundred recordings with his small groups, many of them among the finest of all jazz records. Then, crippled by the popularity of singers and by a thirty-percent wartime entertainment tax, the big bands began to fail, and in 1948 Goodman gave up his band. The most successful part of his career was over; it had lasted just thirteen years. For the rest of his life, he put together a seemingly endless succession of big and small bands for State Department tours, for night-club gigs and television shows, for recording sessions, and even for a fortieth-anniversary celebration of his Carnegie Hall concert. This reconstituted evening remains vivid only because he had three pianists shuttling on- and offstage (Jimmy Rowles, John Bunch, Mary Lou Williams), a girl singer he had first heard a week or so before, and a finale in which he sat down and soloed with his feet up on one end of Lionel Hampton's vibraphone.

Goodman played a demanding instrument with almost unfailing beauty for fifty years—an extraordinary stretch, unmatched by any other jazz musician. Buddy DeFranco once explained why the clarinet is hard to play: "The clarinet's three registers—chalumeau, middle, and altissimo—are built in twelfths. If you press the octave key on a saxophone, you go up or down an octave, but on a clarinet you go twelve tones—from, say, low F to middle C. Saxophones have pads over the air holes. When you press a key, the pad closes the hole and you get a note. Clarinets have seven tone holes and no pads, and you have to close them with the ends of your fingers. So you have to have absolute finger control. If any air escapes, you get a terrible squeak or no note at all. Going from the middle register of the clarinet to the altissimo is very awkward because the fingering changes completely. That's the reason so many clarinettists seem to lose control when they go into the top register, why they tend to shriek." Goodman had a full, even tone in all three registers. But it never got in the way of his playing. It never came first, as it often did in the work of Pee Wee Russell and Edmond Hall and Irving Fazola. He was a melodic improviser, and his attack—the snapping runs, the quick, almost epigrammatic melodies, the carefully screened emotion, the rhythmic surefootedness—invariably implied that he knew where his solo would land long before it got there. Goodman's style

174

changed little. In the thirties and the early forties, he would occasionally growl and carry on, but later he abandoned such emotional yawing and became almost academic. After he married gentry and became a Connecticut gentleman, his playing always had a press.

Sidney Catlett joined Benny Goodman early in June of 1941 and was fired in October. His place was taken by a mediocre drummer named Ralph Collier. When Goodman was asked many years later why he had done something similar to Toscanini's firing Vladimir Horowitz, he said, "It's slways been one of my enigmas—drummers." The band appeared that summer at the Steel Pier, in Atlantic City, at the Hotel Sherman, in Chicago, and at Frank Dailey's Meadowbrook, in Cedar Grove, New Jersey. It broadcast almost every night, and it went into the recording studios in Chicago and New York seven or eight times. From all indications, Catlett, who suddenly found himself in the challenging and auspicious position of being the first black drummer ever hired full time by a white big band, behaved with his customary tact, taste, and brilliance.

Here is what Mel Powell, now a classical composer and professor of music, said of Catlett the other day: "I always thought that this giant of a man had no peer as a percussionist. After all, he was playing on nothing but a set of traps—a snare drum, a couple of tomtoms, a bass drum, and some cymbals. Yet he invariably sounded as if he were playing delicately tuned drums. Where he hit his snare with his stick, how hard he hit it, where and how he hit his cymbals and tomtoms—all these things transformed ordinary sounds into pitches that matched and enhanced what he heard around him. His sensitivity and delicacy of ear were extraordinary. So was his time. He'd nail the band into the tempo with such power *and* gentleness that one night I was absolutely transported by what he was doing. Watching him lift and carry us, I took my hands off the keyboard and missed the beginning of a solo. I don't think I have ever been more awed by a musical performance. Sid's personality reflected his playing. He was lovable and loving. He was gentle. He was compassionate and concerned. He was also vulnerable. I saw tears in his eyes the night he was told, just after he'd joined the band, that his uniform wasn't ready yet, that he'd have to play in his street clothes, and so—to him—look unfinished. He had a wonderful sense of humor, and, among other things, he liked to take off black stereotypes. He had never flown—in fact, he had carefully avoided flying. But the only way to get to a gig we had in Canada was by plane. Sid asked to sit next to me, and when they were starting to rev the engines one of the boys in the band called out, 'Hey! What's that weird noise in the engine?' Sid turned to me and rolled his eyes and said, 'Oh, merciful God!' It was flawless Stepin Fetchit—and it almost hid his fear. I have never been able to figure out why Benny fired Sid. All that comes to mind is that Benny was not a follower and neither was Sid. But Benny was the boss."

Catlett had spent his career in the big black bands of Benny Carter, Rex Stewart, Fletcher Henderson, Don Redman, and Louis Armstrong, and the job with Goodman put him squarely before the white public. It also put him in tacit competition with the celebrated Gene Krupa, who had left Goodman three years earlier to start his own big band. Catlett was thirty-one years old and at the height of his powers. Goodman's dismissal must have stunned him, but it didn't derail him. He returned briefly to Louis Armstrong's unpressed big band and then went with Teddy Wilson's masterly sextet at Café Society Uptown. He was the only drummer at the Metropolitan Opera House concert in January of 1944. (Those present were winners of an *Esquire* jazz poll, and they included Armstrong, Art Tatum, Billie Holiday, Red Norvo, Mildred Bailey, Teddy Wilson, Jack Teagarden, Coleman Hawkins, Roy Eldridge, Lionel Hampton, and Oscar Pettiford.) He had his own small groups in the mid-forties, and he recorded with everyone from Eddie Condon to Duke Ellington to Lester Young to Dizzy Gillespie. In 1946, he became an original member of Louis Armstrong's All Stars. A heart attack in 1949 slowed him down—but not enough—and he died on Easter Sunday in 1951.

Catlett sounds relatively subdued on the eighteen or so studio recordings that he made with Goodman. Recording engineers, still using jumpy pre-tape equipment, were wary of drummers, and often placed them at the back of the studio. And Goodman, the perfectionist, tended to frown on any sort of inspirational waywardness when he recorded. But now, with the release of "Benny and Sid 'Roll 'Em'" (Honeysuckle Rose Records), it is at last clear how Catlett really sounded with Goodman. He drove the band (and Goodman) almost unmercifully, and he demonstrated once and for all how to play big-band drums. The recording consists of twenty-five air checks (one is made up of snippets of "Roll 'Em" taken from four different broadcasts) recorded between July 12 and October 8, 1941. The broadcasts were recorded by a Denver fan and by the New York collector Jerry Newman. The Honeysuckle record was produced by Jerry Valburn, who, with the help of Jack Towers and John T. Gill, has very nearly restored the recordings to what they must have sounded like on a decent radio. The selections include old Goodman material ("Sing, Sing, Sing" and "Ida"), numbers made popular by other bands ("Flying Home," "Tuesday at Ten," "Concerto for Cootie," "One O'Clock Jump"), and tunes that Goodman either had recently recorded or was getting reaaady to record ("A Smooth One," "Benny Rides Again," "The Count," "The Earl," "Pound Ridge," "Clarinet à la King," and "Roll 'Em"). The Goodman band was primarily an ensemble group with one principal soloist—its leader. Other soloists (in order of space given them) were Cootie Williams, Lou McGarity, Vido Musso, Billy Butterfield, and Catlett, who was mainly allotted two- and four-bar breaks. Catlett, though never obtrusive, is everywhere—almost tilting the band on the first "The Earl" and the first "Benny Rides Again"; using luxurious press rolls behind Williams on a languorous, dreaming "Concerto for Cootie"; using three perfectly placed tomtom beats on the final bridge of "The Birth of the Blues"; driving Goodman very hard with his tomtoms on a fast "Sing, Sing, Sing"; and dropping, like mots, his immaculate and unique rim shots. Catlett clearly had a strange effect on Goodman, who solos at great length throughout the recording. The precise, parsed

Goodman of the studio recordings is nowhere to be heard. This Goodman is wild and woolly, and even experimental (the first chorus of "Pound Ridge"). Sometimes, perhaps driven beyond his powers, he is forced and empty. Catlett was over-qualified.

From Joplin to Goodman, and Slightly Beyond

TUESDAY: The 92nd Street Y's second annual mini-festival Jazz in July began tonight in Kaufmann Concert Hall. The advance material has been somewhat overwrought. A concert built around three clarinettists is called "Licorice Shticks," and an evening of jazz-influenced classical music is "Blazing Fiddles: Symphonic Flirtations with Jazz." The concert tonight involved ragtime and the pianist Max Morath, who was the master of ceremonies. Morath is a ragtime historian who likes to make jokes about the music, and whenever he was onstage there was a feeling that someone would run out and hold up a laugh card. But the music survived the gags, thanks to the pianist-bandleader-composer Dick Hyman, who is the artistic director of the festival and also played tonight, and to the tubist Harvey Phillips, who conducted the first-rate eighteen-piece 92nd Street Ragtime Concert Band. (Its members, tuned to the general jocularity, had on bow ties and red silk vests.) Included in the band were the trumpeter Joe Wilder, the trombonists Wayne André and George Masso, the clarinettist Phil Bodner, the banjoist and guitarist Howard Alden, and the drummer Ron Traxler. The best numbers were James Scott's "Grace and Beauty," Joseph Lamb's "Ragtime Nightingale," Scott Joplin's "Maple Leaf Rag," and Adaline Shepherd's "Pickles and Peppers," which brought much merriment from Morath over the fact that it was used as a campaign tune by William Jennings

Bryan when he lost the Presidential election to William Howard Taft. The evening wandered chronologically. Hyman and the band played orchestrations of Jelly Roll Morton's "Grandpa's Spells" and "The Pearls," which revealed how close Morton's music was to ragtime, and Hyman played a solo version of Morton's numbing "Finger Buster," a display piece Morton used to cow competitors with. Phillips also did the "Trombone Blues," a "Walkaround" played by circus bands when acts were being changed. He closed the evening with a ringing "Stars and Stripes Forever," after which the musicians waved tiny American flags and looked sheepish. Earlier, the singer Carrie Smith, who likes to re-create Bessie Smith, did half a dozen red-hot-mama numbers, including "After You've Gone," "Ja-Da," and "Beale Street blues."

The Y festival, it should be pointed out, is self-limiting. Dick Hyman told Jon Pareles in today's *Times*, "Until bebop . . . jazz still played by the rules of songs. It was improvisations on themes people knew, and people could pick up on them, even if they had never thought songs could be done this way. In the newer music, you don't quite know what's going on until you learn the new language—it's a different repertory, a different length of solos and a different goal in performance. . . . Not to be too blunt, but the music takes itself too seriously now. . . . What this festival is not about is music that is somber, perplexing, hostile or boring. It's a festival of hot jazz." In short, a paean to old practices, old principles, old joys.

WEDNESDAY: Dick Hyman put together a model jazz concert tonight. Here is how the first half went: The house band for the evening—Joe Wilder, the tenor saxophonists Buddy Tate and Al Cohn, the trombonist Al Grey, the pianists Derek Smith and Hyman, the bassist Milt Hinton, and the drummer Butch Miles—played a medium-tempo "Perdido." Wilder and Cohn disappeared, and Grey and Tate did a fast "Tangerine." Carrie Smith, backed by Hyman, Hinton, Miles, Wilder, and Cohn, sang "You've Changed" and an Alberta Hunter blues. Hinton played an unaccompanied solo on "Jericho." Tate offered

"Polka Dots and Moonbeams," and Hyman and Smith did unaccompanied duets on "Gravy Waltz," a gospel-like number by the bassist Ray Brown, and on Jerome Kern's "All the Things You Are." Grey appeared with the rhythm section for a very slow "Summertime." This half of the concert was closed by Tate and Cohn, who hustled through a fast Count Basie number and were joined in the last chorus by Wilder and Grey.

The rest of the evening had even more variety. The tap dancers Honi Coles, Bubber Gaines, and Charles (Cookie) Cook did half a dozen numbers. Then Joe Wilder, on flugelhorn, played two a-cappella choruses of "Willow Weep for Me." Cohn and Derek Smith each had a solo excursion, and Carrie Smith returned for the last three numbers of the concert, in company with the whole band, both pianists presiding.

THURSDAY: Vince Giordano and his various bands have been expertly reproducing the jazz of the twenties and thirties for over ten years, and tonight they gave another exhibition of how to do jazz repertory. In the course of fifteen numbers, the band re-created Bix Beiderbecke as he was with the Wolverines, with Jean Goldkette, with Frankie Trumbauer, with Paul Whiteman, and with his own groups. The band included two trumpets, trombone, three reeds, piano, banjo, guitar, drums, violin, a singer, and the leader on string bass, tuba, bass saxophone, and a Bing Crosby vocal, and it swung without being quaint (a common fault among the pioneer repertory groups of ten or fifteen years ago) or too free (young repertory musicians are apt to unconsciously use rhythmic devices unknown in the twenties and thirties). The ensembles, with their intricate saxophone writing and staccato brass, were never stilted, and neither were the solos. Bill Challis's complex, multilayered arrangements ("Clarinet Marmalade," "Lonely Melody," " 'Taint So Honey, 'Taint So") never faltered, and Fud Livingston's 1927 arrangement of his "Humpty Dumpy" was a revelation—its fresh, winding harmonies and voicings presaged the Ellington of the thirties. Beiderbecke's solos were played by Randy Sandke, a trumpeter who has digested the styles of the twenties, thirties, and forties. Beiderbecke has been widely imitated, and among his most persuasive admirers have been Jimmy McPartland, Red Nichols, and the early Bobby Hackett. At first, Sandke's tone was not quite belling enough, and he played too far behind the beat. But halfway through he began punching out his notes and making his tone linger. Dick Hyman played Beiderbecke's "In a Mist" with the seeming casualness that Beiderbecke himself, a come-as-you-are pianist, might have displayed.

During the second part of the evening, Hyman and the violinist Stan Kurtis redid three of the small-band numbers that Joe Venuti recorded in the late twenties and early thirties—"The Wild Dog," "Four String Joe," "Satan's Holiday." Kurtis caught Venuti's sound and came close to his insuperable swing, and all that was missing was the guitar and the bass saxophone that Venuti used on some of his original recordings. The ten final numbers of the concert were given over to a Jelly Roll Morton band, made up of Warren Vaché, on cornet; Phil Bodner; Jack Gale on trombone; Hyman; Major Holley on bass and tuba; Marty Grosz on banjo; and Ron Traxler. They played two of the famous 1926 Red Hot Pepper numbers, and the rest were taken from the often underrated dates Morton did after he moved from Chicago to New York in 1928. Vaché did well with Ward Pinkett's acidic trumpet, and Gale was masterly in recapturing the trombonist Geechy Fields. Bodner, doing Omer Simeon and Albert Nicholas, was uncanny—he poured and mooned and was tonally perfect.

TUESDAY: Jocularity reigned again tonight. We were offered a program of stride piano playing, and the pianists on hand—Dick Wellstood, Dick Hyman, Mike Lipskin, Ralph Sutton, Judy Carmichael, and Jay McShann—played not only as soloists and in duets but in a round robin and six strong at three pianos. (McShann did not really belong. He is a Kansas City blues pianist, and his duets with Sutton were a jarring mixture of Eastern stride and Western blues.) Wellstood and Hyman fashioned two blithe and crowded duets, the second of which, Jerome Kern's "Who," was full of echoes of the version done in

1939 on Bluebird by Frankie Newton, Pete Brown, and James P. Johnson. Mike Lipskin, who studied with Willie the Lion Smith, did four solo numbers (with Butch Miles playing over-fancy wire brushes on a snare drum set upstage front), and got the ho-ho tone of the evening going by making jokes and singing two off-key Fats Waller-type vocals that sounded more like parodies than like the tributes they were meant to be. The round robin, with Lipskin, Wellstood, and Hyman, followed. Wellstood played a fine solo rendition of "Lulu's Back in Town," and Hyman matched him with a solo "Jeepers Creepers." The Classic Jazz Quartet came on for just three numbers. These included "Happy Feet," Fats Waller's "How Can You Face Me," and the Boswell Sisters' "It's the Girl," done without a vocal. Sutton and McShann did "Lady, Be Good," and Sutton, who moves readily between ironbound stride numbers and Debussy ballads, performed by himself, and McShann sang and played a solo blues. Judy Carmichael, a young stride pianist from California, did four numbers and demonstrated a strong left hand and a mechanical, striving right hand. All the pianists appeared in the jam-session finale, and so did the Classic Jazz Quartet.

Two notes: Almost no amplification has been used during the festival (Kaufmann Hall may be the best small auditorium in New York City), and it is marvellous to hear music without distortion of any kind. We have been treated to what is well on its way toward vanishing—unadulterated human music.

Milt Hinton has taken close to thirty thousand photographs of his colleagues during his fifty-year career, and forty-five of his pictures are on display in the gallery adjacent to Kaufmann Hall. Hinton took his pictures at rehearsals, in recording studios, onstage and backstage, on the bus, and on the street—probably out of a need to try and slow down the fluid, evanescent life around him. In one picture, the clarinettist Scoville Browne and the bassists Jimmy Blanton and Al Lucas stand in front of the Hotel Braddock in Harlem in 1940, with the twenty-two-year-old Blanton, who was already on his brilliant way (he died two years later), in snappy chest-high, chalk-striped trousers and a straw hat. In another, Dizzy Gillespie and Charles Mingus are laughing uproariously at a beer stand at the 1971 Newport Jazz Festival. In another, taken in 1967, Gene Krupa is at his drums, the handsome, flamboyant youth still visible in the middle-aged man. Again, Willie the Lion Smith and Eubie blake sit silently side by side, the Lion in his derby and cigar and Blake with his oarlike hands in his lap. And, finally, Tyree Glenn and Chu Berry, Hinton's old mates in the Cab Calloway band of the early forties, stand in their overcoats beneath a sign reading "Hamburgers. Hot Dogs. Lunches. For Colored Only."

WEDNESDAY: "Licorice Shticks" was begun by Kenny Davern, accompanied by Milt Hinton, Howard Alden, Dick Hyman, and Butch Miles. Davern came up in the early sixties, during the last days of the Condon gang, and he has worked frequently with Dick Wellstood and Bob Wilber. Emotion governs his style. He did a medium-tempo "Linger Awhile," a very slow, almost creepy "Summertime," and a medium "Wrap Your Troubles in Dreams," and was joined by the Belgian harmonica player and composer Toots Thielemans for a slow blues, which was distinguished by Alden's solo—particularly his ringing third chorus. Davern closed with a jigging "Jazz Me Blues." Peanuts Hucko, a veteran of the big bands, the Condon gang, the studios, and the Louis Armstrong All Stars, is possibly the best of Benny Goodman's imitators, and he did three gleaming Goodman numbers, the last (with Thielemans) an excited, pressing version of Goodman's old flag-waver "The World Is Waiting for the Sunrise." The festival poked its nose carefully into modern times in the person of the clarinettist Eddie Daniels, a Juilliard graduate who worked in the sixties and seventies with the Thad Jones–Mel Lewis band and is stylistically in the mode of Sonny Rollins and John Coltrane. He played three partly written, rather monotonous numbers that moved between jazz and classical music ("Alone Together," Gershwin's Second Prelude, and a C. P. E. Bach solfeggietto), and a very fast "I Want to Be Happy," on which he and Milt Hinton played a duet. In the evening's last number, the three clarinettists plus Thielemans did a rummaging, rampaging "Sheik of Araby."

THURSDAY: It is strange that jazz and classical music got in each other's hair for so long—the one sneering at the old bore and the other at the messy upstart. Improvisation was part of European formal music well into the nineteenth century, and virtuosity has long been one of its guidons. And jazz musicians were quick to absorb European harmonic methods and forms. European composers were beguiled by jazz rhythms, and jazz musicians readily admired the pastels of Debussy and Ravel. Whether classical composers were much influenced by jazz when it first became widespread has never been clear, and it wasn't any clearer after tonight's attractive concert, the last of the festival. A twenty-nine-piece orchestra, under the direction of Maurice Peress, played seven formal compositions (one was an excerpt) supposedly influenced by jazz. Five were written in the twenties, when jazz began to take hold, one in the thirties, and one just ten years ago. The most impressive of the early pieces were George Antheil's "A Jazz Symphony" (1925) and James P. Johnson's "Yamekraw: A Negro Rhapsody" (1927). Antheil's composition boils with Stravinsky dissonances and has the staccato weight of Soviet industrial music. There are jazz touches—a sounded regular beat, a wa-wa trumpet solo over a ground bass, and crashing piano interludes (played by Ivan Davis) that predict the Cecil Taylor of forty years later. The composition ends, however, with a heady, swirling waltz—the lady of the house sweeping out the poker players at one in the morning. Johnson's piece, probably written in reaction to Gershwin's "Rhapsody in Blue" (the first formal piece to truly reflect jazz), is genteel and primitive and sentimental. There is a stride-piano passage (Dick Hyman was on piano) and a flash of boogie-woogie and several choruses of the blues, swathed in strings. It is a timid, inert piece. Bohuslav Martinu's short "Le Jazz" (1928) resembles a Paul Whiteman orchestration of the period, and a suite from Darius Milhaud's ballet "La Création du Monde" (1923) resembled Debussy and had a long, melancholy alto-saxophone solo (played smoothly by Jack Kripl) that had a peculiar and oblique jazz feeling—almost akin to one of Charles Mingus's meditations. Hyman appeared in his own "Ragtime

Fantasy," for piano and orchestra (1976), a sedate and polished reflection of that elegant music which came to life in a rattling Baby Dodds-style drum passage and in direct ragtime allusions by the pianist. The most unusual selection of the evening was John Alden Carpenter's "Krazy Kat," in which the orchestra played melodic string passages while George Herriman's "Krazy Kat" cartoons were shown on a screen at the back of the stage and a narration was read by June Le Bell. (The narration and the music worked at cross-purposes.) It was good to see Herriman's surreal drawings blown up, but the music had little or nothing to do with jazz. The program was closed by Gershwin's "'I Got Rhythm' Variations" (1934). The orchestra and the piano (played by Ivan Davis) exchanged fragmented variations on Gershwin's famous song (where would bebop have been without it?), and there were suggestions—they resound all through Gershwin's later orchestral works—of "Rhapsody in Blue."

1987

The Keynotes _____

Supervising jazz recordings in the days of the 78-r.p.m. recording was delicate and demanding. The A. & R. (artists and repertoire) man, as the recording director is called, was responsible for choosing congenial musicians, for getting them into the studio on time, for helping them pick apposite material, for somehow softening the frigid atmosphere of most recording studios, for making the musicians' improvisations fit the three- or five-minute time limit of the 78 without deflating them, and, most difficult of all, for deciding immediately just how good a take was. One of the sharpest of the old A. & R. men was Harry Lim, a Dutch-Javanese jazz fan and organizer of jam sessions in Chicago and New York, who, in the mid-forties, supervised fifty or so small-band sessions for the Keynote label, nearly a third of which are among the best of all jazz recordings. (Keynote, begun in 1940 by Eric Bernay as a left-wing folk-music operation, became in Lim's hands the equal of such other pioneer independent jazz labels as Milt Gabler's Comodore and Alfred Lion's Blue Note.) All but two or three of Lim's classic sessions were done in 1944, when he was in his mid-twenties. Small-band swing had suddenly risen to a kind of pre-bebop climax, and recording companies were frenetically attempting to fill the vacuum left by the just ended sixteen-month recording ban. Lim directed no fewer than twenty-one sessions between the end of 1943 and the end of 1944, five of them in a two-week burst in late spring. He had an unerring and daring sense of whom to record and in what combinations. He put Lester Young, who was in loose, superlative form, with the sparkling, chameleon pianist Johnny Guarnieri (who could paraphrase Teddy Wilson, Count Basie, and Fats Waller), the humming bassist Slam Stewart, and Big Sid Catlett. He put three trumpeters (Roy Eldridge, Joe Thomas, Emmett Berry), four trombonists (Benny Morton, Vic Dickenson, Bill Harris, Claude Jones), and four saxophonists (Coleman Hawkins, Tab Smith, Don Byas, Harry Carney) with rhythm sections. He put Coleman Hawkins and Teddy Wilson together four times (both were at their most commanding), and mixed them, on two of the sessions, with either Roy Eldridge or Buck Clayton. He put Joe Thomas with the ex-Lunceford trombonist Trummy Young and with the still imperious Earl Hines. He turned eight times to Thomas, a beautiful, aphoristic, little-known player, mixing him also with the huge, jumping alto saxophonist Pete Brown, with Red Norvo and Vic Dickenson, and with Jack Teagarden and the pianist Herman Chittison. He used small groups from the big bands of Cab Calloway, Count Basie, Duke Ellington, and Woody Herman. The Basie session turned out to be the best small-band date the pianist ever made. Lim went West and recorded Nat Cole and Benny Carter. He recorded George Barnes' sleek sextet in Chicago and the New Orleans clarinetist Irving Fazola.

Very little that Lim did in 1944 went wrong, but early in 1945 he began to change direction. Always attentive to little-known players, he became obsessed by them. He recorded saxophonists like Herbie Haymer and Babe Russin and Corky Corcoran, and trumpeters like Clyde Hurley and Manny Klein and Dick Cathcart. He used pianists like Bernie Leighton and Tommy Todd and Skitch Henderson. He made his first second-rate recordings. There were notable exceptions: the Nat Cole date; a couple of sessions with the trombonist Bill Harris; Joe Thomas's elegant "Black Butterfly" session; and Lennie Tristano's first recording date under his own name. In 1946, the label got into financial difficulties, and the next year Lim quit, leaving his invaluable masters behind. Keynote was bought by Mercury Records, which in time was absorbed by Phonogram, which became Poly-Gram. Mercury reissued some of the Keynotes in helter-skelter fashion in the fifties, and some came out on the Trip label in the seventies. Then, for a long time, nothing happened, and it began to seem that the great early Keynotes, like the great early Blue Notes, had disappeared.

But now the Japanese jazz expert Kioshi Koyama, working in conjunction with PolyGram and with the Japanese branch of Phonogram, has brought forth the entire Keynote catalogue in a boxed set of twenty-one L.P.s, as "The Complete Keynote Collection." The reissue includes almost three hundred and fifty performances, a third of them alternate takes and previously unreleased masters. The first twelve L.P.s, which go through 1944, are essential, and the bright spots carry most of the remainder. Here are four classic numbers from the early sessions. The first is the fast blues "Afternoon of a Basie-ite," recorded on December 28, 1943, by the Lester Young Quartet. Johnny Guarnieri, doing his Basie, plays three choruses, backed by tight, pushing Catlett high hat. (High hat of this kind is invariably associated with Jo Jones, but Catlett recorded some in 1933, when Jones was still to be heard from.) Young takes five choruses, using every swinging trick he knew: honks; lazy nasal figures; marvellous short, tucking runs; half-time swoops. Catlett backs him with a panoply of snare and bass-drum accents that the early bebop drummers must have listened to. Slam Stewart appears for two choruses, and on the first of the two takes of the number Guarnieri spices Stewart's solo with some wild upper-register figures. Catlett solos for one chorus, using his high hat and snare on the first take and mainly snare figures on the second. Both solos crackle and jump. Young returns for two more choruses, and the number ends. Young and Catlett recorded together only twice, which is a pity. They worked like birds and air.

The second number, recorded a month later, is "Fiesta in Brass," by Little Jazz and His Trumpet Ensemble—Eldridge, Thomas, and Emmett Berry, joined by Guarnieri, Israel Crosby on bass, and Cozy Cole on drums. It is a study in brass textures. Eldridge, though muted, is rough-toned and hurrying; Berry is querulous but patient; the gentle Thomas soars and ponders. The number is a medium blues, and consists of identical opening-and-closing unison annunciatory ensembles enclosing two-chorus solos by Guarnieri, again doing his Basie, and El-dridge, Thomas, and Berry. Thomas, with his ballooning tone and his exquisite choice of notes, takes the honors.

The third and fourth numbers are part of the Joe Thomas–Trummy Young–Coleman Hawkins–Earl Hines date, on February 22, 1944. Sam Coslow's "Just One More Chance" is built around Hawkins, who plays a chorus of embellished melody (backed by lovely ascending organ chords), gives way to a chorus of Earl Hines (with a bridge by the guitarist Teddy Walters), and returns for a closing twenty-four bars of improvisation. There are two takes, and both match the best of Hawkins' recorded ballads. He sounds as though he had finally decided to wipe out all those impinging Lester Youngs and Ben Websters and Don Byases with one majestic, obliterating number. His tone is enormous, his vibrato surging. He plays with power and deli-cacy and lyricism. "Thru' for the Night" is the fourth number. Its attractive melody, written by Trummy Young, is based on "Honeysuckle Rose." The band does the melody in a swinging, medium-slow tempo, with Hines providing icing. Then, cush-ioned on a repeat of the melody, he splits a chorus with Walters. Hines' solo is full of tremolos and glisses and runs, topped by upper-register diamonds. His dynamics are the breezes presag-ing a storm. Thomas takes an empyrean half chorus, and Trummy Young, very delicate and nasal, takes the other half. Hawkins plays twenty-four resounding bars, and there are eight measures of closing ensemble.

Traps,
the Drum Wonder

When Buddy Rich first recorded his "West Side Story" medley, late in 1966, his solo, surrounded by eight minutes of instrumental framework, lasted just under two minutes. When he made what turned out to be his final recording of the number, in April of 1985—Rich died early this spring, at the age of sixty-nine—he took two solos, the first four minutes long, and the second six minutes long. His life—though dogged by chronic heart trouble, by financial difficulties, by a wild temper, and by a boundless ego—seemed, like his solos, to gain momentum. The pianist Mel Powell appeared with Rich on a jazz cruise in the fall of 1986. "He was playing superbly," Powell said recently. "He was relaxed, and not in a show-business mood. He sounded sturdy but subtle. Working with just small groups and without any pressures must have been a joy to him. He didn't much want to take solos, and when I gave him the signal for four-bar exchanges he barely agreed. His playing demonstrated what it might have been like throughout his career if he had been able more often to play in such convivial, low-key situations. Working with big bands was a kind of theatre that he both loved and loathed and never got free of. He looked marvellous on the cruise. His hair was whitish, but he had a Palm Springs tan, and there wasn't a wrinkle in his face. We had a kidding relationship, and when I asked him how he managed to keep so well he said, 'By staying on the road,' which is indeed where he spent most of his life."

Rich was born in Brooklyn, and he had two sisters and a brother. His parents were in vaudeville. He once described his mother as "a singer and a heavy-made woman and very pretty," and he went on to say, "My father was a soft-shoe dancer and a blackface comedian. He was strong and nice-looking and had a great sense of humor. But when you stepped out of line you got a shot in the mouth and that straightened you out." Rich's parents brought him into their act when he was a toddler, and at the age of seven he travelled around the world as Traps, the Drum Wonder. For a time, in the early thirties, he was making a thousand dollars a week singing, dancing, and drumming, and was the second-highest-paid child star, after Jackie Coogan. But in 1936, to his father's chagrin, he turned his back on vaudeville. The clarinettist Joe Marsala hired him, and, two years later, gave him the space on "Jim Jam Stomp" for his first recorded drum solo, a seventeen-second explosion—on snare, snare rims, woodblock, cowbell, and bass drum—that must have turned heads. In 1938, Rich took a job with Bunny Berigan's big band, then he moved on to Artie Shaw and, later, to Tommy Dorsey. He formed his own big band in the mid-forties, but that was a shaky time for big bands, and it went under. During the next twenty years, he patched together a career with Jazz at the Philharmonic, with Harry James' and Les Brown's big bands, and with various small groups. He formed another big band in 1966, and he kept it off and on until he died.

New York was full of great drummers when Rich came up. He listened to Tony Briglia with the Casa Loma band, to O'Neil Spencer, to Dave Tough, to Lester Young's brother Lee, to Sidney Catlett, to Gene Krupa, to the singer and drummer Leo Watson, and, above all, to Chick Webb, the tiny, amazing hunchbacked drummer from Baltimore. (With the exception of Catlett, who was well over six feet, all the master swing drummers were small. Napoleons of Noise, a contemporary dubbed them.) Webb's driving, on-the-beat snare-drum figures reappeared again and again in Rich's solos. Though totally untrained, Rich became a virtuoso and, like most virtuosos, he became a captive of his technique. His technique was his style, for he had no style in the conventional sense. He could play what amounted to a single-stroke roll with one hand, and he could very nearly do the same thing with one foot, on the pedal of his bass drum. He could move between his tomtoms and his snare drum and his cymbals with such speed that he gave the impression he was playing simultaneously on three different parts of his set. His long solos were not rhythmic investigations as much as avalanches—he wanted to bury his listeners with his brilliance, with crushing rolls and rimshots, with round-the-set rocketry and bass-drum thunder. Occasionally, he relented. He would take a funny wire-brush solo, or fool around a long time on his cymbals. That's what he does through much of his second solo in his 1985 "West Side Story" recording. He begins with a hard right-and-left Chick Webb figure on his snare, and switches to his cymbals (he was using four, plus his high hat), making breeze noises, chime sounds, all the while growing softer and softer. Then he moves to his snare rims for a ticking mile-a-minute roll, carries the roll to his closed high hat, inserts a couple of offbeat rimshots on his snare and a tomtom, drops some jolting bass-drum bombs, returns to his cymbals, rolls again on his rims, and settles onto his snare for some broken-field figures, interspersed with cymbal splashes and bass-drum accents. He closes with one of his great showoff feats: a single-stroke roll, gradually slowed down to alternate individual strokes, then just as gradually speeded up until it returns to a full, creamy roll. He mixes in his cymbals and his bass drum and, sharply increasing the volume on his snare drum, brings the solo to a climax.

Rich did not get a particularly attractive timbre on his drums—they always sounded gray and matter-of-fact. Nor did he have much taste. He kept excellent time behind whomever he was accompanying, but how he did his accompanying—whether to back a trombonist with a ride cymbal or a high hat, say—didn't seem to matter to him. Instead of carrying a band from within, in the subtle, insinuating manner of Webb and Tough and Catlett, he pushed it before him, like a man throwing someone out of his house. And it was never certain—except in his sometimes exhilarating four- and eight-bar breaks—that he could swing. He had a metronomic quality—an inability to move his time back and forth within a beat. There are several passages in the two long solos that Catlett took during Louis Armstong's Symphony Hall concert in 1947 ("Satchmo at Symphony Hall"; MCA records) which are so rhythmically infectious they make you dance. Rich never did that; he wowed you but rarely moved you.

Rich was compact and slightly below medium height. He had close-cropped hair, battered-handsome looks, and what he would have described as a Charlie Glamour smile—although, dead serious on the stand, he did not often show it when he played. He was a sharp dresser, and he liked to drive fast. He was sardonic and unpredictable, and he affected a slightly belligerent air. He had a caustic show-biz wit; when he didn't strain, he could hold his own with Johnny Carson. As a bandleader, he was something of a martinet. He was not a blowhard, but he did not have any false modesty. He once said, "I'm told I'm not humble, but who is? I remember being interviewed by a college kid once, and he said 'Mr. Rich, who is the greatest drummer in the world?' and I said 'I am.' He laughed, and said 'No, really, Mr. Rich, who do you consider the greatest drummer alive?' I said 'Me. It's a fact.' He couldn't get over it. But why go through that humble bit? Look at Ted Williams—straight ahead, no tipping of his cap when he belted one out of the park."

Rich demonstrated where he was headed when he was with Artie Shaw's band. Shaw said of him not long ago, "When Buddy came in the band, in 1939, he couldn't read music—and, for that matter, I don't think he could read any better at the end of his life. I told him that some of our arrangements were pretty complex. He asked me if he could sit out front a couple of nights and learn the arrangements. He did, and said he was ready, and he was—amazingly so. He was an amusing, ebullient kid, and sometimes he'd get so excited when he was playing that he'd yell and rush the beat. Near the end of the year he was with the band, he began going off on his own in his playing, doing things that were good for him but not for the band. I sat him down and told him what he had begun doing, and not long after we parted amicably. He went with Tommy Dorsey, which was just right, because Tommy had a big show band. The vitality and exuberance that poured out of Buddy were endless."

Virtuosos share one nightmare. "When I think that I can't play the way I want to play," Rich once said, "I'll hang up my sticks. That'll be it. There'd be nothing more horrible than to hear some guy say, 'Poor Buddy Rich, he doesn't have it anymore.'" He needn't have worried.

John Hammond
and Dick Wellstood

With his customary princely aplomb, John Hammond wrote in his autobiography, *John Hammond on Record,* "Death has never frightened me. I have led a full life, one I have enjoyed, and when it ends it ends." It did early this summer, when he was in his seventy-seventh year. Although he was slowed by repeated heart attacks, Hammond never stopped going. He explained in his autobiography what drove him: "It will always be difficult for me to sit still, to wait a moment or a day before setting out to discover the world all over again. I am an early riser, among the first to buy each day's *Times,* and my daily armful of new magazines is as much my trademark as my crewcut. . . . This compulsion to see, to read, to hear everything as soon as possible is as strong now as it ever was, and to be the first to know—or, certainly, never the last—is vitally important to me. To allow the events of a single day to reach me second hand, to miss my morning call at the newsstand, to drive without the car radio turned on, to pass by a marquee announcing a show or a movie or a jazz player unknown to me will never be possible. I try to be careful, but I cannot stop."

Hammond was a great discoverer and champion of American musical talent. His most adventurous and influential years lasted from early in the Depression to the first of the recording bans in the forties. Here are some of the things he did during that exhilarating time: took a *mixed* band (Frankie Newton, Benny Carter, Pee Wee Russell, Fats Waller, Eddie Condon, Artie Bernstein, and Zutty Singleton) to the staid Mt. Kisco Golf and Tennis Club for a 1932 Saturday-night dance; recorded such relatively unknown masters as Fletcher Henderson, Carter, Coleman Hawkins, Red Allen, Chu Berry, Roy Eldridge, Dicky Wells, Teddy Wilson, Sidney Catlett, Benny Goodman, Red Norvo, Artie Shaw, Bud Freeman, and the boogie-woogie pianists Meade Lux Lewis, Albert Ammons, and Pete Johnson;

drove down to Kentucky (in the indomitable Hudson he used in scouring the country for talent) to help Malcolm Cowley, Quincy Howe, Edmund Wilson, and Waldo Frank hand out food to striking coal miners in a time when strikers and their supporters were often beaten up, or even killed; tracked down an out-of-fashion Bessie Smith in Philadelphia, brought her to New York, and gave her her last recording session, a glorious affair in which the great singer, still in fine voice, was backed by Newton, Goodman, Berry, and Jack Teagarden; covered two of the Scottsboro trials in Decatur, Alabama, for *The Nation*, and joined the board of the N.A.A.C.P. (Hammond was one of the most incisive civil libertarians of his time); supervised many of the incomparable recordings Billie Holiday made between 1935 and 1941; got the Benny Goodman band on its feet and helped record the first Goodman Trio sides (Goodman, Teddy Wilson, Gene Krupa); put Harry James in a recording studio with Wilson, Norvo, and the bassist John Simmons for a classic six-minute slow blues that covered both sides of a ten-inch 78-r.p.m. record, anticipating the spacious pastures of the L.P. recording; brought the Count Basie band out of Kansas City and sent Basie on his way; gave Lester Young and Charlie Christian their first recording dates (Young with Basie, and Christian with Goodman), débuts that changed forever the way the tenor saxophone and the electric guitar were played; and, in 1938 and 1939, presented the two "Spirituals to Swing" concerts at Carnegie Hall, in which he offered to the world the gospel singers sister Rosetta Tharpe and Mitchell's Christian Singers, the blues singers Sonny Terry, Big Bill Broonzy, Ida Cox, Joe Turner, and Jimmy Rushing, the pianists Ammons, Johnson, and Lewis, the Count Basie band, the Benny Goodman Sextet and the Kansas City Six (in which he put Charlie Christian and Lester Young side by side), and a kind of New Orleans band made up of Tommy Ladnier, Sidney Bechet, and James P. Johnson. And all the while, when he had the chance, he was tooling around in his Hudson in the Midwest or the Deep South, searching for genius.

Hammond was distracted in the forties. He was drafted into the Army, where he fought racial battles with various redneck superiors, and he had personal problems. But he came storming back in the fifties with a series of often brilliant recordings built around Vic Dickenson, Mel Powell, Ellis Larkins, Jimmy Rushing, Jo Jones, Emmett Berry, Buck Clayton, Ruby Braff, and Count Basie. The records, done for Vanguard and Columbia, were distinguished not only for their music but for their natural sound and for their pioneering use of the L.P.'s extended time. A surprisingly different Hammond appeared in the recording studios in the sixties and seventies. He was still Hammond the Discoverer, but the discoveries—Aretha Franklin, Bob Dylan, Paul Winter, Denny Zeitlin, George Benson, Bruce Springsteen—had a pop flavor. The old purist had begun doctoring his soup.

Hammond had an American patrician background and American patrician looks. His mother, Emily Vanderbilt Sloane, was a great-granddaughter of the Commodore, and his father, John Henry Hammond, was the son of a Union general. Hammond's mother was imperious, religious, philanthropic, energetic, asocial, and a de-rigueur racist. She was also extremely wealthy. His father, about whom he says comparatively little in his autobiography, did not have money but became a successful banker, lawyer, and railroad man. He was far more flexible than his wife, and, Hammond suggests, had the makings of a closet liberal. Hammond had four older sisters, one of whom, the rebellious Alice, managed to marry both a British M.P. and Benny Goodman. Hammond grew up in a lordly mansion on East Ninety-first Street, and, after Hotchkiss and a brief stint at Yale, moved to Sullivan Street, in the Village, and began making jazz recordings. (He started out with a private income of twelve thousand a year, much of which went to needy musicians, to pay for recording sessions no one else would pay for, and to civil-rights causes.)

Hammond changed very little over the years. He was around six feet tall. He had a high forehead, an elegant, slightly hooked nose, and a blistering constant smile. His effusive graciousness made it seem as if he were always holding court. He had an onrushing way of talking, made up of bursts of superlatives connected by deep hums. He tended to use his listeners as sounding boards. The trumpeter Ruby Braff, whom Hammond began boosting in the mid-fifties, likes to tell of a telephone conversation he once had with Hammond:

"Hello, Ruby, This is John. How are you!"

"Well, I'm in bed with pneumonia and I feel awful."

"Wonderful, Ruby. Now, what I called about . . ."

Hammond's image was boyish. He wore Ivy League clothes, but in a careless, teen-age way, and he invariably affected a crewcut. And he drove a car with abandon, throwing more looks at his passengers than at the road.

But this image was deceptive. The writer and critic James T. Maher has said this about Hammond: "I always loved John's enthusiasm. It was constantly reinforcing. He could get so cranked up about some new musician—once, it was this 'perfectly extraordinary' Yugoslavian trumpet player—that resisting him was like standing up to a tidal wave. He had an angelic enthusiasm, which found improbable perfections. John's nervous energy was such that no sooner had he arrived somewhere with some new intelligence than his foot was out the door—you caught him on the wing. He laughed a great deal, but he was not a witty man. Alec Wilder, who knew him well, could never resist putting him on. Once, John told a girl singer he was recording that title of Alec's song 'Who Can I Turn To?' was ungrammatical, that it should be '*Whom* Can I Turn To?' News travels fast in the jazz world, and when Alec ran into John a few days later he asked him if he had seen the new Broadway hit musical 'Better Foot Forward.' John didn't get the joke. He was, I suppose, the ultimate connoisseur—one who comes to think that he knows more than the objects of his veneration. He became rather infamous for telling people how and what to play. And in the days when he was still a sort of adviser to the Goodman band he became known as 'John the undertaker.' Whenever he appeared at a rehearsal or a recording session, the musicians knew that one of them would probably be replaced by his newest enthusiasm. His 'discoveries' became graven in stone in his mind—perhaps because he was over-interviewed when he was young. It seems fairly certain, to cite an example, that Red Norvo and Mildred Bailey took John to Harlem to hear the young Billie Holiday rather than John having found her himself. But he was unique and a good man—a patrician bad boy who turned left and became both a realist and a romantic."

Like most enthusiasts, Hammond sometimes missed the mark. He never understood the majestic complexities of Louis Armstrong and Duke Ellington—possibly, it has been suggested, because neither man ever sought his help. (He rated the Fletcher Henderson trumpeter Joe Smith higher than Armstrong.) He felt that Coleman Hawkins stopped developing in 1933, when Hawkins had just begun the supernal ascent that he would not complete until the late forties. He did not consider Benny Carter's compact, lyrical trumpet playing first-rate. Bebop never reached him, and he was rarely interested in white musicians. And many of his enthusiasms of the sixties and seventies have proved less than stunning.

Hammond's autobiography was perverse. It was warm and expressive about his family, and defensive and oblique about music and his life as a civil libertarian. But there are patches of eloquence, and one of them serves him well: "I still would change the world if I could, convince a nonbeliever that my way is right, argue a cause and make friends out of enemies. I am still the reformer, the impatient protester, the sometimes-intolerant champion of tolerance. Best of all, I still expect to hear, if not today then tomorrow, a voice or a sound I have never heard before, with something to say which has never been said before. And when that happens I will know what to do."

Not long after eight o'clock on the evening of July 21st, Dick Hyman and dick Wellstood opened the 92nd Street Y's "Jazz in July" festival by sitting at two grand pianos in Kaufmann Hall and playing three intricate, charging stride-piano duets. Hyman, with his slender, delicate attack, provided the tracery, and Wellstood, with his Germanic sound, provided the thunder.

They backed the singer Carrie Smith for three numbers, and Wellstood joined Vince Giordano & the Nighthawks for a set of early Benny Goodman music. Then, got up in an unaccustomed tuxedo, he went off to the Bemelmans Bar in the Carlyle Hotel, where he was spelling Barbara Carroll. (Wellstood said that although he was born in Greenwich he was born in "clam-digging Greenwich, not backcountry Greenwich," and wearing a tuxedo at the Carlyle made him feel easier with the swells who came to hear him.) Three days later, he died suddenly, of heart failure, in Palo Alto, where he had gone for a week-end Jazz gathering. He was fifty-nine.

Wellstood is not mentioned in John Hammond's autobiography. He was white, and it is likely that Hammond regarded him merely as a skilled copyist, an assiduous re-creator of Fats Waller and James P. Johnson. But Wellstood was a great deal more. He regarded himself as "a contemporary musician who uses tools that are out of fashion," and he was right. In the last decade or so of his life, however, he moved forward stylistically, folding bits and pieces of Count Basie and Thelonious Monk and Bill Evans and Cedar Walton into his playing, and broadening his repertory to include Monk and the Beatles and Wayne Shorter. He also gained self-confidence, eventually deciding that he had become "quite excellent" and wondering why he didn't work steadily. Wellstood was witty, sardonic, acute, and matter-of-fact. (He claimed that he liked working in a cha-cha band as much as he liked playing jazz.) In the fifties, he went to law school during the day and played at night, and passed his bar exam. (He finally joined a law firm several years ago, and practiced for ten claustrophobic months before returning to the piano.) He was a good, piquant writer. (From a set of liner notes for a Donald Lambert album: "In a world full of pianists who can rattle off fast oom-pahs or Chick Corea solo transcriptions or the Elliott Carter Sonata, there are perhaps only a dozen who can play stride convincingly at any length and with the proper energy.") He thought things out. (He once said, "Audiences are rarely on the same wavelength as performers. In fact, two very different things are going on at once. The musician is wondering how to get from the second eight bars into the bridge, and the audience is in pursuit of emotional energy. The musician is struggling, and the audience is making up dreamlike opinions about the music that may have nothing at all to do with what the musician is thinking or doing musically. If audiences knew what humdrum, daylight things most musicians think when they play, they'd probably never come.")

Wellstood was a bearish, tousled, guttural man. He had a shy smile, which embraced him as much as his listeners, and laughing eyes, cleverly hidden behind glasses. Over the years, he became an endearing figure, onstage and off—a description that might have either pleased or horrified him, depending on how ferocious he felt he should be that day.

Ellington Slips By

It is not likely that anyone will write a good biography of Duke Ellington. Like many prominent blacks in his day, he developed a subtle and largely impenetrable series of disguises. These included his orotund conversation, often delivered in the form of put-ons, which ranged from mock unctuousness to high flattery (to a female guest at the close of the seventieth-birthday party given him at the White House: "I'm so glad you could come. You looked so beautiful, and you brought such dignity to my party"); the amused expressions that flickered across his seignorial (sometimes masklike) face; his Technicolor written efforts (as in his autobiography, *Music Is My Mistress*); his double-entendre song titles ("Warm Valley" and "T.T. on Toast"); his almost foppish way of dressing (six-inch trouser cuffs, ruffled shirts); and the Ellington band itself, which was the secret and spacious house in which—blinds drawn—he spent so many nourishing years. Eventually, all these camouflages became automatic, and it was increasingly difficult to tell where they stopped and Ellington began. Of the half-dozen or so biographical efforts that have been published since his death, in 1974, only *Duke Ellington in Person*, a sharp, pained memoir by Ellington's son, Mercer, penetrates any of the Ellington veils. (Mercer Ellington's book was done with Stanley Dance, who also helped the Duke assemble his autobiography.) Certainly James Lincoln Collier's new book, *Duke Ellington* (Oxford), built squarely on Mercer Ellington's effort, doesn't bring us much closer to the Master. Collier trots through the now standard résumé of Ellington's life: his genteel, middle-class upbringing in Washington, D.C., his lifelong devotion to his mother, his playboy ways and early-and-only marriage, his prolonged love affairs, his more or less accidental entry into music as a pianist, his first fame as a bandleader at the Cotton Club, his manipulation of and slyness with people, his consuming hypochondria, and his gradual acceptance of the belief that he was an important composer, with the concomitant need to hear every new piece performed by his band, which it sometimes seemed he kept in existence just for that purpose.

What Collier principally wants to get across is that Ellington was *not* the great American composer, as many have claimed—that, indeed, he was not a composer at all in the conventional sense. Collier points out that many of Ellington's best-known numbers were written partly by Ellington and partly by members of his band, in what proportions we may never know. Oftentimes, Ellington arrangements did not exist on paper but were worked out in recording studios and commited to memory by the band. (Many of the Ellington numbers played by repertory groups use arrangements that have been transcribed, note by note, from Ellington recordings.) Sometimes Ellington harmonized and orchestrated his pieces, and sometimes these essential tasks were done by others. Collier suggests that Ellington was, above all, a synthesizer, who saw to it that all the requisite parts of a big-band jazz number—the song, its orchestration, the proper soloists, the tempo—were aligned and ready to go. Collier compares Ellington's methods to those of a master chef:

"The chef does not chop all the vegetables himself or make the sauce with his own hands. But he plans the menus, trains the assistants, supervises them, tastes everything, adjusts the spices, orders another five minutes in the oven for the lamb. And in the end we credit him with the result. So it was with Duke Ellington: wherever he got the ingredients, it was his artistic vision that shaped the final product."

But it wasn't as simple as that. Ellington's greatest numbers, written and recorded between 1940 and 1942, were fluid and ongoing collective improvisations that began with the invention of a melody and ended by shaping the section work that surrounded and supported the soloists. Some of these group improvisations were never finished; Ellington tinkered with them off and on for thirty years. The results, when everything fell into place, were masterpieces of "composed" improvisation, unmatched in American music.

Collier moves swiftly through the last thirty years of Ellington's musical life (he seems to get stuck forever in the years around 1930), dismissing most of Ellington's concert pieces, secular and sacred, and passing lightly over the hundreds of short, workaday numbers turned out between the longer ones. This is too bad. Despite their episodic nature, some of the concert pieces have merit, and much close listening needs to be done to the late short numbers. (What of the two dozen or so funny and ingenious parodies he recorded of the theme songs of other bandleaders?) Collier is troubling in other ways. He likes to insult his readers' intelligence (Washington, D.C., is "a short distance from Baltimore"), and he is often careless with facts (John Hammond did not organize Benny Goodman's 1938 Carnegie Hall concert, and Ellington's "Controversial Suite," a kind of parody of Dixieland and Kenton music, was being played several years before 1951). And he gives us slow, unenlightening musical analyses of such Ellington classics as "Ko-Ko" and "Harlem Airshaft"—numbers long since taken apart and put together again by Ellington musicologists. He likes to call Ellington's sidemen "virtuosos," thereby revealing that he does not understand the unique and fragile home-brewed nature of many of the musicians who inhabited Ellington's band. At the same time, he scants certain Ellington musicians. He dismisses Sonny Greer outright, claiming that Greer did not drive the band but played alongside it. Greer *was* a homegrown drummer and a showoff, as many drummers of his generation were, but he swung, he had decent time, and he had great style. He got a wake-up, morning tone out of his drums, and he was a first-rate cymbal player. He had much to do with establishing and preserving the Ellington *sound*. Greer was with the band thirty years, and it was never the same after he left. Collier is also off the mark about Ray Nance, a gifted violinist and jazz singer, and a trumpeter of knotted, complex emotions, who had a way of playing slow blues that made you sit very still.

Collier fails to grasp Ellington's polarities. At one end was the pure humor that aerated much of his music (Collier tends to take Ellington far too seriously), and at the other end the ghostliness, so beautifully described in Mercer Ellington's book: "[Ellington] sought a sensuality in the way his music was expressed; there was always an emotion attached to the sound. Or I might say that he was always very conscious of the need to make the listener *feel* experiences with the sound, almost as though he were creating apparitions within the music."

Jazz musicians write good books—not as-told-to or tape-recorded books but books they write themselves. These include Ellington's *Music Is My Mistress*; Charles Mingus's ribald memoir, *Beneath the Underdog*; Danny Barker's salty *A Life in Jazz*, finally published last year; Rex Stewart's portraits of his peers, *Jazz Masters of the Thirties*; Artie Shaw's epigraph-laden *The Trouble with Cinderella*; and Max Gordon's *Live at the Village Vanguard*, Max being as close to a jazz musician as you can get without actually playing an instrument. (Max's instrument is the Vanguard.) And now Marian McPartland, the English-born Renaissance person (pianist, composer, record-label owner, teacher, and radio producer and personality), has put out a collection of descriptive and biographical sketches, *All in Good Time* (Oxford). The book contains, among other things, portraits, written between 1960 and 1983 for music magazines, of Paul Desmond, the bassists Ron McClure and Eddie Gomez, Mary Lou Williams, Bill Evans, Benny Goodman, and Alec Wilder. McPartland keeps herself out of the way much of the time (although she is a born self-publicizer, an ability few jazz musicians have and all need), and is nowhere in sight in her highly effective chapter on Desmond, a witty man, who tells her, "I'm glad [Ornette Coleman] is such an individualist. I like the firmness of thought and purpose that goes into what he's doing, even though I don't always like to listen to it. It's like living in a house where everything's painted red." She is equally good on her old friend Alec Wilder, who wrote music for her and marvelled at her improvisations. ("God! That would have taken me a week to write and she played it in five seconds!") She says in a postscript to the piece that Wilder's "greatest gift and the most lasting one of all was his music." I'm not sure that Wilder's greatest gift wasn't his complex, brilliant, echoing self. Look at the hole he's left.

1988

Cruising _____

SATURDAY: Jazz festivals of various sorts were held in Australia and France in the forties, but the first permanent festival took place in mid-July of 1954 on the grounds of the small, rickety, fashionable tennis Casino in Newport, Rhode Island. By the late fifties, the Newport Jazz Festival, as it was called, had become a fixture, and its countless spinoffs cover the earth. But many of them, including the various permutations of the Newport Festival itself, have grown faddish and overweight. Jazz flourishes in small, heedless situations. It also depends on its entrepreneurs. Two of the most imaginative (and least well-known) are Hank O'Neal and his wife, Shelly Shier. For the past five years, they have run a series of mini-festivals on the S.S. Norway, which cruises year-round between Miami and the Virgin Islands. The O'Neals invite about fifty musicians (and their families) for one- or two-week stints, and the musicians play in two comfortable cabaretlike rooms and in an eight-hundred seat theatre. The programs are varied and loosely shaped. There are one-hour afternoon recitals, and evening jam sessions that stretch into the morning hours. The sets are easygoing and uncrowded, and the musicians are arranged in congenial, non-competitive groups. The audiences never have to travel more than a couple of football fields to get to the music, and there are no tickets or cover charges or minimums or hassles about seats. The audiences also have two simultaneous (and very different) events to choose from each evening.

The Norway sailed at four-thirty this afternoon, and after two days of open sea it will stop for day visits at St. Marten, St. Thomas, and Great Stirrup Cay, returning to Miami early next Saturday—a round trip of over two thousand miles. The music began at nine o'clock in the Club Internationale, a plush, high-ceilinged room filled with sofas and overstuffed chairs. A small bandstand and a small dance floor are at one end, and a bar is at the other. Life-size plaster statues of Bacchus and Triton are set in niches at the bandstand end. A group made up of Buddy Tate on tenor saxophone, Al Grey on trombone and bass trumpet, Jay McShann on piano, Major Holley on bass, and Oliver Jackson on drums did six numbers, most of them blues. It was good shake-down music. Grey, a slender man with a smile slightly wider than his face, played an agile bass-trumpet solo on "Days of Wine and Roses" and got off some heavy muted wa-wa trom-bone on "St. James Infirmary." Tate, as always, slid up and down his special emotional slopes. The Tate-Grey group alternated with the tenor saxophonist Don Menza, the pianist Roland Hanna, the bassist Milt Hinton, and the drummer Louis Bell-son. Menza is a hard-blowing player who works largely on the West Coast. He has a shouldering attack and a perfervid sound. Hanna is a beautiful player whose improvisations emerge in bursts—a train passing under a series of bridges. This fitfulness fell away in "Satin Doll," and he got off a sweeping single-note line. It is a comfort to hear Bellson, a taut, precise drummer in the Buddy Rich mold. He has a dry, almost baked, tone, and his breaks and solos are flawlessly designed.

The Checkers Cabaret, a low-ceilinged red-and-black room with a long bar and a spacious dance floor, will be offering big bands during the week, and tonight we heard Panama Francis and the Savoy Sultans. The original Sultans, one of the house bands at the Savoy Ballroom in the late thirties and early forties, had two purposes—to play for dancing and to swing ferociously. They used a lot of riffs broken by short solos, and they blew whole bands away. Francis resurrected the Sultans in the late seventies, and although his personnel has changed, his straight, hot Chick Webb drumming keeps everything at a boil.

SUNDAY: This morning a marvellous Caribbean cloud show was mounted on the horizon, with white thunderheads standing to the left, a frieze of sheeplike black clouds moving swiftly between the thunderheads and the ship, impenetrable deep-gray rain clouds directly opposite, and slim silvery ball-gown clouds to the right. The entire show was sandwiched by a high cobalt-blue sky and the royal blue of this tropical ocean.

The *Norway*, originally the *France*, is something of a white elephant. Her keel was laid in 1957, the first year that more people crossed the Atlantic by air than by sea. She was, and is, the largest of all passenger ships. She is one thousand and thirty-five feet long, and she weighs over seventy thousand tons. The *France*'s essential, tourist-class passengers began to desert her for the air in the early seventies, and the French government, which had been subsidizing her, abandoned her, and she was tied up indefinitely at the Quai de l'Oubli in Le Havre. In 1979, the Norwegian Caribbean Lines bought her, and she was converted from a fast, indoor North Atlantic ship into a sedate, outdoor Caribbean ship. Her famous silhouette, with its two huge winged stacks (*grandes cheminées à ailerons*), was left intact except for a couple of touches of giantism: two one-story-high signs, reading "NORWAY," were installed between the stacks, and a pair of enormous tenders, ninety feet long and capable of holding four hundred passengers apiece, were installed on the foredeck, between dinosaurlike davits. So the France-Norway has been given a second chance, even though she draws too much water (thirty-four feet) for the harbors she visits and is a little grand for the small seas she sails.

At two o'clock, there was a parade of pianists in the Club Internationale. Roland Hanna did three numbers—a dramatic (yet oblique) "Love for Sale," a slow Debussy ballad, and a blues. The Chicago pianist Eddie Higgins played two Clare Fischer pieces and a Jobim, and he was inconclusive. Art Hodes, looking frozen in such fast company, got himself through "Tennessee Waltz," "Summertime," and "It Ain't Necessarily So," and a jumpy reading of "St. Louis Blues." Jay McShann did three blues, was followed by the Japanese pianist Makoto Ozone, a brittle player in the florid, Corea-Hancock mold. His four numbers, including a "Someday My Prince Will Come," left little to the imagination. Mel Powell wound up the recital with two disappointingly brief numbers. He also served as the master of ceremonies, and he was at his mock-professorial best, filling the room with his big laugh and rumbling mots, and coating all the pianists who preceded him with buttery compliments.

Late in the afternoon, a program called "Meet the Stars" was held in the Checkers Cabaret. Six of the bandleaders on board talked about themselves, then answered questions from the audience. On hand were Cab Calloway, Panama Francis, Benny Carter, Buck Clayton, Jay McShann, and Erskine Hawkins. Calloway tended to hog the proceedings, ending his perorations with "I've had a wonderful career, and you [the audience] made it possible. So the money's there. I'm pretty well heeled. I enjoy it." Panama Francis, who once worked for Calloway, added this observation, which is shared by other Calloway alumni: "You hit on time. You quit on time. You got your money on time." The leaders were asked to divulge their ages, and, considering their vitality and unflagging abilities, their revelations were buoying. Calloway is seventy-nine, Francis sixty-nine, Carter eighty, Clayton seventy-six, McShann seventy-eight, and Hawkins seventy-three.

The vibraphonist Gary Burton appeared at nine in the Club Internationale with his Berklee Ensemble, which consists of Makoto Ozone (a graduate of Berklee College, in Boston) and four Berklee students—the alto saxophonist Doug Yates, the tenor saxophonist Donnie McCaslin, the bassist Gildas Boclé, and the drummer Marty Richards. Burton is a rococo vibraphonist who uses four mallets and floods every number with notes. His figures behind the other soloists let no one rest, melodically or harmonically, and the result was a dissonant, vertical music. The group played a Chick Corea, a John Scofield blues, Victor Young's "Beautiful Love," and Billy Strayhorn's "Isfahan." Richards is a tidy relentless drummer, but he plays thunderously, as is the custom with contemporary drummers.

The alternating group in the Club I. had Flip Phillips on tenor saxophone, Kenny Davern on clarinet, Roland Hanna, Howard Alden on guitar, Milt Hinton, and the drummer Chuck Riggs. The materials ("Sometimes I'm Happy," "Cotton Tail," "Sweet Georgia Brown") have been played so often and so affectionately by jazz musicians that they seem to swing by themselves. Phillips, an amalgam of Ben Webster, Don Byas, and Lester Young, was particularly acute, and right behind were Hanna and Alden, a Red Norvo graduate and post-Charlie Christian guitarist with a lovely tone, an advanced harmonic sense, and an infallible sense of structure. The comedian and singer Martha Raye is on board, and halfway through the group's celebration she sat in and sang "I Remember April," "The Man I Love," and "The Sunny Side of the Street." She has a reputation among older jazz musicians as a good, swinging singer, and in the thirties she used to sit in up in Harlem. Even so, she was a surprise. Her singing verged on the surrealist extravagances of Betty Carter and Leo Watson.

The Chicago-style cornettist Wild Bill Davison, who is as snappy and tart as he was forty years ago (he is eighty-two), was sitting out front during the Burton set, and, deep in his jowls, was listening to Burton's quite modern alto player with the same blank intensity that Winston Churchill must have given the paintings of Francis Bacon.

MONDAY: Eight A.M. again. The ship moving gently over gray water, through gray fog, and under gray rain. The horizon was about three hundred yards away, and there was rain overhead on the Oslo Deck (the boat deck). Fifteen minutes later, the horizon retreated several miles, the rain stopped, and the water turned its customary resounding royal blue. There were small whitecaps, and they broke into Queen Anne's lace. The ship took on speed, slowly passing in the far northeast a black Martin Johnson Heade storm.

There was a jam session in the Saga Theatre after lunch. Buck Clayton conducted loosely, and present were the trumpeter Eddie Allen, Al Grey, Kenny Davern, the Danish violinist Svend

Asmussen, Roland Hanna, Milt Hinton, Howard Alden, and Oliver Jackson or Louis Bellson. "Jumpin' at the Woodside," "Moten Swing," a ballad medley, and "Lester Leaps In" went by. Hanna and Asmussen turned up bright things on "Woodside," and Alden played another closely reasoned statement on "Lester Leaps In." Clayton led a series of studio jam sessions for Columbia Records in the fifties, and they are classic recordings. He had with him the likes of Trummy Young, Coleman Hawkins, Jo Jones, Billy Kyle, Urbie Green, Lem Davis, and Julian Dash—to say nothing of his own eloquent playing. Clayton's last flowering as a player took place in the sixties, but his teeth and gums and other health problems were already bothering him, and by the mid-seventies he had all but retired. He made several attempts at comebacks in New York, and they were encouraging. His lip was weak, but his warmth and lyricism were intact, and it seemed that it would be only a matter of weeks before he was in top form again. But he did not play again, and eventually word came that he was hopelessly discouraged and would play no more.

In the fifties and early sixties, Buddy Tate led a Count Basie-type band at the Savoy Ballroom and the Celebrity Club, on 125th Street. Tonight, he took a new Celebrity Club band into Checkers, and it had the Basie trumpeter Harry Edison, the Ellington alto saxophonist Norris Turney, Al Grey, Jay McShann, Major Holley, and Oliver Jackson. Edison, who often plays the trumpet the way Basie played the piano, was at his languorous best in "Things Ain't What They Used to Be," and Tate took a lonesome, blue clarinet solo in "Hootie's Blues."

Two groups appeared in the Club Internationale tonight. One was a maroon velvet quartet made up of Benny Carter, Makoto Ozone, the bassist George Mraz, and Marty Richards. Among their numbers were "Green Dolphin Street," "Honeysuckle Rose," "Lover Man," "You'd Be So Nice to Come Home To," and "Secret Love." Mraz excelled in "You'd Be So Nice," and Carter constructed solo after perfect solo, and even played trumpet on two numbers. Carter, heaped with awards and medals and honorary degrees in recent years, shows no age or swelling of the psyche. The brilliant teeth shine, lighting his impeccable manners and dress. His alto-saxophone playing is as gracious and obliging as ever, and he has returned to his trumpet.

The other group was led by Wild Bill Davison. With him were Kenny Davern, Eddie Higgins, Howard Alden, the bassist Bob Haggart, and Chuck Riggs. Wild Bill likes to rampage, but tonight, tiring by his second set, he slowed down and was lyrical in "Do You Know What It Means to Miss New Orleans," "Love Is Just Around the Corner," and Fats Waller's lovely lullaby "Blue Turning Gray Over You."

TUESDAY: Chip Hoehler is the bandmaster of the *Norway*, and he has a pool of thirty-nine musicians who play dance music, music to swim to, cocktail music, music for shows, country-and-Western music, and big-band jazz. Born in New York in 1941, Hoehler is a cool, compact man who came up through Marshall Brown's Newport Youth Band in the late fifties (he is a trombonist) and through the road bands of Charlie Spivak and Warren Covington. He had his own band in the Bahamas for eleven years and put together his present aggregation in 1979. He has several excellent soloists in his jazz band: Fred Norman on piano; a Paul Gonsalves tenor saxophonist, Larry Spivak; the trumpeter Tom Swayze; and the alto saxophonist John Lux. Hoehler's jazz band has the rare ability to jump into the skins of other bands. Tonight, in the Checkers Cabaret, it became the old Erskine Hawkins band, which flourished in Harlem in the late thirties and early forties. Primarily a dance band, it used a relaxed mixture of riffs, call-and-response patterns, organ chords, and wa-wa brass figures. Its secret was playing a fraction behind the beat; this gave it a rubato swing, a knee-action motion. It had three good soloists: the trumpeter Dud Bascomb; his brother Paul, a tenor saxophonist; and Julian Dash, another tenor saxophonist. Hawkins himself played harum-scarum trumpet, and you were never sure what you would hear—a Harry James style, a Rex Stewart style, a Snooky Young style. He has led a hotel band in the Catskills for twenty-

217

five years, and has retained all his eccentric verve. (Many of the old big bands linger on, but in strange and parlous ways. Some are "ghost" bands—those once led by Glenn Miller and Tommy Dorsey and Count Basie and Duke Ellington—and some, like Erskine Hawkins', go on in the outlands and are still led by their originators.) Hoehler's men caught much of the quality of the original band, and they were particularly apt in "Weary Blues," "Tuxedo Junction" (one of Hawkins' big hits, later made bigger by Glenn Miller), "Gin Mill Special," and "After Hours," Avery Parrish's classic hymn to the slow blues.

Hoehler's band rested, then did a set of Buck Clayton's originals and arrangements, with Clayton conducting. Clayton fell into an acedia after he stopped playing, but lately he has been doing a great deal of big-band writing. Ten of his numbers were played tonight, and they demonstrated that he has somehow transposed his trumpet playing into his writing. His melodies are occasionally irresistible ("Yorkville," "Beaujolais," "Nancy's Fancy"), and his arrangements are graceful enlargements. His saxophone writing winds around like Benny Carter's, his trumpets shout. Finest of all tonight was a long slow blues, called "Homeless." Each soloist takes two choruses, the first backed by the rhythm section and the second by lovely countermelodies or organ chords. It is one of the rare instances in which a piece of program music works as music and as metaphor. Clayton, as thin as a pin and as dapper and handsome as ever, conducts by not conducting. He cups his hands like jai-alai racquets, faces them toward the floor, and moves them almost imperceptibly up and down. Or he holds his hands flat, palms up, and raises them an inch or two to signify more steam. When he wants a certain soloist, he points a crooked finger at him and lifts his chin just above the horizon.

WEDNESDAY: Hank O'Neal created a stir last year by persuading Mel Powell to come on a cruise and play jazz in public for the first time in thirty years. This afternoon, Powell, who is scheduled to appear tonight, rehearsed in Checkers with Benny Carter, Howard Alden, Milt Hinton, and Louis Bellson. They rolled through "Stompin' at the Savoy," a slow "Makin' Whoopee," Eubie Blake's "You're Lucky to Me," and "What Is This Thing Called Love?," and betweentimes Powell was ornate and witty. The quintet's appearance in Checkers tonight was frequently brilliant. Powell got off some Hindemith chords on the bridge of his first chorus on "Stompin' at the Savoy" and some Milton Babbitt chords on the bridge of his second chorus on "What Is This Thing Called Love?" Carter was a marsh hawk in flight throughout, and Bellson was crisp and luminous. Alden played with great invention, and stands a good chance of being voted M.V.P. at the end of the week.

The evening ended in the Club Internationale with a good set by Kenny Davern, Svend Asmussen, Alden, Bob Haggart, and Chuck Riggs and a middling one by Carter, Tommy Flanagan, Hinton, and Bellson. There was some nice counterpoint in the first between Davern and Asmussen, who swings in a curved, willowy way, but the Flanagan-Carter-Hinton-Bellson group never seemed to reach its proper propulsiveness.

Mel Powell was sitting outside Checkers before his rehearsal this afternoon and said that he had a cold—his first "since Muggsy Spanier."

Walking is wonderful on the *Norway*. Seen broadside, she is slightly swaybacked, so no matter which end you start at on the International Deck (enclosed) and the Oslo Deck (open), which contain the longest unobstructed stretches on board, you get a downhill start. If you walk in the direction the ship is going, you really fly.

THURSDAY: A tour of the engine room this morning. The temperature sometimes reaches a hundred and thirty degrees and the noise a hundred and thirty decibels. It is an astonishing concatenation of pipes (some like hoses, some like Roman columns), boilers (the two main ones, painted silver, tower out of sight), drive shafts (they are two hundred and fifty feet long and at least two feet thick), turbines, valves, tanks, pumps, stairways, grid passageways, and torpedo-size fire extinguishers. It is about eight hundred feet long and seven stories high. A feast for Demuth and Sheeler and Crawford; a fantasy for Coleridge and Kafka and Cocteau! After an hour of more or less steady descent (some of the railings on the ladderlike stairways were too hot to hold), we ascended in an elevator to the International Deck, which was freezing and very quiet.

Gary Burton and Makoto Ozone played an hour duet in the Club I. this afternoon. They did two Chick Coreas, two Ozones, a Steve Swallow, and a couple of standards. Burton uses a lot of resonator and Ozone a lot of loud pedal, so they shimmered, sometimes in harmony, sometimes in counterpoint, sometimes in unison.

A pleasant approximation of the first concert last Saturday took place tonight in the Club I., and included Buddy Tate, Norris Turney, Al Grey, Jay McShann, Major Holley, and Oliver Jackson. Jackson uses drumsticks the size of logs, but he showed verve and imagination and kept the proceedings moving. Wild Bill Davison led the alternating band, and said just before he went on the bandstand, "Drinking almost killed me and quitting drinking almost killed me, too. One morning after my wife, Anne, made me stop, I was having breakfast at home in Santa Barbara and I heard birds singing outside for the first time. I told Anne, 'I hear birds singing,' and she said, 'Bill, those birds have been singing at breakfast as long as I can remember.'"

According to John Maxtone-Graham, the elegant historian of ocean liners, the custom of being invited to have dinner at the captain's table began in the nineteenth century when immigrant passengers, required to feed themselves, ran out of food and were given free company rations. The free rations at the Captain's dinner tonight included marinated and smoked salmon, cream-of-ratatouille soup, sliced beef tenderloin with morels, duchesse potatoes, snow peas, chayote and bean sprouts, chocolate mousse, and coffee and cognac. The wines were from California—a Chardonnay from Château St. Jean and a cabernet from Clos du Val. The ship had begun rolling noticeably by ten-thirty, and the captain, making a jest, said we were going through "a little hurricane."

Time stopped a couple of days ago. It is difficult to remember what day it is, and appointments don't seem terribly important. The music moves in slow motion, no matter the tempo.

FRIDAY: We went through the captain's little hurricane all night, with the ship doing a lot of thrashing about. Clouds had moved back in by morning, and the seas were heavy and white-haired—too heavy, it turned out, for us to stop at Great Stirrup Cay, a big sandbar a hundred and fifty miles east of Miami which the Norwegian Caribbean Lines owns and which is used for swimming and picnicking. There was a good deal of grumbling, so Hank O'Neal put together a jam session in the Club I. It began around two o'clock, and present were Benny Carter, Don Menza, Gary Burton, George Mraz, and Oliver Jackson. They played half a dozen numbers and were joined along the way by Flip Phillips, the trumpeter Ed Allen, and one of Chip Hoehler's tenor saxophonists. Carter—dressed in wrap around shades, a raspberry shirt, black pants, and white shoes—played trumpet. His solos on a couple of medium blues and on "Stompin' at the Savoy" and "Body and Soul" were spare, delicate, and singing. Panama Francis sat in and played with an even four-four Sid Catlett beat. Burton took a beautiful ad-lib, a-cappella solo on "Body and Soul," and elsewhere supplied a billowing field of background chords for his compeers.

There is a small observation deck directly over the bridge and just forward of the mast, and it's a good place to get some air. Tonight, wind—a combination of the easterlies and the ship's motion—was so strong it was impossible to stand there for more than ten seconds. It was a malevolent wind, and would have flicked us overboard, given the chance.

SATURDAY: The ship docked in Miami at 6 A.M. on a placid, sunny sea. The musicians went ashore around ten o'clock, and were surprised to feel the concrete pier rock gently under their feet. Wild Bill Davison was sitting on a bag waiting for a taxi, and he said, "Now she wants me to quit smoking."

Jimmy Knepper, Peggy, and the Duke

For the past couple of years, Bradley Cunningham, of Bradley's, on University Place, has been adding a horn player to his customary Sunday-night piano-and-bass duo. One Sunday not long ago, Bradley—at the behest of Sue Mingus, the widow of Charles Mingus and the manager of the Mingus ghost band, Mingus Dynasty—hired the master trombonist Jimmy Knepper, a former Mingus sideman and the leader of the Dynasty. He was accompanied by the pianist Kenny Barron and the bassist Buster Williams, both Bradley's regulars. Barron, a heavy, percussive player, pushed Knepper, a lyricist and thinker, in most of the right places. And Williams, one of the fashionably florid, bamboo-toned bassists, kept his accompanying more or less in the background and the length of his solos within sight.

Knepper is tall and thin and laconic. (He said at Bradley's that he's been losing a pound a year and if he lives long enough—he is sixty—he will disappear.) He has a small face, afterthought hair, and long, trombone arms. He wears glasses and looks like the class brain. Knepper came up at the end of the big-band era and during the early years of bebop, and one can hear in his work considerations of J. C. Higginbotham and Dicky Wells and Lawrence Brown, and also the melodic lines and expanded harmonies of Charlie Parker. He is one of the few musicians of his generation who successfully combine the rhythmic tensions of swing and the rococo melodies of bebop. He is an original. He has a casual trombone tone, neither voluptuous nor nasal, and he avoids the bag of tricks that the instrument sometimes induces—growls, smears, shrieks, roars. He is a limitless improviser. Many improvisers rely on patterns they hit upon early in their careers: they play variations on their own frozen variations. They make it easy for the listener, who comes to count on these set phrases. But Knepper, in his oblique way, constantly

222

needles us. Each solo is full of fresh phrases, fresh rhythmic turns, and fresh melodic insights.

For all that—or perhaps because of it—Knepper has never got his due. He is one of those superior jazz musicians who, for whatever reason, rarely win polls, don't grow rich, never rock the boat. He isn't even easy to find. He doesn't make many records, and all his regular jobs—with the Mingus Dynasty, with Buck Clayton's new big band, with Loren Schoenberg's big band, with the American Jazz Orchestra—are part time. Hearing him at length at Bradley's was a choice event. He opened his first set with three easy choruses of "Stompin' at the Savoy" and then went into a fast "What Is This Thing Called Love?" He began his solo in the second number with a sixteen-bar phrase of such subtlety and dexterity that notes seemed to be hidden behind notes, and he ended the number with an eerie, rolling-back-the-beat legato passage. In a slow "Out of Nowhere" he was as smooth as Tommy Dorsey, and he used a lot of triplets and the sort of odd, outside-the-chord notes that Duke Ellington loved and that give improvised melody nubble and texture. Knepper closed his first set with a medium-tempo "Autumn in New York," in which he demonstrated his agility and his melodic invention (though Knepper doesn't really *demonstrate* anything; he simply does difficult things with ease).

Peggy Lee came back to the Ballroom this winter. Her voice and phrasing were as crafty as ever—lithe, laid-back, spacious, dark, rhythmically flawless. She likes to wear costumes when she sings, and this time she was a polar bear. She wore a white silk gown, a patterned white silk jacket trimmed with marabou feathers, a platinum fall, and large, round, tinted rhinestone glasses. She did her anthems—"Fever," "Is That All There Is?," "Johnny Guitar," and "Them There Eyes"—but she also did Duke Ellington's buoyant "Jump for Joy" and three blues. She sings the blues in the same sad, easy way as Billie Holiday. Peggy Lee is a terrific performer. All her moves are miniature—a lop-sided smile, a low laugh, a floating hand—but all have purpose and weight. She makes her listeners feel cherished. Her singing lulls you, and it is easy to forget how daring it still is.

The American Jazz Orchestra completed its third season in the Great Hall at Cooper Union by giving an Ellington evening. The centerpiece of the concert was "Black, Brown and Beige," Ellington's first voyage into extended composition. The piece, which runs about fifty minutes, was written in late 1942 and early 1943. It had been played before in its entirety only three times: at a warmup session at the Rye (New York) High School on January 22nd, 1943; at Carnegie Hall the following night; and at Symphony Hall in Boston a week later. The New York newspaper reviewers gave it poor marks, and Ellington, dismayed, never played the piece again. But he recorded parts of it, and dipped into it from time to time ("Come Sunday," "The Blues") for special recordings and for his sacred concerts. The newspaper boys were right, but for the wrong reasons. Ellington was not working within the symphonic form, or within any kind of European form. He had written a piece which consisted of half a dozen or so episodic, semi-programmatic sketches mourning the travails and celebrating the triumphs of the American Negro. And he had written it not for a symphony orchestra but for his unique jazz-dance band. Considered in such terms, "Black, Brown and Beige" was a startling musical act. No other bandleaders until Woody Herman and Stan Kenton, several years later, pressed a dance band into such high-flown duty. The notion of a "Black, Brown and Beige" had been in Ellington's mind for at least ten years, and its completion was, among other things, a sociopolitical act: he was issuing a kind of musical Emancipation Proclamation—the title, indeed, of a section of the "Brown" movement.

Beside the small concertos Ellington set down between 1940 and 1942, "Black, Brown and Beige" seems pompous and over-blown. The *sound* of the music, like some of Berlioz, is more persuasive than the music itself. But the piece has beauties. One is the spiritual "Come Sunday," played at Carnegie Hall by Johnny Hodges as an ethereal alto-saxophone solo, full of god-like glissandi and sighing, almost lachrymose whole notes. If it is possible to make religious music cool and sweet, Hodges did it that night. (Fortunately, the concerts at Carnegie Hall and Symphony Hall were recorded, and the patched-together result can be heard on the Prestige label as "The Duke Ellington Carnegie Hall Concerts: January 1943.") Other, lesser beauties include an ad-lib a-cappella trumpet-section passage in "Black"; Harold Baker's lilting solo just after "Come Sunday"; and an odd, dissonant reed-and-trombone passage just after Rex Stewart's solo in the same section. Also to be noted throughout the piece is Ellington's revolutionary use of tempo. He shifts speeds constantly, sometimes even using accelerando and decelerando. He lapses into ad-lib again and again. He uses waltz time and jumpy six-eight. This is where Charles Mingus came from.

Maurice Peress conducted "Black, Brown and Beige" at Cooper Union, and it was a spirited and idiomatic performance. Mel Lewis captured many of Sonny Greer's effects, especially Greer's slogging afterbeat rim shots, and Loren Schoenberg moved handsomely between Ben Webster's style and his own. Norris Turney, who was with Ellington in the band's later years, approximated Hodges' solo, and Jimmy Knepper was admirable, even doing a little plunger-mute work. The first part of the evening was given over to interpretations of half a dozen or so of Ellington's short masterpieces, among them "Main Stem," "All Too Soon," "Bojangles," and an eighteen-minute version of "Mood Indigo" put together by Ellington in 1950. (There was also one number by Billy Strayhorn, whose best work equals and sometimes surpasses Ellington's). John Lewis, the music director of the American Jazz Orchestra, conducted this part of the concert and, as is his wont when he conducts, set some disastrously slow tempos. The "Mood Indigo," which had lovely things in it, went by like a swaybacked horse.

Stéphane Grappelli
and Warne Marsh

The eightieth-birthday celebration held in Carnegie Hall in April for Stéphane Grappelli involved the cellist Yo-Yo Ma, the singer Maureen McGovern, the Juilliard String Quartet, the harmonica player Toots Thielemans, the dancer and singer Harold Nicholas, the New York rhythm team of Mike Renzi, Jay Leonhart, and Grady Tate, and the pianists and composers Michel Legrand and Roger Kellaway, the last of whom doubled as musical director for the evening. Aside from an occasional Gallic touch (a couple of Legrand songs, the first movement of Debussy's String Quartet in G Minor), the concert had nothing to do with Grappelli until it was well into its second half. Then three things happened: Grappelli, appearing for the first time, did an easy "Sweet Lorraine" with Yo-Yo Ma, Kellaway, and the rhythm section; swam through a P. T. Barnum "Pennies from Heaven," in which he was teamed with Legrand and Kellaway, the string quartet, Yo-Yo Ma, Thielemans, Nicholas, and the rhythm section—all of them, at one point, sawing, blowing, tinkling, thumping, and plucking; and played several liquid, jumping numbers with his trio (Marc Fosset on guitar and Jon Burr on bass.) He has lost nothing: his melodic lines arch and float and skim. Grapppelli believes that performers should dress dramatically onstage, and he was in one of his famous warring outfits—a light-colored, open-neck flowered shirt and Black Watch pants. You could hear him before he made a sound.

The tenor saxophonist Warne Marsh died late last year, at the age of sixty. He died in California, where he was born and raised. He had distinguished Hollywood antecedents. His father, Oliver H. T. Marsh, was a well-known cinematographer (*David Copperfield, A Tale of Two Cities*), and his aunt Mae Warne Marsh, after whom he was named, was a silent-film star. Marsh came up under the tutelage of the brilliant, relentless pianist and teacher Lennie Tristano, whom he considered nonpareil. His friend the alto saxophonist Gary Foster once said of him, "His sound on the tenor is completely untenorlike, just as Jimmy Knepper's sound on the trombone is completely untrombonelike. Both men seem to use their instruments simply as vessels to contain their notes. They could be playing any instrument." His tone was brown and thick, and he used almost no vibrato. His melodic lines were Proustian. He was an intellectual improviser, who played intensely complex melodic lines, which demanded complete concentration and offered no over-the-counter emotions. He was never a popular player: he never courted his audience when he performed. He disappeared inside his music. He was a shy, hidden, restless man who waited for the world to come to him and, when it did, returned the compliment in full. Marsh might have been a cult figure but wasn't. Cult figures often leak; Marsh was watertight.

1989

The Swing Era_____

Gunther Schuller's *The Swing Era: The Development of Jazz,
1930–1945* (Oxford) has at last arrived. The second volume of a
projected three-volume history of jazz, it has taken twenty years
to write and is over nine hundred closely printed pages long.
(The first volume, the comparatively slim *Early Jazz: Its Roots
and Musical Development*, is also available from Oxford.)
Schuller tells us that in the course of his research he listened to
over thirty thousand recordings, and that there are over five
hundred pieces of musical notation in the book, which "required many, many hundreds of hours of laborious transcribing
from recordings." He also tells us in a publisher's biographical
note, that he was the "artistic director" at Tanglewood for
almost twenty years and the head of the New England Conser-
vatory of Music for ten years. He could have swelled the flow
with these stats: born in New York in 1925, he was a horn player
with the Metropolitan Opera in the forties and fifties, he is a
classical composer and conductor of note, he coined the term
"third-stream music" in a lecture at Brandeis in 1957 (third-
stream music attempts to fuse jazz and classical music), and in
the late fifties he was one of the leaders in writing and performing such music. In short, Schuller is an adventurous musician,
uniquely at ease in every quarter of European and American
music (except, possibly, as an improvising musician). Who else
could hand down these Olympian statements?

[*Duke Ellington's 1933 "Delta Serenade"*] *contains moments
of timbral and harmonic inspiration which had never been*

produced before by any composer, including Ravel or Schoen-
berg.

The remaining parade of stellar soloists includes Hodges,
Stewart (who begins his improvisation with a mighty half-
valve yelp, unknown to music theretofore) . . .

In the thirties and early forties, jazz came close to being a popular music. There were hundreds of big bands, ranging from nondescript local groups to the great bands of Duke Ellington, Count Basie, and Jimmie Lunceford. The big bands could be heard in ballrooms, hotels, theatres, and roadhouses and also on nightly network radio and in countless recordings. Most of them were dance bands that played occasional jazz numbers; the rest were jazz bands that also played for dancing—people danced then almost as often as they went to the movies. At the same time, there was a subculture of small bands that flourished in night clubs. These clubs were scattered from coast to coast, but the most famous were on West Fifty-second Street in New York. Few of these clubs had room for dancing, and it was in them that jazz changed from a dance music to a reluctant art music. Swing, as all this music came to be called, rose magically from the rhythmic and melodic chunkiness of the twenties and early thirties. Its characteristics were a four-four beat, the ability to swing, truly improvised solos, the wide use of arrangements, a deepening harmonic sense, an endless variety of tones and timbres, and a reverence for melody, written and invented. (Schuller points out that the recent discovery of thousands of alternate takes makes it clear that some soloists used the same solos over and over. Still, such solos *were* improvised the first time they were played.) It was an accessible, lyrical music that could be fiery and serene, raucous and romantic. At its best, it had no pretensions or self-consciousness. Bebop elbowed swing aside in the mid-forties, but swing went on into the seventies, when its great originators started to falter and die out.

For a long time, swing was segregated. Few white bands hired black musicians (Goodman, Shaw, Charlie Barnet, Gene Krupa, and Joe Marsala were exceptions), and few black bands hired white musicians. Blacks, of course, invented jazz, and whites, in rapacious admiration, stole freely from them, diluting and smoothing what they took. Some white bandleaders became rich; no black leaders did. Many white bands grew out of black ones. Benny Goodman came out of Fletcher Henderson, Charlie Barnet and Hal McIntyre out of Duke Ellington, Will Bradley out of the boogie-woogie pianists, Tommy Dorsey and Stan Kenton out of Jimmie Lunceford, and the rhythmic impetus of a dozen white bands out of the old Basie rhythm section. Many white players grew out of black players. Georgie Auld, Vido Musso, Flip Phillips, and Corky Corcoran learned from Ben Webster; a crowd of white tenor saxophonists, among them Stan Getz, Zoot Sims, Al Cohn, Allen Eager, Herbie Steward, Bill Perkins, and Jimmy Giuffre, learned from Lester Young; Benny Goodman learned from Jimmie Noone, and Harry James from Louis Armstrong and Red Allen, Jess Stacy from Earl Hines, and Gene Krupa and Buddy Rich from Chick Webb. Segregation died out in jazz in the late forties, but by the late fifties reverse segregation had set in. Black bands rarely hired white musicians and, when they played, turned their backs on their predominantly white audiences.

Gunther Schuller's book is not so much a history of swing as a string of highly subjective critical assessments, arranged more or less chronologically. The parade goes like this: Benny Goodman; Duke Ellington (Schuller's beau ideal: a hundred and eleven pages); Louis Armstrong, who stood outside the swing era as a kind of lyrical minister without portfolio; the black big bands (two hundred and twenty-five pages); the great soloists beginning with Coleman Hawkins and closing with Red Allen (two hundred and six pages); the white big bands (a hundred and thirty-eight pages); the so-called territory bands (groups mainly from the Midwest and Southwest who never got to New York: thirty-six pages); and the small bands (thirty-eight pages).

Writing about an evanescent music like jazz is like trying to sculpt air: it is there, but you can't feel it, or smell it, or see it, and it keeps leaking through your fingers. Schuller goes at the problem in two ways, both musicological. He transcribes solos and ensembles (he admits that such notation is severely limited, because there is no way of designating blue notes or timbre or tone or the various rhythmical urgencies of jazz), and he parses the music verbally, as in this passage on Ben Webster's celebrated solo on Duke Ellington's "Cotton Tail":

His stealthy entrance on "Cotton Tail" is in its subtleness and surprising understatedness one of the all-time hair-raising moments in jazz. It also embodies one of Webster's other favorite devices, a descending chromatic line, usually evenly spaced and often set in cross-rhythms. In mm. 1–4 we hear one of Webster's smoother versions of this configuration; we shall encounter it again later in this solo in a more flamboyant form. In mm. 5–7 a more varied (and concealed) use of the same idea follows, lining out the notes A flat G G flat F E E flat (incidentally almost all of these by chance doubled in [Jimmy] Blanton's high register walking bass). More of the same occurs in mm. 13–16, as the G in m. 13 works its way down to the D four bars later.

But such techniques exclude the musical illiterates of the world. So Schuller occasionally aerates his musicology with metaphors and impressionism. He almost describes the indescribable—a Pee Wee Russell solo:

Starting in the fifth bar, Russell takes that F, bends and twists it in quarter tones: this over the E flat chord, the flattened F, almost an E sharp, producing some anguished dissonances with Joe Sullivan's piano background. Russell continues to worry this note to death, irreverently pulling and tugging at it like a cat playing with a mouse. Adding to the slightly uneasy effect are Sullivan's soft tremolo accompaniment and Zutty Singleton's somber, mournful drum press roll, the contrast heightened by Russell's insistent agitated double-time over the accompaniment's rather more serene single-time.

The Swing Era is full of surprises. Schuller likes to praise figures who have been ignored or discredited by the jazz critical fraternity. Some of his rescue operations are invaluable, and some are romantic. Ennobled are the tenor saxophonist Dick Wilson; the trumpeter and arranger John Nesbitt; the trumpeters Red Nichols, Bunny Berigan, Harry James, Charlie Shavers, Emmett Berry, and Charlie Teagarden; Red Norvo; the trombonists Lawrence Brown, Bobby Byrne, Bill Harris, and Sandy Williams; the accordionist and pianist Joe Mooney; Benny Carter's clarinet playing; Pee Wee Russell; and the drummers Chick Webb and Moe Purtill. (It is difficult to agree with his feelings about James and Brown. Both were superb technicians who didn't always swing, and who seemed to work on the dressy fringes of jazz.) Schuller also praises Cab Calloway and Woody Herman's singing and such white big bands as those of Bob Crosby, Bob Chester, Charlie Barnet, Isham Jones, Hal McIntyre, and Glenn Miller (but he never mentions Bobby Hackett's immortal cornet solo in Miller's "A String of Pearls"). He is even kind to such sharkskin "sweet" bands as those of Jan Garber and Alvino Rey and Shep Fields.

Just as surprising are the superior players Schuller puts down, barely mentions, or bypasses. These include the trumpeter Joe Thomas and such scarcely less valuable brass players as Hackett, Bill Coleman, Sidney de Paris, Frankie Newton, Dicky Wells, and Benny Morton. He also skirts Django Reinhardt, Joe Venuti, Sidney Bechet, Jess Stacy, the boogie-woogie pianists, and Fats Waller. (He explains his neglect of Waller by saying he simply ran out of gas when it came time to do him.) And he dismisses Count Basie's piano playing.

The most startling inequity in the book, though, has to do with the space accorded big bands and small bands—almost five hundred pages versus less than forty pages. Fewer than a dozen of the hundreds of big bands were first-rate. The rest were, in varying degrees, bland, repetitive, and unswinging. From the mid-thirties, small jazz bands—either working groups or groups put together for recording—preserved the heart of jazz. It was their music that was so often deep and exhilarating. (Ellington, Basie, and Andy Kirk made their bands seem more like small ones than big ones. None depended on massed sounds.) Beyond the half-dozen or so groups that Schuller does study, these small bands make a handsome list: the Goodman septet; many of Lionel Hampton's 1937–40 Victor recording groups; Teddy Wilson's Café Society Uptown band; the Blue Note recording groups led by James P. Johnson, Edmond Hall, Sidney de Paris, and Ike Quebec; the small Ellington groups; Sidney Bechet's New Orleans Feetwarmers; Lil Armstrong's bands; the Bechet-Spanier Big Four; Fats Waller's little bands; the Mary Lou Williams Trio; Joe Marsala's various groups; Zutty Singleton's Chicago band; the Delta Four; the Coleman Hawkins–Red Allen sides and those done by Allen himself; Frankie Newton's various groups; the Spirits of Rhythm; Stuff Smith's band and trio; the recording groups assembled by Harry Lim in 1944 for his Keynote label and by Bob Thiele for his Signature label; Mel Powell's band with Benny Goodman; Eddie Heywood's band; Hot Lips Page's sides for Savoy and Commodore; Rex Stewart's Big Seven and Jack Teagarden's Big Eight; and the Eddie Condon groups, which at their best provided some of the most headlong and joyous collective jazz ever played. One more inequity must be mentioned. Schuller writes that Chick Webb was "virtually the only swing era drummer on whose recordings one can aurally shut out the other instruments and still have a consistently rewarding musical experience." He also says that "very few [swing] drummers—Chick Webb was a notable exception—could hold a sophisticated listener's attention in a long *a capella* drum solo." Almost all the recordings Sidney Catlett made are worth listening to simply for his playing. And his long solos (see the Louis Armstrong 1947 Symphony Hall concert and the 1944 Metropolitan Opera House concert) are as exciting and beautifully turned melodically and rhthmically now as they were forty years ago. Catlett began where Chick Webb left off.

Schuller disarmingly apologizes at the outset of his book for his "German-bred verbosity and love of long sentences." It is true that his prose, with its clause-upon-clause roll and its verbal garnishes, must sometimes be pushed through. Also distracting are such phrases as "woefully neglected," "we must factor in," "veneered over," and "winnowed down." (And who was minding the spelling shop at Oxford? "Medlies," "be-knighted," and "antidated"!)

Schuller has promised a third volume of his history, and, to judge by the number of eager mentions in "The Swing Era" of modernists like Charlie Parker, Dizzy Gillespie, Charles Mingus, Thelonious Monk, and John Lewis, he must already be on his way. Schuller has been deeply involved in modern jazz as a composer, arranger, leader, and close colleague, and perhaps these firsthand immersions will sharpen his vision and tighten his prose.

Max

Max Gordon had reached the great age of eighty-six when he died. He was still at the helm of his beloved Village Vanguard, which, at fifty-five, is probably the oldest night club in the world. Standing row upon row in the sizable space of his past were the performers whose careers he had started or furthered—an extraordinary group, which includes Woody Allen, Pearl Bailey, Bobby Short, Wally Cox, Comden and Green, Leadbelly, Nichols and May, Harry Belafonte, Judy Holliday, Barbra Streisand, Mort Sahl, Mildred Bailey, Lenny Bruce, the Weavers, Carol Sloane, Aretha Franklin, Josh White, and almost every jazz musician from Zutty Singleton to Albert Ayler.

Max backed into his life. He was brought to this country from Svir, Lithuania, in 1908, and in 1926 he moved to New York from Portland, Oregon, where his family settled. He studied law at Columbia, but he lasted only six weeks. Greenwich Village was full of poets and writers and painters, and, drawn by its ferment, he took a furnished room near Washington Square. Max's Village was made up of writers and vagabonds like Harry

Kemp, Maxwell Bodenheim, Joe Gould, and John Rose Gildea—
not the tony group that included Edmund Wilson, Elinor Wylie,
Edna St. Vincent Millay, and E. E. Cummings. Kemp, who was
big, loved Max, who was small. "Kemp lived on the dunes at
Provincetown," Max said once, "and he helped start the Provincetown Playhouse. When he came back to town, he'd look for
me in the coffeehouses and he'd shout, 'Max! Where are you? I
have a new poem to read to you!' and crush me with an
embrace."

For five years, Max worked at odd jobs, read at the Public
Library, and hung out with the poets at the coffeehouses. In
1932, at the insistence of a friend named Ann Andreas, he
opened his own place, the Village Fair Coffee House, on Sullivan
Street. The poets came to drink, and declaim their poetry, but
the club lasted only a year. ("Unbeknownst to me, one of the
waitresses got caught trying to sell liquor to a cop in plain-
clothes, so they put a cop on the premises every night, and there
he sat in his uniform, and it put a pall on the place," Max
explained.) In 1934, Max opened another place, on Charles
Street, and called it the Village Vanguard, for a reason that he
could never remember. In February of 1935, he moved a couple
of blocks north, without skipping a night's work, to the Vanguard's present site, on Seventh Avenue between Eleventh
Street and Waverly Place.

No architect would design a place like the Vanguard, which,
in its accidental way, is a perfect union of form and content. A
pie-shaped basement some sixty feet long, it has a small bandstand at its south end, or apex, and a small bar at the other end. A
passageway behind the bar leads to a disused kitchen, which
became Max's office, a dressing room, and a gathering place for
jazz musicians. The walls of the main room were once covered
with murals and are now covered largely with photographs.
When someone asked Max who decorated the Vanguard, he
replied, "It decorated itself." Max was married and had two
daughters, but, in truth, he was married to the Vanguard. He
once said, "This place has been like a love match to me. I've
probably spent more time in it than anywhere else. I've even

slept here, stretched out on a couple of tables. I've learned that if you're good to the Vanguard, the Vanguard will be good to you." He often spoke of the place as if it were flesh and blood. "The Vanguard has a life of its own. It's nice to people. It doesn't push them around. It doesn't make them feel it's trying to inveigle them into more drinks. It doesn't hustle. If people want a drink, they get it. If they don't, they don't." Max was revered by the people who worked for him, and although he had a sharp ear and eye, he never tried to shape his performers. If they met expectations, they were asked back. He said, in a resigned way, "I never got to know a lot of the people who appeared at the Vanguard. Maybe they were scared of me, maybe I was scared of them. Maybe they were like John Coltrane, who was always surrounded by worshippers. I loved his music, but I never said four words to him."

The Vanguard was not Max's only invention. From 1943 to 1963, he was co-owner, with Herbert Jacoby, of the Blue Angel, on East Fifty-fifth Street. Jacoby was a supercilious Frenchman who had started out in the Paris *boîtes*, and Max was, in his own cheerful estimation, a Village bumpkin. Once Max got his bearings in the rarefied atmosphere that Jacoby moved in, the two got on well enough, and eventually worked out a smooth system. They tried out new acts at the Vanguard and, if they went over, shipped them to the Blue Angel. Max often claimed he was not a businessman; what he really meant was he wasn't greedy. Whatever profits he made were the result of offering a pure product in decent surroundings at a reasonable price. Ambition got the better of him only twice, with disastrous consequences. In the late forties, he and Jacoby bought the faltering Café Society Uptown from Barney Josephson and, at enormous expense, converted it into the posh Le Directoire. After a deceptive early success, it foundered, and they sold it back to Josephson, for five thousand dollars. In 1955, Max and Michael Field, the cookbook writer and classical pianist, opened a fancy ice-cream parlor, Maxfield's, near the Paris Theatre, on West Fifty-eighth Street. It had tile floors, marble counters, red velvet walls, brass chandeliers, homemade ice cream made with cream, and coffee brewed every twenty minutes. The Bergdorf's crowd found it outrageously expensive, and the after-theatre crowd stayed away because it didn't have a liquor license.

In the early sixties, the Vanguard, long neglected for Max's uptown interests, nearly went under. Max had to sell his car and his house on Fire Island. He borrowed ten thousand dollars ("One of the axioms of the night-club business is you have to have somebody to lean on for money") and, by dint of shrewd booking (quality jazz acts that might become popular; popular jazz acts that had quality), pulled the Vanguard through. Max was of two minds about money. He knew it was essential, but he also knew how ephemeral it was—which is probably what made him carry a comforting roll of bills, bills that fluttered like leaves onto the table and the floor when he pulled them out of his pocket to pay a restaurant check.

In the early seventies, he moved back to the Village from the Upper East Side, and after that his life became simpler. He lived in a small apartment on Lower Fifth Avenue, and he ate dinner at Joe's, on MacDougal Street, or at Pirandello, just east of Washington Square. He went to the Vanguard twice a day—in the afternoon to do his booking, take reservations, and replenish his stock, and in the evening to watch the cash register, talk to friends, and listen to the music. He'd sit at his desk in the back or at a table near the door: an owlish man with receding white hair, heavy-rimmed glasses, and a big cigar. Clothes puzzled Max. For much of the year, he wore a chamois shirt, open at the neck, a corduroy suit, and, when he went out, a shapeless black hat, pulled so low that only tendrils of white hair showed. He liked to talk, in his casual, enunciatory way ("I feel all right. I feel pretty gude"), and he loved to laugh. At a memorial service for Max, Katy Abel, the Vanguard's longtime doorkeeper, reported that once two men appeared at the top of the steps leading down to the club and started fencing with loaves of French bread. She asked Max what to do, and he looked up the stairs and said, "Ask them if they want some butter."

In a nonchalant way, Max eventually began to take himself as seriously as he took the Vanguard. In 1980, he published a memoir, *Live at the Village Vanguard*. He wrote it himself, page by page, over a period of seven years, and it is a funny, literate book. Here is his caption for a photograph of the singer Betty Carter at the Vanguard: "I happened to walk in on her last show. It was late, it was February, the snow was on the ground; there was nobody in the joint. And there she was, singing to a lot of empty chairs and tables. I could never get that picture out of my mind. She used to come around, looking for work. 'Let's wait and see,' I'd say. Then finally she said, 'You should hear me again, hear me somewhere else, hear me in a place other than the Vanguard.' So I went all the way up to Harlem to hear her at a place called Wells's. I heard her and put her to work. And today she's Betty Bebop, the greatest bebop singer of them all. And do you know what? I can't afford her anymore; she now sings in arenas and does concerts in college gymnasiums. But she comes down to see me. We sit in the kitchen and talk." He kept a pile of his books at the Vanguard, and he estimated he had sold two thousand copies. This is what he said about the techniques he used in the book: "I kept trying to find a way to get my ideas across, and I hit on dialogues, sometimes with real people, sometimes with people based on real people. Some of the dialogues are fictional, but it's fiction borrowed directly from life. Life fiction, you might call it."

Max was the last of the old-style New York jazz-club owners, who not only operated honest places but loved the music. Others, down through the years, have included Nick Rongetti (Nick's), Jimmy Ryan and Matty Walsh (Jimmy Ryans), Barney Josephson (Café Society Downtown and Café Society Uptown, the Cookery), Ralph Watkins (Kelly's Stable, Basin Street East, the Embers), Art D'Lugoff (the Village Gate), the Canterinos (the Half Note), the Termini brothers (the Five Spot), Gil Wiest (Michael's Pub), and Bradley Cunningham, (Bradley's). Josephson, who ran the Café Societies from 1938 to 1948 and the Cookery from 1971 to 1982, died last September, and Cunningham, who opened Bradley's in 1969, died in November. Barney, Bradley, and Max lived and worked within a three- or four-block area, but they didn't commingle much. Max sometimes ate dinner at Bradley's (Bradley was rarely there that early), and Bradley would turn up at the Vanguard when Max celebrated an anniversary of some sort. Barney, a stylish, elegant man, tended to stay on his own turf. They were of a kind in their different, rebel ways. New Yorkers aren't heavy mourners, but they have long memories.

Mixed Blessings

Grove's Dictionary of Music and Musicians has embraced jazz. Grove first approached the music with some sort of seriousness in 1980, when the *New Grove Dictionary* included not only articles on jazz but almost two hundred entries on jazz musicians. It came even closer in 1986, in the *New Grove Dictionary of American Music*—more than four hundred entries on the music and its makers. Now the *New Grove Dictionary of Jazz* has arrived, and it attempts to encompass all the jazz literature that has accumulated since the mid-thirties, when Hugues Panassié published the first critical book on jazz (*Le Jazz Hot*), Charles Delaunay published the first discography (*Hot Discography*), Louis Armstrong the first jazz autobiography (*Swing That Music*), Dorothy Baker the first jazz novel (*Young Man with a Horn*), and Otis Ferguson the first more or less regular jazz criticism in a national magazine (*The New Republic*).

Here are some of Jazz Grove's particulars. It comes in two volumes, each measuring eight and a half inches by eleven inches, and each just shy of seven hundred pages. There are two broad columns to a page, set in readable type on good stock (there is no indication of whether or not it is acid-free), and surrounded by generous gutters (there is no rule between the columns, and none is needed). Of the forty-five hundred entries, three thousand deal with individuals, and among them are musicians, composers, arrangers, record producers, editors, discographers, impresarios, and writers. The rest of the entries have to do with such subjects as jazz notation, the beat, bands of whatever size and disposition, harmony, improvisation, arrangements, recording, transcription, synthesizers, festivals (two hundred listings), night clubs (nine hundred listings), jazz libraries and archives, the instruments peculiar to jazz, record labels, jazz groups, jazz films, and jazz terms. Each entry on an individual gives his working name, his real name, his nickname, his date and place of birth (and death), a summary of his career, a selective discography and bibliography, and the repository of any oral history he may have done. Most of the musicians are American, but there are also hundreds of international players, ranging from the Turkish trumpeter Maffy Falay to the Argentine bassist Alfredo Remus to the Dutch reed player Jan Morks. The volumes contain a couple of hundred apt and often unfamiliar photographs, taken mainly from the collection of Frank Driggs, and there is a twenty-page bibliography in small type at the back of the second volume, just before a list of the names and origins of the dictionary's two hundred and fifty contributors, many of whom are unknown academics who are not always as hip as they might be. The relatively few well-known contributors include Danny Barker, Joachim Berendt, Edward Berger, Ran Blake, John Chilton, James Lincoln Collier, Frank Driggs, Leonard Feather, Mark Gridley, Lawrence Gushee, André Hodeir, Felicity Howlett, Michael James, Dan Morgenstern, Paul Oliver, Henry Pleasants, Lewis Porter, Brian Priestley, John Rockwell, Bill Russell, Gunther Schuller, Ernie Smith, Richard Sudhalter, J. R. Taylor, Michael Ullman, Martin Williams, and Valerie Wilmer. The largest number of entries are by Barry Kernfeld, who edited the dictionary and is a musicologist.

Chief among Jazz Grove's blessings is bringing under one cover the biographical entries that for so long have been buried in the six volumes of Leonard Feather and Ira Gitler's *Encyclopedia of Jazz*, in John Chilton's *Who's Who of Jazz*, in Roger

Kinkle's *Complete Encyclopedia of Popular Music and Jazz,*
and in Al Rose and Samuel Charters' directories of New Orleans
jazz. It is fine, too, to have the entries on films, night clubs,
record labels (nothing is more fleeting in jazz), jazz festivals, and
jazz archives and libraries; the essays on jazz (almost novella
length), jazz forms, harmony, arranging, rhythm, and improvisation; and the histories of the instruments used in jazz, some of
them almost invented by jazz musicians (the drum set, many of
the saxophones, the vibraphone, the electric guitar).

In many ways, jazz has been a hand-me-down, word-of-mouth
music, often unchronicled, unfilmed, and under-recorded, at
least until recent times. Jazz Grove, in trying to get the specifics
of this ephemeral music on paper, has made a good many
mistakes, some of them wild, some of them minor. A selective
list, in alphabetical order: Despite his occasional association
with jazz players, the harmonica player Larry Adler is not a jazz
musician. James Lincoln Collier, in his Louis Armstrong entry,
scants the celestial Victors Armstrong recorded late in 1932 and
early in 1933. Astonishing statement No. 1: Daniel Zager
claims that Amiri Baraka (LeRoi Jones), an emotional, highly
politicized writer, has had "a profound influence on jazz criticism." Gene Bertoncini and Michael Moore's beautiful, unclas-
sifiable duo cannot in any sense be considered a "bop duo." Art
Blakey did not learn how to use "his elbow on the tom-tom to
alter the pitch" in Africa; he learned it from his master, Sidney
Catlett, who used the device long before Blakey went abroad.
Bob Brookmeyer was not the first important valve trombonist
after Duke Ellington's Juan Tizol—Brad Gowans was. There is
no mention in the Tina Brooks discography of the comprehensive Mosaic Blue Note reissue brought out several years ago.
(The discographies following the biographical entries tend to be
poorly chosen.) Nor is there any mention in Ray Charles' entry
of his being a great jazz singer. Three things are wrong in this
sentence from the long and comprehensive entry on drums:
"Many drummers from the 1950s onwards—notably Sonny
Greer, Chick Webb, Chico Hamilton, and Elvin Jones—have
also employed timpani mallets." Webb died in 1939, Sid Catlett

used mallets extensively in the early forties, and Greer and Jones have rarely, if ever, used them. The entry on Art Farmer is simply inadequate; it does not place him in modern jazz or describe his original and exquisite style. Astonishing statement No. 2: James Lincoln Collier claims that "jazz usually takes place in the context of an actual or simulated jam session, which has some aspects of a ritual." Jam sessions, which have nearly died out, were manhood-testing rituals; they stood to one side of the nightly, almost blue-collar business of jazz as, first, a dance music and then as an art music. If Gus Johnson's "aggressive but fluid and dance-like style made him the best drummer (Count) Basie had after Jo Jones," then what about Shadow Wilson, Buddy Rich, and Sonny Payne? The sublime tap dancer Baby Laurence is no longer alive; he died in April of 1974. There is no mention that the recording director Harry Lim was responsible in 1944 on the Keynote label for some of the best jazz recordings ever made. Astonishing statement No. 3: Barry Kernfeld writes in his essay on Charles Mingus that "Mingus's accomplishments surpass in historic and stylistic breadth those of any other major figure in jazz." Including Louis Armstrong, Charlie Parker, Thelonious Monk, and Mingus's acknowledged master, Duke Ellington? The New York night-club listings are far from complete. (See the priceless glossary of Harlem clubs in the booklet prepared in the early sixties by George Hoefer for the Columbia boxed set called "The Sound of Harlem"—a booklet nowhere mentioned in the bibliography. And where in the New York listings are such clubs as Pookie's Pub, Bourbon St., Buddy's Place, the Back Porch, Frank's Place, the Royal Box, Plaza 9, Hopper's, the Composer, the Limelight, the Roosevelt Grill, the Rainbow Grill, Shepheard's, and the Guitar?) We are never told what instrument the Chicago clarinettist and alto saxophonist Joe Poston played. This meaningless description appears in the entry on Mickey Roker: his drumming "draws upon the inherent impetus of the blues." Leonard Feather leaves out Leo Watson, Jelly Roll Morton, and Hot Lips Page in his essay on jazz singing. And in the brief paragraph accorded the trumpeter Joe Wilder nothing is said about his style or the fact that he was one of the first jazz musicians to function on both sides of the jazz-classical fence.

Three more quibbles: (1) Although the bibliography at the end of Volume II appears fairly complete, the bibliographies appended to many of the biographical entries are at best haphazard. (2) These figures have been unfairly omitted from Jazz Grove: the baritone saxophonist Gil Mellé; the pianist Dorothy Donegan; the drummers Victor Lewis and Baby Lovett; the tubist-bassist-bandleader Vince Giordano; the bassist Ray Drummond; the jazz singers Barbara Lea, Carol Sloane, Peggy Lee, Sylvia Sims, and Nellie Lutcher; the record producer Milt Gabler; and the night-club owners Barney Josephson and Max Gordon (mentioned in passing in the night-club listings). (3) In his preface Kernfeld declares that he has purposely left out gospel singing. Too bad. Such gospel singers as Mahalia Jackson, Marion Williams, Dorothy Love Coates, and Claude Jeter are, their idiom notwithstanding, among the greatest of jazz singers.

Many of Jazz Grove's short biographies are admirable. These stand out: J. Bradford Robinson's on Red Allen and on Buddy Bolden; Barry Kernfeld's on John Coltrane and on Freddie Hubbard; John Chilton's on Bobby Hackett; Michael James' on Warne Marsh; Bob Zieff's on Bobby Stark; Lawrence Gushee's on King Oliver and on New Orleans jazz; and Gunther Schuller's on Ornette Coleman.

James Lincoln Collier is a born revisionist. His latest effort is a ninety-five-page pamphlet, "The Reception of Jazz in America" (Institute for Studies in American Music, Brooklyn College), in which he attempts to demolish the old belief that jazz, neglected in its own country, was first appreciated by Europeans. Collier claims that Americans have always been knowledgeable about jazz and that they began to write intelligently about it in the twenties and early thirties, long before the Europeans knew what was happening. Two of the early American critics he advances for attention are familiar: the novelist and photographer Carl Van Vechten and the blues specialist Abbe Niles. He pulls the third out of his hat—R. D. Darrell, long a critic of and handyman writer about classical music. Darrell, it turns out, wrote about jazz for small-circulation music magazines from the mid-twenties to the early thirties. Collier quotes Darrell persuasively on Ellington; he understood what he was hearing. Collier points out that in 1937 *Time* estimated that there were half a million "serious jazz fanciers" in this country. (Benny Goodman was riding high then and the swing craze had begun, so *Time*'s guess might have been somewhere near the mark. But such widespread jazz admiration has never been evident since. When two or three jazz fans find each other anywhere, they consider themselves a crowd.) Collier also argues that the belief in European clairvoyance was started by American leftists who wanted the American establishment to look reactionary. He claims that Hugues Panassié's *Hot Jazz*, which is generally credited with turning us on to jazz in this country is emotional, inaccurate, and irresponsible. (Panassié, of course, had not yet been to America, and had based his book on recordings.) But for all its ineptness Panassié's book had an enthusiasm and love for the music which jarred and excited the American young. (Gunther Schuller says that Panassié brought him to the music.) Collier is not convincing when he attempts to pooh-pooh the Swiss conductor Ernest Ansermet's astonishing description of Sidney Bechet, written in 1919, when jazz was largely sequestered in New Orleans. Nor does he explain why there have always been so many people in this country who cannot even tell you what jazz is.

Mingus Regained

Charles Mingus's two-hour assemblage, "Epitaph," was given its première early in June at Alice Tully Hall by a thirty-piece jazz orchestra conducted by Gunther Schuller. It marks the first advance in the composition of large-scale jazz works since Duke Ellington's 1943 "Black, Brown and Beige," a fifty-minute piece that can now be considered an overture to Mingus's leviathan, which is full of Ellington devices and Ellington melodies.

Although money problems forced Mingus to work with small groups most of his life, his head was always full of big sounds. These took the form of works for large jazz bands, and they were realized perhaps half a dozen times either on recordings or at concerts. One of the concerts, given at Town Hall in 1962, with thirty all-star musicians on hand, was meant to be a summation of Mingus's work, but, as so often happened in his involuted life, it went wrong. The concert, moved forward five weeks at the behest of the company that was to record it, became a four-hour rehearsal, in which copyists were still at work onstage and almost nothing was played in its entirety. The most command-ing music was Mingus's various harangues—to his musicians, to the recording technicians, and to the restive audience. But the concert has turned out to be the acorn from which "Epitaph" grew. More than half of the eight or so numbers played that night in 1962 appeared in different form at Alice Tully Hall. They became part, it is now clear, of a large work that Mingus completed sometime in the early seventies and set aside be-cause he was convinced that, in the rock climate of the time, he would never be able to raise the money to have it properly performed. As Mingus the master ironist knew, its title would mean nothing unless he was dead and the piece was discovered and played.

"Epitaph" was turned up by the musicologist Andrew Homzy while he was cataloguing the bags and boxes of music Mingus left behind when he died, ten years ago. Homzy writes in the program notes, "Approximately twenty scores for a large jazz orchestra written on oversized, frayed, and yellowed paper were discovered in the collection. On some of these scores the title 'Epitaph' was written; on others, 'Epitaph' appeared as a subtitle for what at first looked like independent compositions. Signifi-cantly, all the measures on all of the scores were successively numbered. . . . Further study . . . led Gunther Schuller to the conclusion that Mingus's hope 'was to find improvisation and spontaneity and freedom, and at the same time compose a large extensive frame of reference. That's the problem . . . that in jazz has not yet been solved. Only Duke Ellington really tackled it. But Ellington was still writing songs and fashioning suites around them. ["Epitaph"] has nothing to do with thirty-two-bar-song forms. It is composition in the true sense.'" Homzy said just before the concert, "It's not the kind of piece where the themes are connected. It's more of an anthology, a panorama complete in itself. When I found the score, I felt the energy coming up from the pages, as if they had a life of their own. Friends have told me they had the same sensation when they looked at Mozart scores in Salzburg."

It took five months for twenty copyists and two computer programs to assemble a five-hundred-page score, containing over four thousand measures of music. It could not have been easy. Here are some of the instructions that Mingus left about how he wanted one of the parts, "Please Don't Come Back from the Moon," scored: "We usually extend the E-flat-minor-A-flat-seven sound together—more or less with arabic harmonies gradually sneaking in . . . the piano gives a two-bar cue and we're back at the top again. . . . Perhaps the brass or other section could have a cue chord that one of the section men could conduct in for two or more bars. This cue can be used throughout the piece. Since there is no time bars after we reach the minor mode, I would like to have section or sections, 'pattern' riffs, that space themselves spasmodically, so the piece won't have that four-bar-eight-bar feeling. 'Like' the trpt plays the melody on the E-flat-A-flat part in harmon mute close to a mike. . . . He begins with just rhythm—then little things sneak in on the third and fourth beat. Then out some bars—then in on the beat."

"Epitaph," as played at Alice Tully, contained nineteen sections, over half of them reworkings of pieces that Mingus had written and/or played from the late thirties to the early seventies. These included "Started Melody" (an improvisation on "I

Can't Get Started," a song Mingus often played), "Moods in Mambo," "The Self-Portrait—The Chill of Death" (from 1939), "O.P. (Oscar Pettiford)," "Please Don't Come Back from the Moon," "Monk, Bunk and Vice Versa," "Peggy's Blue Skylight," "Better Get Hit in Your Soul," and "Noon Night." There were five balladlike sections, the mambo, four blues, two improvisations on standard tunes, and six uncategorizable sections, a couple of them over ten minutes long. In "Epitaph" Mingus uses every device known to jazz—and to him. The tempo doubles and is halved, decelerates and accelerates. There are accented and unaccented four-four beats, and two-four beats. There are lengthy sections without any sounded rhythm. There are ritards and places where the beat is at the very front of each note. There are riffs and ostinatos. There are breaks and stop-times and chase choruses. There are growl trumpet and growl trombone solos, pizzicato and arco bass solos, a bassoon solo, a recited poem, and chanting by the orchestra. There are all sorts of melodic interpolations—a bugle call, bits of "Tea for Two," an Ellington band call and echoes of Ellington's "Happy Go Lucky Local," a riff from the "One O'clock Jump." At the end of the final number, the entire orchestra improvises at once.

The harmonic pallet moves from huge unison chords to impenetrable dissonances. The great trombonist Jimmy Knepper, a longtime, long-suffering Mingus sideman and the present leader of Mingus Dynasty, the Mingus revival band, once said about Mingus as an orchestrator, "I never felt he was as great an orchestrator as some people made out. For instance, in 'Cumbia' he would use the trombone with the bassoon and the bass-clarinet. If you put them all together, it just sounds like mud. There are at least half a dozen places where Mingus has four or five ensemble voices going at once—mass counterpoint that is so dense that the ear can't take it all in.

The most complicated movements—the two parts of "Main Score," and "Main Score Reprise," "The Self-Portrait—The Chill of Death," and "The Children's Hour of Dream"—are in constant motion. No phrase lasts more than two or three measures. The music resembles the way Mingus talked—in

fast, irregular, often slurred bursts. The wild, acidulous, melancholy "The Children's Hour of Dream" went like this: A heavy
bass ensemble chord slid into a brief, sorrowing melody, echoed
by a solo alto saxophone, then by a flute; a walking-bass ostinato
began and was joined by stabbing offbeat chords, played by the
brass; still other instruments (it was impossible to tell in what
combinations) thickened the ostinato, and there were more
offbeat stabs; a reed figure shot past; a trombone figure entered
and was opposed by high, light trumpet sighs; timpani strokes
introduced a melody for the brass, the reeds played a balancing
melody, backed by a piano tremolo and a new, very fast ostinato,
and muted trumpets floated above; a short, muttering trombone
figure anchored an oboe; the ostinato slowed, and a muted
trombone and a tenor saxophone soloed against swelling brass
and drums. Then the drums went into a kind of "Saber Dance"
rhythm, there were more of the earlier, giant offbeat chords, and
the mournful opening melody rolled by again. Everything
speeded up, and in quick succession we heard more brass;
heavy, descending, steplike unison figures played by what
sounded like the entire orchestra; the opening melody replayed
with its alto-saxophone flourish, again the steplike unison
figures, the opening melody with its flute flourish, and—
bang!—it all ended. There had been no consistent beat, yet the
timbres, the accents, the phrasing were jazzlike. "The Children's Hour of Dream" is part jazz, part Stravinsky modern, part
Ellington, part Mingus—a new music.

The orchestra was made up of six trumpets, six trombones,
three alto saxophones, two tenor saxophones, two baritone
saxophones, a bassoon, a contrabass clarinet, a tuba, two pianos,
two basses, a vibraphone, a guitar, drums, and percussion.
Present, among many others, were John Handy, George Adams,
and Jerome Richardson on reeds; Roland Hanna and John Hicks
on pianos; Urbie Green, Britt Woodman, and Eddie Bert on
trombones; Randy Brecker, Lew Soloff, Wynton Marsalis, and
Joe Wilder on trumpets; and Victor Lewis on drums. The soloists, battling huge sounds on every side, were adept, and four in
particular shone: the trumpeters Soloff and Brecker; Michael

Rabinowitz, who played five lyrical choruses of the blues on his bassoon; and the canny Jerome Richardson, who began an alto-saxophone solo with half a dozen eerie, falsetto, strangely placed, descending bent notes that settled into a fine Charlie Parker-like chorus. The musicians, with only a week of rehearsals behind them, were, clams easily accepted, heroic. Columbia recorded the concert, and at the end, when two sections had to be redone, Gunther Schuller told the audience, "This music is so difficult—you have no idea."

A Hostile Land

The big news in jazz during the strange, suspended summer of 1941 was that some of the best and most successful white bands had again begun to hire black musicians. Benny Goodman, who already had Charlie Christian and Cootie Williams, took on Sidney Catlett and John Simmons. Artie Shaw, who had once employed Billie Holiday, recorded four numbers with Red Allen, J. C. Higginbotham, the pianist Sonny White, and the guitarist Jimmy Shirley. Later in the summer, he hired Hot Lips Page. Perhaps the biggest news was that Gene Krupa, still rising as a leader, had brought in Roy Eldridge. (Krupa had previously used Leo Watson on several recordings.)

Eldridge, who was thirty, was little known outside jazz circles, where he was regarded with awe, but he was famous when he left Krupa, in 1943. Aside from a spell with Fletcher Henderson's band, those two years were his first big-league experience. "Riding up on that stage at the Paramount Theatre with the Krupa band scared me to death," Eldridge once said. "The first three or four bars of my first solo, I'd shake like a leaf, and you could hear it. Then this light would surround me, and it would seem as if there wasn't any band there, and I'd go right through and be all right."

Eldridge played melodramatic fast solos with Krupa ("After You've Gone," "Twelfth Street Rag") and dramatic slow solos ("Rockin' Chair," "Georgia on My Mind"). He delivered hip, funny vocals ("Let Me Off Uptown," "Knock Me a Kiss"). And sometimes he sat in on drums while Krupa fronted the band. A short, bristling, jumping man with a two-hundred-watt smile and snapping eyes, Eldridge astonished the white audiences who flocked to hear him. He continued to wow them when he joined Artie Shaw, in 1944, and he wowed them throughout his career. His love-hate relationship with these audiences was the central paradox of his life. "Droves of people would ask him for his autograph at the end of the night," Shaw has said, "but later, on the bus, he wouldn't be able to get off and buy a hamburger with the guys in the band. He thought he was travelling through a hostile land, and he was right." The life of the great black soloists was a constant scuffle, compounded by racism. After a short European tour with Benny Goodman, in 1950, Eldridge stayed on in Paris almost a year—presumably to catch his racial breath—and when he came home he made a hair-raising début at the old Stuyvesant Casino. He then joined Norman Granz's Jazz at the Philharmonic, where he stayed for much of the fifities. He accompanied Ella Fitzgerald in the early sixties, flickered through Count Basie's band in 1966, and, after endless gigging, settled into Jimmy Ryans in 1970.

For a long time, Eldridge was said to be the link between Louis Armstrong and Dizzy Gillespie. But it has gradually become clear that although he stands between them, he was linked only to Gillespie, and was Gillespie's chief model. Eldridge had ferocious pride, and he would never admit that he had heard Armstrong any earlier than 1931 or 1932, when Armstrong, having passed through his first, rough-and-ready revolutionary phase, suddenly became a player who lived in his upper moonlit register. Eldridge must have studied this Armstrong, particularly his fondness for O altitudo notes, but he and Armstrong had very different natures: Armstrong went where the waters took him, while Eldridge invariably headed upstream. Armstrong was a melodic player who used silence and whole notes; Eldridge loved speed and lightning and noise. He told the jazz writer John Chilton, "I had this thing about playing as fast as I could all the time. I double-timed every ballad I did, and never held a long note." Eldridge listened closely to the wild men of the music. One of these was the breakneck trumpeter Jabbo Smith, who, presaging Dizzy Gillespie, stampeded the New York brass players in the late twenties before moving to the Midwest, where Eldridge had a run-in with him in Milwaukee. "We met at a place called Rails," Eldridge said. "We played fast and slow. The crowd thought I had cut Jabbo, and he didn't talk to me for two weeks, but I didn't fool myself. I knew he had cut me." Another player Eldridge studied and did combat with was the cornettist Rex Stewart, who always went after notes that no one had played before. And Eldridge must have listened to Red Allen when Allen was with Fletcher Henderson, in the mid-thirties. Allen was a one-man avant-garde, who played "strange" notes and had a revolutionary sense of time. He stretched regular four-four time to make it accommodate his melodic inventions without losing the rhythmic pulse. But Allen also had a dark, turning-away sound, and it was that elusive quality which Eldridge absorbed. Of course, one of Eldridge's first and greatest admirations was the garrulous Coleman Hawkins of Fletcher Henderson's 1926 recording of "The Stampede." (Later, he and Hawkins became fast friends, and worked, drove, and drank together until Hawkins' death, in 1969.)

The intensity and energy of Eldridge's mature style gave it a bas-relief effect. His tone was heavy and irregular. His growling and rough low register often had an angry cast, and as he grew older it became even more plangent. You wondered, when you went to Jimmy Ryans in the seventies, how he could get his massive style airborne yet again. There were two Eldridges—fast and slow. The fast Eldridge was wild and even maniacal. He might start a solo with an ascending shriek that was part run, part glissando. Then he'd drop, in a dodging run, through three registers and play a low long note, capped with a brief, hurried vibrato. He would leap to the top of his middle register and issue five strutting staccato notes, placed slightly behind the beat, and whistle back into his high register. He'd move rapidly between two high notes the way most trumpeters move between middle C and E, and pass through a two-octave interval and into a simple middle-register figure. A pause, and he'd go down another octave, to his sad low register, and close the solo with a glancing high note. Eldridge was erratic. Either his adventurousness would carry him off the deep end or he might find himself in a situation that made him uncontrollably nervous—playing in front of a congregation of his peers, as he had to do several times in 1957 on the television show "The Sound of Jazz." Then he'd blare and show off and play empty, gesticulating things. His best slow ballad numbers were anthems. He would generally stay in his middle or low register and play ceremonial embellishments on the melody before moving into a full improvisation. This would involve sizable melodic fragments separated by frequent rests and sounding like the original melody turned inside out. Eldridge's slow ballads had a cathedral quality that no other jazz trumpeter—even the 1932 Armstrong—has surpassed.

Eldridge died last winter, at the age of seventy-eight. He had quit playing in 1979, when his health began to deteriorate. "I don't miss the music anymore," he said several years after he had stepped down. "I've had enough fun and praise and ovations to keep me. I played fifty years, and that was long enough. Anyway, I found out the main doors were always locked. The color thing. I also found out I'd never get rich." For the last thirty or so years of his life, Eldridge lived, when he was off the road, in a small house in Queens, not far from the Nassau border. He lived with his wife, Vi, who had been a hostess at the old Savoy Ballroom, and whom he had married in 1936, and with his only child, Carole, a legal secretary. Very little in his house suggested what his life had been. In a small alcove off his living room he kept awards from the magazines *down beat* and *Esquire*, one from 1945 and one from 1946; a certificate of appreciation from Mayor John V. Lindsay; and a letter from President Jimmy Carter, thanking him for appearing at the jazz concert given on the South Lawn of the White House in June of 1978. Eldridge never changed much in appearance. His hair whitened and his glasses thickened, but his high, scrapy voice was full of pep and laughter. He would have been pleased by a summation of his work offered the other day by a fervent admirer: "Eldridge was a player of great magnitude."

Goodbye, Michael

For the past seven years, one of the best open secrets of New York night life was the nearly year-round Sunday concerts given by the duo of Michael Moore (bass) and Gene Bertoncini (guitar) at Zinno, in Greenwich Village. But last spring Moore—some think he is the greatest living contrabassist of whatever kind—sold his house, in Bangor, Pennsylvania; had its contents packed in a forty-foot container; collected his portable bass and his wife, Meena, who is Indian, and their six-year-old son, Matthew; and moved to India, thereby leaving an irreparable hole in American music.

Moore talked about his move a few days before he left: "The packers came yesterday, but they didn't have enough boxes or tape, and one of them was drunk. Then, in the middle of it all, we had to close on the sale of the house. This all began one day at home when I was working on a piece I had written with Mick Goodrick, and I said that we should go and live in India and do nothing but sit and write music. I said it as a lark, but I had been to India with Meena to visit her family, and I knew how pleasant the hill stations are and how great the schools are. I had seen how far ahead of Matthew scholastically his Indian cousins were. Meena was born in London of Indian parents, but she was educated in Darjeeling, and I knew what a joke my own education was in comparison with hers. We had already been having trouble in Bangor. The officials decided to close our small local school and put all the kids—including Matthew—in a huge school an hour away by bus. We were very much opposed, and we got very much involved, and if we hadn't been perhaps we wouldn't have experienced the seamy things we did. Meena, not being white, became the center of the battle, and people threatened to burn us out. That made us think seriously for the first time about moving to India. Another thing was my career. I've been making a living mostly in night clubs as a bass player for over twenty years, and I'm tired of it. Anyway, I've never been that fond of performing. Being on a stage in front of people makes me nervous. I get *agita* in the stomach, as the Italians say. I was attracted to the bass in the first place because it was a background instrument—so what happened but I ended up playing mostly in duos and trios. I've also come to hate travelling. I don't intend to spend my sixties and seventies carting a bass up and down the country. I want to do more studying and writing. I've become a born-again Christian in the past seven or eight years, and I've been writing songs based on the Bible. I want to use my talents in a spiritual way, and writing spiritual songs comes easily to me. I clothe the words in the Bible with my melodies, which frees me from the thirty-two-bar standard-song box. I've written about thirty of these songs, and I'm hoping to get them published. I have also written a long piece for the bass, at the Eastman School, where I've been teaching summers. So I've gotten my feet wet in composition. I've always idealized the life of a painter and the writer and the composer. I've idealized the life of being alone in a room with nothing but yourself and your work.

"I've also been playing a lot of piano. I wouldn't feel comfortable yet about playing in public here, but over there I can work at it without embarrassment. Accompanying pianists like Jimmy Rowles and Roger Kellaway and Tommy Flanagan taught me an incredible amount. I'd go home after working with them and try and incorporate in my piano what I had heard that night. A lot of the improvised music I like is endangered. It's gotten to the point where if you don't take care of it it'll go away, it'll disappear. At the same time, everything in jazz has gotten compartmentalized. You have to play a certain way to get anywhere. That freedom of the sixties and seventies is gone. Look at Jimmy Rowles. He's a timeless player, but there's no place for him. He should be playing in New York, where he's scarcely ever been, and he should be recorded every day. This is all part of the feeling I have that our values are out of whack in this country, that something is seriously wrong. So, at forty-five, I have to look elsewhere.

"I met Meena in 1981, in Edmonton. She owned part of a jazz club there, and she also managed it. She's a painter and a cordon-bleu chef. Her mother and brother live in Edmonton, and the rest of her family is in India. Her great-grandfather was one of the last rajas. She grew up in an extended family where the cousins are all like sisters and brothers. I like that family feeling. We're planning to rent a house in the Nilgiri Hills, the spice hills, south of Bangalore. There are four or five little towns up there, and we're leaning toward Kotagiri, which was a British hill station, seven thousand feet up. We're going to live on the money from the house, and I'm going to teach in a college nearby. I'll be out from under the constant financial pressure I've had here. I'm making just about the same money I was making ten years ago, and there was a nine-week period last summer when I didn't have any work at all. I've never been able to put together a retirement plan, and I don't have any medical insurance. Meena's family is excited that she is married to an American jazz musician. Artists are next to God in India. I've heard that the alto player Charlie Mariano is in Bombay, and I know that Maynard Ferguson lived in India for a while. He told me there are a lot of Indian jazz musicians. I loved the peaceful feeling I had when I was there.

"I feel bad about Gene. We've been playing together off and on for seventeen years. I had more trouble telling him I was leaving than telling my own parents. I told him that I had given him the best years of my life, and that even if the duo was to get busier it would mean a lot of travelling and being away from my family, and I didn't want that. Meena and I are homebodies. I told him that he'd be a lot freer now, that he'd have a chancc to do all kinds of things he'd never done before. Gene's a worrier, and I told him he wouldn't have to worry about me anymore."

Michael Moore was born in Cincinnati, and came to the duo via the Cincinnati College-Conservatory of Music, the big band of Woody Herman, the Marian McPartland trio, and the Ruby Braff-George Barnes quartet. Gene Bertoncini, born in the Bronx in 1937, came to the duo via the architecture school of Notre Dame and the television bands of Merv Griffin and Skitch Henderson. Bertoncini and Moore first met in Salt Lake City twenty years ago, and played together soon after, in New York. Here is what Moore said about Bertoncini several years ago: "He never plays for himself, the way most guitarists do. He wants people to like his music, but without his having in any way to sell out. He's not fettered by what's hip. He hasn't listened widely in jazz. Sometimes when he solos, I don't hear *any* influences. It's all him. He has a great ear and perfect pitch and he can read anything. He does harmonic things I've never heard any other guitarist do. Improvisation used to be a means for him, but it has slowly become an end. What he's after is beautiful melody. He's a melodic improviser. He's moved by all good melody—that strain is in everything he does." And here is what Bertoncini said about Moore at the same time: "There is nothing about him as a player that I don't admire. Years ago, when I worked in the Philharmonic Café after concerts, Michael used to sit in and play the arco parts. I was bowled over by the warmth of his sound, and I still prefer him to any classical bassist. He is also a great pizzicato accompanist, and a brilliant improviser. I don't know anyone on any instrument who takes you on a melodic trip the way Michael does. I love to watch people responding to his solos. I consider him one of the great living jazz musicians. We've always thought of the music as being bigger than either of us. I've seen a dark side of Michael on occasion, but he cares about my feelings and I care about his."

Bertoncini does not overpraise Moore. His pizzicato solos, delivered more and more frequently in his upper registers, consist of ecstatic melodic lines, each line flowing into the next, and each bearing little flags of the original melody, which orient us and sharpen the freshness of the surrounding improvisations. These melodic flights have an urgency that no other bassist has matched, with the possible exception of the Charles Mingus of the early sixties. Mingus's solos had a bravura exuberance, a here's-how quality, while Moore's are dedicated to the proposition that beautiful melody can be wrested from even mediocre songs. Mingus bullied you; Moore takes you by the hand. Moore's pizzicato tone has the even, deep *string* sound of such earlier bassists as Jimmy Blanton and Oscar Pettiford and Mingus, and it is an antidote to the fashionable overamplified tone of most contemporary bassists. And Moore is an immaculate timekeeper. He chooses the right notes in every chord, and he lands at their center or just forward of their center in such a way that the time never sags or races. Somewhere along the line, Moore grew courageous about his arco playing, and he began to take almost as many arco solos as pizzicato solos. His bowed-tone is rich but delicately edged—it doesn't have the insistent, mahogany sound of, say, Gary Karr's—and, unlike that of most other arco players, it never goes flat. He rarely improvises with his bow; instead, he plays straight melody or choice melodic variations. These last are paeans to the almost impossible art of instantly making up beautiful melody.

Neither does Moore overpraise Bertoncini. He is an original jazz guitarist. Most of the guitarists who have appeared during the past forty years have been offshoots of Charlie Parker, or offshoots of his offshoots—handing down dazzling eight- or sixteenth-note arabesques, showers of notes that give the listener no chance to pick and choose and breathe. They have also developed an interchangeable tone: electric, twangy, cheap—a neon sound. Bertoncini uses very little amplification, and comes as close as Jim Hall to a pure acoustic sound. His solos are constantly surprising, because they are free of licks. He is as much a celebrator of melody as Moore is. His solos, though less intense (guitar intensity is to bass intensity what a tenor is to a basso), are subtle investigations of the undersides of melody. (Moore works on top of his melodies.) His solos are full of short runs, placed unexpectedly; silences; dodging, behind-the-beat phrases; and easy connective passages. Bertoncini never belabors. He invites the listener in—just once—and if he hesitates goes on without him.

One of Moore and Bertoncini's last sets at Zinno took place a week before Moore left for India. The mournful news of his actual departure date had spread fast, and the little room at Zinno where they played—a wide hallway between the bar and the main dining room—was packed. Most professional musicians are hard, punctilious workers, and everything appeared to be business as usual. Moore, tall and trim, with his pleased, round burgher's face, was standing with his back to the left-hand wall of the room and holding his new portable "stick" bass, made specially for him by David Gage. Bertoncini, short, gray, handsome, with his guitarist's stoop and his sabrelike right thumbnail (he doesn't use a pick), was seated on a stool just in front of Moore. They opened with Denny Zeitlin's "Quiet Now," a blues with a bridge, and that was followed by Antonio Carlos Jobim's "Quiet Nights." Both numbers were warmups for a swinging "Sweet and Lovely," in which Bertoncini balanced runs with reining-in ritards. Alec Wilder's "Winter of My Discontent" was a bowed bass solo. It hummed and sang, moving elegantly through the thickly carpeted rooms where bowed basses live. Clare Fischer's "Pensativa" preceded a superb "My Funny Valentine" arco solo played partly against romantic Bertoncini chords. The duo ended the number with a chorus of counterpoint, the two instruments knocking heads, straining to get away from each other, embracing, arguing, harmonizing, creating a new, near-perfect music. A bossa nova had a lingering Bertoncini solo and a wild round of four-bar exchanges. The set ended appropriately, with a medium-tempo blues. Bertoncini soloed, and Moore issued a series of high melodies, each more radiant than the last.

Several weeks after Moore's departure, Bertoncini talked about his friend and colleague: "The nature of being a bass player is you have to have a lot of clients. You have to take a lot of work that isn't that great. Mike often had to play with musicians who were supposed to be good but who he didn't think *were* that good. He had a thing about pianists who played too many notes, who didn't play melodically or didn't keep good time. Sometimes he spoke of getting home after a gig and having a backache from working so hard to keep time. Years of schlepping a bass for not all that much money got to him. So did being treated just as any old bass player instead of as a major soloist, which he is. He would say to me that performing didn't mean that much, which was the opposite of the way he looked and acted on the stage. In fact, I never saw anyone who seemingly loved to play more than he did. He always denied it, but I think he revelled in people's attention. If he didn't get attention, it upset him. As a bass player, he got more acclaim than most. For him to say he was tired of it all doesn't make sense.

"The duo would have gone on forever. I think it was the best jazz duo, and we were on the verge. We were getting calls from festivals in Norway and Brazil and Canada. Three years ago, we did ten concerts, and the next year fifteen. This past year, we did more than twenty, and that doesn't count the Sundays at Zinno and the occasional night-club gigs and private parties. And there was always the possibility of working off and on with another musician—a horn player, say, like Chet Baker, whom we played with in a club in Annapolis.

"I started on my own as a guitarist, but I always had a duo in mind. I feel honored that Mike chose me as his partner. He seemed to respect me as a musician. I felt that my reputation as a musician was that much better for working with him. After a while, I guess I got to rely on him. There was no question we'd be safe, his playing was so dependable. The challenge for me is to go out there and grow. I just came back from a festival in Norway, and I used a Norwegian bass player, and it worked O.K. Anyway, I can't imagine things working out in India for this great musical force. I can't imagine him hiding his gifts in a culture where he can't make that much of a musical contribution. His gift is needed here. Mike started reading the Bible several years ago, and he changed totally. He used to get angry and be critical about almost everything, but he gradually became a model of patience. I'd be concerned about a certain job situation, and I'd run it past him, and he'd say, 'Sure! Let's do it!' I think he prayed about his decision, and I feel good about that. It was nice to be around the high values in his life and in his music. He never played a note he didn't mean. He never joked with the music.

"But there was always something lurking in Mike—a weariness of the music business, of I don't know what. His living way out there, near the Delaware Water Gap, didn't help. Neither did the fact that he *always* had his answering service on. You have to be accessible in the music business."

Odysseys are never simple, and Moore's is not over. Word has come to Bertoncini in a roundabout way that Moore and his wife have left India and are living in England, where she is working and he is writing a string quartet. The only letter Bertoncini has got from Moore was written in India, and in it Moore said that a restaurant they had eaten in had a lot of flies but that the carbonara sauce wasn't bad.

Miles _____

Miles Davis has led a bedevilled life. He was born in 1926 in Alton, Illinois, and raised in East St. Louis. He has an older sister, Dorothy, and a younger brother, Vernon. His father was a dentist who eventually retired to a two-hundred-acre farm he owned, in Millstadt, Illinois. His mother was beautiful and stylish and idle. He got on well with his father, but found his mother, whom he loved, possessive, peevish, and heavy-handed. He took up the trumpet at ten, and by the time he was in high school he had been given his second trumpet and had met his first idol, Clark Terry. He worked in a local band led by Eddie Randle, then, at eighteen, he suddenly accelerated. He had the first of two children by a woman whom he never married; he graduated from high school; he worked for two weeks in Billy Eckstine's legendary bebop band, with Charlie Parker, Dizzy Gillespie, and Art Blakey; he moved to New York and enrolled in Juilliard; and he began hanging out with Parker and Gillespie and Fats Navarro. A year later, his attractive aura already working, he was on one of the earliest and most famous bebop records ("Billie's Bounce," "Now's the Time"), with Parker, Gillespie, and Max Roach. And he appeared on Fifty-second Street with Parker and Coleman Hawkins. His style, though still hesitant, began to emerge.

In the late forties, inspired by Claude Thornhill's big band, he organized the nonet (among the players Lee Konitz, Gerry Mulligan, Kai Winding, John Lewis, Max Roach) that made the celebrated Capitol album "Birth of the Cool." The nonet's laid-back quality and calm, intricate, deep-red arrangements made it the most adventurous small band since the Ellington small bands and some of the Woody Herman Woodchopper sides of 1946. (The typical small bebop bands of the time were not ensemble groups, like the nonet. They used leaping, tongue-tying unison opening-and-closing collective passages, but the often long solos that came between carried the musical weight.) Davis also began taking drugs. He describes what happened in his new autobiography, *Miles* (Simon & Schuster): "I lost my sense of discipline, lost my sense of control over my life, and started to drift. It wasn't like I didn't know what was happening to me. I did, but I didn't care anymore. I had such confidence in myself that even when I was losing control I really felt I had everything under control. But your mind can play tricks on you. I guess when I started to hang like I did, it surprised a lot of people who thought I had it all together. It also surprised me." (The book, done with a poet and teacher named Quincy Troupe, is petulant, outspoken, defensive, honeyed, error-filled, and impressionistic—and loaded to the gunwales with four-letter words. Davis uses them more as hammer blows than for their literal meanings, and they soon become a dull barrage, which, for whatever reasons, gradually abates as the book goes along.)

Davis takes pains to point out that he was not alone in his addiction. Many of the best young musicians of the late forties—black and white—became heroin addicts, and he needlessly names them. Here, in the late fifties, is Billie Holiday, one of the most famous victims of this devastating plague: "She was looking real bad by this time, worn out, worn down, and haggard around the face and all. Thin. Mouth sagging at both corners. She was scratching a lot." (There are other eloquent patches in the book, but it is difficult to tell whether they are Davis's or Troupe's doing. Listen to this description of the church music Davis heard early in his life: "We'd be walking on these dark country roads at night and all of a sudden this music would seem to come out of nowhere, out of them spooky-looking trees that everybody said ghosts lived in. Anyway, we'd be on the side of the road—whoever I was with, one of my uncles or my cousin James—and I remember somebody would be playing a guitar the way B. B. King plays. And I remember a man and a woman singing and talking about getting *down!* Shit, that music was something, especially that woman singing. But I think that kind of stuff stayed with me, you know what I mean? That *kind* of sound in music, that blues, church, back-road funk kind of thing, that southern, midwestern, rural sound and rhythm.") Davis began stealing and even pimping to support his heroin habit. He was busted on the West Coast. He was busted again when he went home, ostensibly to give up drugs. He quit heroin in 1953, backslid, and quit for good in 1954.

Almost immediately, his professional life turned around. He led two classic recording sessions in 1954. The first consisted simply of two blues, the medium-tempo "Walkin'" and the faster "Blue 'n' Boogie." Each took up one side of a ten-inch LP, and both were played by Davis, Lucky Thompson, J. J. Johnson, Horace Silver, Percy Heath, and Kenny Clarke. Davis's mature style—annunciatory, clipped, vibratoless, singing—dominated both numbers and both recordings. The second recording had three originals and one standard tune, and on hand were Thelonious Monk, Milt Jackson, Heath, and Clarke. (Davis, along with Charles Mingus and Duke Ellington, has always chosen musicians who can both obey and enrich his sometimes abstruse musical designs.) Davis was in a paradoxical mood. Although he loved Monk's playing, he made him lay out behind his solos on three of the numbers. Both recordings were hailed as bellwethers; actually, they marked an enlightened reshaping of the straight-ahead, uncluttered swing of Red Norvo and Count Basie and the trumpeter Joe Thomas. Davis and his men set aside the eccentricities and excesses of bebop (in whose house most of them had been raised) while retaining its broadened harmonic base. A year later, Davis appeared at the second Newport Jazz Festival with a pickup group consisting of Gerry Mulligan, Zoot Sims, Monk, Heath, and Connie Kay—all musicians he had worked with. He played three numbers—open-horn versions of "Hackensack" and "Now's the Time," and a muted, inner-ear "'Round Midnight." His from-the-mountain-top, time-stopping open-horn solos made it clear that Davis, who had been struggling for much of the time since he came East, had arrived. Columbia Records agreed, and before the year was out had signed him to a contract he says was worth three hundred thousand dollars a year. (He stayed with Columbia until 1985, when he went to Warner Brothers Records.) Davis's comments in *Miles* on the Columbia signing are far from the it's-not-my-fault defensiveness of the artist who has had a windfall: "And yes, going with Columbia did mean more money, but what's wrong with getting paid for what you do and getting paid well? I never saw nothing in poverty and hard times and the blues. I never wanted that for myself. I saw what it really was when I was strung out on heroin, and I didn't want to see it again. As long as I could get what I needed from the white world on my own terms, without selling myself out to all of those people who would love to exploit me, then I was going to go for what I know is real."

Davis had entered his great period. He assembled the first of two working bands, and it included, at various times, John Coltrane, Cannonball Adderley, Red Garland, Bill Evans, Paul Chambers, and Philly Joe Jones. Davis, like Mingus, began experimenting with different kinds of improvisation, and he made the album "Kind of Blue," in which he gave his players modal sketches to work their variations on, and set them loose, one take per number. The results are cool, subtle, edgeless music. Davis was also busy in the Columbia studios making three concerto albums—"Miles Ahead," "Porgy and Bess," and "Sketches of Spain"—in which, accompanied by a big band playing Gil Evans' velvet arrangements, he was the only soloist. (Would that Louis Armstrong had had such cosseting when he was at his height, in 1933!) Davis's second famous small working band arrived in the sixties and had Wayne Shorter, Herbie Hancock, Ron Carter, and Tony Williams. Its repertory moved between mooning, muted ballads and furious up-tempo numbers, in which Davis, always a middle-register player, ventured into the upper regions and used unaccustomed avalanches of notes.

Davis's life since the early sixties has been hill-and-dale. He has been married to and divorced from the dancer Frances Taylor and the actress Cicely Tyson. He has been plagued by medical problems, among them hip operations, a stroke, two broken ankles, pneumonia, and diabetes. From 1975 to 1980, he dropped out. He gave up playing and retired to his house, on West Seventy-seventh Street. Here, brutally, is what he did: "I just took a lot of cocaine (about $500 a day at one point) and fucked all the women I could get into my house. I was also addicted to pills, like Percodan and Seconal, and I was drinking a lot, Heinekens and cognac. . . . I didn't go out too often and when I did it was mostly to after-hours places up in Harlem where I just kept on getting high and living from day to day. . . . The house was filthy and real dark and gloomy, like a dungeon." George Butler, of Columbia Records, got Davis back on the track, and he began coming out again in 1981. Since then, he says, he has given up drugs and drinking. He has also given up his house, and now divides his time between Malibu and an apartment on Central Park South.

Although Davis has tinkered endlessly with his music (various types of improvising, odd time signatures, synthesizers, an electric trumpet), his playing, which resides at the still center of all these experiments, has changed little. He has never been much of a technician, and he has been clever enough to keep his style within his abilities. When he came East in the forties, he ignored his limitations, and his solos were sometimes a string of clams. He ignored them again when he had the Shorter-Williams band and began shooting wildly into the upper register, with nerve-racking results. Many people have influenced Davis—Louis Armstrong, Clark Terry, Shorty Baker, Fats Navarro, Ahmad Jamal, Bobby Hackett, Gil Evans, Lester Young, Charlie Parker, and Dizzy Gillespie. Perhaps the heaviest hand on his playing was that of an early teacher who told him never to play with a vibrato, that he'd have plenty of time for a vibrato when he grew old and could no longer control his lip. His no-vibrato attack sometimes gives his playing an abrupt, telegraphic air, but he softens this by using a lot of rests and long notes. He also softens his attack with his tone. It is full, but it is not a brass tone, a trumpet tone. It is human sound compressed into trumpet sound. His solos in the Gil Evans "Sketches of Spain" album have a unique pleading, sorrowing quality. There have been many other players who have got a human sound—Johnny Hodges, Ben Webster, Red Allen, Pee Wee Russell—but their tonal qualities have never superseded the basic sound of their instruments. Davis has succeeded in making almost visible the emotions—longing, sadness, pity—that move just beneath his complex surface. But his eerie, buttonholing sound is not as common on his recent, synthesizer-controlled recordings, where electronics and odd time signatures dominate the surroundings, and cause him to sound removed and disjointed. The great Davis still resides in his recordings of thirty years ago.

Davis has become a business. On one of his Warner Brothers Records release, "Amandla," he lists his production coördinators, his tour manager, his business manager, and his personal manager. The cover of the album is a semi-abstract self-portrait. (Like such earlier worthies as Pee Wee Russell and George Wettling, Davis has taken up painting.) Beneath Davis's head are the bell of a trumpet and a globe, with the African continent thereon. Davis's eyes, looking into the middle distance, are cold and furious, as if he were tallying the various imponderables that have kept him from becoming the genius he believes himself to be.

1990

Max
and Kit

The 92nd Street Y, famous for its "Lyrics and Lyricists" series, its poetry readings, and its Schubertiade, hasn't paid a great deal of attention to jazz, and, perhaps because of that and to balance Dick Hyman's conservative "Jazz in July" concerts, it inaugurated late in January a three-day festival of modern jazz, called "Jazz in January." It was subtitled "The Worlds of Max Roach," and was organized by the drummer himself.

Roach, now sixty-six, made his mark in the mid-forties with Dizzy Gillespie, Charlie Parker, and Bud Powell. Working under the suns of Kenny Clarke and Sid Catlett, he has gradually evolved a revolutionary style that is melodic and multi-rhythmic. He no longer simply accompanies other instruments but plays melodically alongside them. His drumming has become largely abstract; he improvises rhythms in the ensembles and in his solos which may have no discernible pulse and nothing to do with the underlying beat. Instead of swinging, the way Catlett did, he fills his listeners' heads with a succession of timbres that reach from the treble of his cymbals to the subterranean movements of his bass drum. It is possible to marvel at Roach's complexities without tapping your foot once.

Roach is a polymath. In 1960, he and Charles Mingus put together a brilliant rump festival in Newport to protest George Wein's behemoth (which, ironically, was shut down during the weekend by rioting kids). Two years later, he made a tempestuous trio album with Mingus and Duke Ellington. (Ellington sailed serenely over the surrounding temperaments.) He has written, and performed in, several large pieces dedicated to anti-racist causes. He started a percussion group, called M'Boom, and his Double Quartet, which consists of trumpet, tenor saxophone, bass, drums, and a string quartet. He has recently recorded with such avant-gardists as Anthony Braxton, Archie Shepp, and Cecil Taylor. He is a professor of music at the University of Massachusetts, and he was awarded a MacArthur Foundation fellowship.

Roach made only cameo appearances at the first two "Jazz in January" concerts. Then, on the third night, he and the video artist Kit Fitzgerald filled Kaufmann Hall for an hour and a half with drums and pictures. Roach's drums were set up center stage on a dais, and behind the dais was a sizable movie screen. As Roach played, a mobile television cameraman shot him from every angle. The images appeared on a small monitor in front of Kit Fitzgerald, who sat behind a battery of television equipment at the foot of the stage. Using a computerized keyboard—a kind of video synthesizer—she improvised on what she saw on her monitor, and her improvisations were relayed to a projector behind the screen. Roach improvised on what was in his head, and Fitzgerald improvised on Roach. The images Fitzgerald created were never still, and were avant-garde "painting." You saw Rorschach blots; kaleidoscopic images; recollections, here and there, of the work of Morris Louis, Marsden Hartley, and Richard Diebenkorn; Roach's head and hands, frozen and in motion; drumsticks turning into descending stairs; drumsticks fracturing into hundreds of highly colored cubes; cymbals shining like moons, then melting into Daliesque watches; Roach enormous and Roach in the distance, ghostly and indistinct. Surprisingly, his sounds and Fitzgerald's pictures did not war, as the aural and the visual so often do. You heard what you saw, and saw what you heard. Roach's performance was broken into ten sections, and he started many with a deceptively simple rhythm on his high hat and bass drum. This might be made up of a high-hat whole note and two bass-drum quarter notes, and it would become an ostinato over which he would improvise his abstractions—a formidably difficult patting-your-head-and-rubbing-your-stomach exercise. As each section built, Roach used all his melodic devices: he rattled his sticks ferociously on his snare and tomtom rims; he got round booms with his mallets on his snare (its snares had been released) and on his tomtoms, and ocean swells on his cymbals; he used only wire brushes on a snare drum set up at stage right, and sticks on a high hat at stage left.

The memory of the first two "Jazz in January" concerts was nearly obliterated by the Roach-Fitzgerald duet. On the first night, the Uptown String Quartet—half of the Double Quartet—composed of Diane Monroe (violin, and a teacher at Swarthmore), Lesa Terry (violin, and a member of the Broadway "Black and Blue" band), Eileen Folson (cello, and a former member of the New York Philharmonic), and Maxine Roach (viola, Max's daughter, and a graduate of Oberlin), played eleven numbers, including ragtime pieces, spirituals, a couple of blues, a semi-tonal piece, and a piece in which the group first strummed their instruments and then plucked them. Everyone soloed, and the quartet, despite some pitch lapses, had a nice ecumenical lilt.

The second night, the trumpeter Lester Bowie brought on his Brass Fantasy, which consists of four trumpets, a horn, two trombones, a tuba, drums, and percussion. Bowie, who is just shy of fifty, has been an avant-garde terror for twenty-five years. He was a founder of the Association for the Advancement of Creative Musicians and a founder of the Art Ensemble of Chicago. Ten years ago, he gave a pair of concerts at Symphony Space in which he led a band called the Sho' Nuff Orchestra that included sixty avant-garde stars. He is also a comedian. He wears a doctor's white coat onstage, and he likes to use his horn for blats, growls, squeals, and half-valve effects—sounds first floated by the Ellington cornettist Rex Stewart in the early forties. The Brass Fantasy did a kind of gospel blues, three songs associated with Billie Holiday ("God Bless the Child," "Strange Fruit," and "Good Morning Heartache"), a Whitney Houston ("Saving All My Love for You"), and a number called "The Emperor," in which the trombonist Steve Turre soloed on small and large conch shells, separately and then together, and achieved an alto, calling-over-the-flats sound. The band moved between glutinous dance-band harmonies and dissonant ensembles. Bowie's solos, barring melodic patches, were full of barnyard sounds. His doctor's coat used to be made of cotton, but he wore satin at the Y.

The afternoon before "Jazz in January," WNYC presented the first of this season's "New Sounds" concerts at Merkin Hall, and it served as a preamble to the Y festival. The jazz minimalist, reedman, and composer Jon Gibson had Martin Goldray on piano, Blue Gene Tyranny on synthesizer, and Bill Ruyle on percussion. Gibson has worked with Philip Glass, and his four pieces were filled with the Raymond Loewy effects of the minimalists—one-two-three melodies, ostinatos, repetition, and a dull glossiness. The Les Misérables Brass Band followed. Made up of two trumpets, horn, trombone, alto saxophone, baritone saxophone, tuba, drums, and percussion, it is an excited, hybrid group: it played a merengue, an East European march, David Byrne's "In the Future," a Pakistani meditation, and Jimi Hendrix's "Manic Depression." The phenomenal tubist Marcus Rojas danced while he played; the trumpeter Frank London, who is the leader, made Lester Bowie sounds; and the trombonist David Harris blew so hard he quivered. The Les Misérables band made Bowie's Brass Fantasy and the much touted Dirty Dozen, from New Orleans, seem peaked.

The concert was closed by the World Saxophone Quartet, which, when it started out, in the mid-seventies, liked to parody everyone. But it has grown sedate, and it spends much of its time celebrating its own sumptuous sound. (David Murray is still on tenor saxophone, Oliver Lake on alto, and Hamiet Bluiett on baritone, but the alto saxophonist Julius Hemphill has been replaced by Arthur Blythe.) The group, which seemed off center, played six unidentified numbers. Murray did a lullaby and Lake a long a-cappella passage. There were bits of free ensemble, and some chocolate harmonies on a fast riff tune. In the fifth, and best, number Bluiett played Duke Ellington's "Sophisticated

Lady," holding himself to the sort of reverential melodic embellishments and transcendent basso-profundo tones that Harry Carney used when Ellington featured him on the song. Carney loved to boost other baritone saxophonists, and Bluiett's performance would have pleased him.

Keepers of the Flame

In 1938, Jelly Roll Morton, upset by a Robert Ripley "Believe It or Not" radio program in which W. C. Handy was credited with having invented jazz, sent a long letter to the Baltimore *Afro-American* and to *down beat* saying, "It is evidently known, beyond contradiction, that New Orleans is the cradle of *jazz*, and I, myself, happened to be the creator in the year 1902." Morton was a famous braggart, and the letter was hooted down; everybody knew—or thought he knew—that Morton had not done anything important in jazz until the mid-twenties, when he recorded with his Red Hot Peppers. But hyperbole often dances on fact. Twenty years after Morton wrote his letter, the stride pianist and composer James P. Johnson told an interviewer named Tom Davin that he had heard Morton at Barron Wilkins' club in New York in 1911. Morton "had just arrived from the West and he was red hot," Johnson said. "The place was on fire." So Morton may well have been playing some sort of jazz around 1902, and Johnson himself, with his Harlem confrères the pianists Luckey Roberts and Willie the Lion Smith, was probably playing a music akin to jazz not long after Morton came through town. All of which is to say that jazz pianists, extracting the choicest juice from ragtime, did help to invent jazz; and when the music has been struck by fads or fickleness they have preserved its lyrical essence.

It is surprising that pianists should be the keepers of the

flame, for the piano—inflexible and percussive and vibrato-less—does not transmit emotion easily. But jazz pianists, re-peatedly beating back the army of broken, out-of-tune pianos which has besieged them since the beginning of the century, have learned how to circumvent the instrument's coldness. By raising and lowering their volume in strategic places, they startle the listener and italicize their phrases. They get vi-bratolike effects by holding certain notes, and by using the little tremolos that Earl Hines invented. And they place notes, and even chords, in unexpected spots—a rhythmic juggling that creates a fine tension. These devices are all in evidence in an excellent new recording by Tommy Flanagan ("Jazz Poet"; Timeless), and on three equally valuable, previously unreleased albums by Erroll Garner ("Easy to Love," "Dancing on the Ceiling," and "Too Marvellous For Words"; EmArcy).

Flanagan is still blooming at sixty. He arrived in New York in 1956 from Detroit. He had listened to Art Tatum and Teddy Wilson and Hank Jones and Bud Powell, and also to Dizzy Gillespie and Charlie Parker. For almost ten years, he was a journeyman, who worked with everyone from Miles Davis and Sonny Rollins to Coleman Hawkins and Harry Edison. But by the mid-sixties he had slipped into the semi-oblivion of the accompanist, turning up briefly with Tony Bennett and lasting more than a dozen years with Ella Fitzgerald. In 1978, exhausted by touring, he decided to go out on his own. He soon pulled even with such solo pianists as Dave McKenna, Hank Jones, and Jimmy Rowles. Then, about five years ago, his work took on a new subtlety. He began to play with a delicacy and steadiness that infused everything—his ballads, his blues, and his up-tempo numbers. He was continually refreshing, continually surprising. (Flanagan has never allowed himself to lean on pat phrases when his inspiration flags.)

Flanagan's recordings of the last decade—they include "Giant Steps" (1982), "Thelonica" (1982), and "Nights at the Van-guard" (1986)—are of the same high order. (He is accompanied on all three by George Mraz on bass and by either Al Foster or Art Taylor on drums.) But "Jazz Poet" (with Mraz and the drummer Kenny Washington), made just a year ago, reveals his present brilliance—or, at least, four of the eight tracks do. These are J. J. Johnson's "Lament," taken at a slow tempo and notable in the second chorus for an airy, beautifully spaced melodic line; a fast version of Juan Tizol's indestructible "Caravan," in which Flanagan places new melodies across the original in a legato half-time, and, moving into tempo, a series of runs that spin away into the upper register; Matt Dennis's "That Tired Routine Called Love," complete with a quiet, restless, hornlike passage and a no-hands double-time run; and a "Glad to Be Unhappy," filled with melancholy, shadowy minor chords. As for the remaining tracks on the album, Flanagan's own "Mean Streets" is a runaway display piece for the drummer, but "Willow Weep for Me," "St. Louis Blues," and Billy Strayhorn's "Raincheck" are only inches below the best numbers. Because jazz pianists ordinarily don't carry their instruments with them, they are at the mercy of strange pianos—pianos whose action is too loose or too stiff, pianos whose high registers are shrill, or low registers are murky, pianos that simply seem hostile. As a result, there are very few successful solo recordings by jazz pianists. This one is an exception.

Erroll Garner died in January of 1977, at the age of fifty-three. From the mid-forties, when he first arrived in New York from Pittsburgh, until 1975, when he gave his last public performance, in Chicago, he travelled around the world, obsessed by his music, delighted, inexhaustible, casting his shadow over almost every pianist who heard him, and making his audiences marvel at his ebullience and his melodic invention. Garner, who never learned to read music, could reportedly reproduce the styles of all the great pianists who preceded him, but his own style was inimitable, no matter how often it was copied. He liked to open a number with an ad-lib cadenza, lasting eight or ten bars and giving no indication of what was to come. Then he would drop his volume and go into tempo, his right hand embellishing the melody with behind-the-beat notes broken by offbeat chords, and his left hand keeping strict time with on-the-beat guitarlike chords. He would take the volume up slightly at the bridge and shift into double-time octave chords, lower his volume again, and close the chorus with staccato notes that gave the impression they were wildly trying to break off from the melody they were a part of. The rest of the number would be a constant round of raised and lowered volumes, doubled or halved rhythms, staccato and legato passages, and boiling chordal interludes that wiped his melodic slate clean and prepared the listener for his next surprise. Garner's fast numbers skimmed the earth, and his slow ballads were stately, ceremonious dances.

Garner made countless recordings. Whenever the spirit moved him, he'd rent a studio, summon his bassist and drummer, set down a dozen or more numbers—usually one take apiece. For years, there have been rumors of a trove of unreleased Garner material, and at long last Martha Glaser, his manager and producer, has begun to issue what she believes is the best of it. The first two albums include twenty numbers and are drawn from five different sessions—three in 1961, one in 1964, and one in 1965. The third includes fourteen numbers, set down during one session in 1954. Almost all are prime Garner. (Of course, he had off days. There are missed notes, chords that don't quite land where they should, and endings that don't return to earth.) On the first album, "Easy to Love," he plays a slow, dancing "September Song"; a hustling "My Blue Heaven," its second bridge constructed of an exuberant boppish trumpet line; a "Somebody Loves Me" that includes an even more rakish single-note passage; a medium "As Time Goes By," with a laughing Debussy introduction; and a very fast "Lover Come Back to Me," with a bridge in which his hands invent totally different melodic and rhythmic lines in exhilarating counterpoint.

The second album, "Dancing on the Ceiling," is memorable for a seesawing staccato line in "It Had to Be You"; for a rocking, medium-tempo "After You've Gone," in which Garner takes the breaks—miniature wonders in themselves—and moseys along behind the beat; a strange, slow, rhapsodic gospel blues,

"Like Home," played largely with the loud pedal and with heavy, damask chords; and a stomping, new "Ain't Misbehavin'." The third album has at least six marvels. There are an easy "Margie," an unexpectedly fast "Way Down Yonder in New Orleans," and a medium-tempo "Louise," full of delayed notes, and double-time chords. There are a fast, ripping "My Gal Sal," a sly "Too Marvellous For Words," and a virtuosic reshaping of Zez Confrey's brittle 1921 "Kitten on the Keys." Audible on all three albums are the hums, grunts, "myeh"s, and "oh-oh"s that Garner uttered as he played, the sounds of a man leaning deliriously into his work.

Imagining Music ———————————————

For a long time, jazz fans were idolaters, who enshrined their Louis Armstrongs and Billie Holidays and Charlie Parkers. This defensive zealotry was particularly apparent when the music was still regarded as mean and primitive. Early jazz writers were even more protective. They made such troubled heroes as King Oliver (down and out in Savannah in 1938, aged sixty), Bix Beiderbecke (dead of drink in 1931, aged twenty-eight), and Bunk Johnson (toothless and hornless in New Iberia, Louisiana, aged forty-five) into tragic figures and wrote about them with an "O lost, and by the wind grieved, ghost" sentimentality. This sentimentality leaked into the first full-length jazz movies in the fifties, and it's still in evidence, despite such heavy lumber as *'Round Midnight* and *Bird*. (The best feature film about jazz is the little-known, low-budget *The Gig*, written and directed in the mid-eighties by the playwright Frank Gilroy. It deals with a group of white amateur musicians—and a black professional ringer—who play a summer gig in the Catskills, and it explains for the first time the blue-collar ethos of the average jazz musician.) The same myth-making has also affected most of the fiction written about jazz since 1938, when Dorothy Baker published *Young Man with a Horn*, a pioneering, worshipful novel based on Beiderbecke.

But how *do* you write fiction (or poetry, for that matter) about painters and dancers and writers and musicians? The jazz fan's idol-making is common to all the arts. Perhaps there are three ways to write about Picasso or Balanchine or Horowitz: ennoble him; reduce him to life-size; try to show him as the obsessed, gifted drudge most artists are. Laboriously spinning their works out of themselves, artists are desperate more often than exultant. They take no vacations: one invention leads to another, and the iron must never be allowed to cool. All camouflage themselves. Writers pretend to be inarticulate, painters speak in symbols or hyperbole, musicians gossip and tell jokes, dancers talk about their bodies and about food. There is an added difficulty in writing fiction about jazz: The music is ephemeral. A novelist can describe the "Appassionata" and tell you exactly how his pianist hero plays it, but a jazz novelist must describe a music that is gone the instant it is played. Nowhere else does invention turn into memory so quickly. (Playwrights have an edge in writing about jazz: plays are a performer's art, like jazz. Witness Jack Gelber's *The Connection* and August Wilson's *Ma Rainey's Black Bottom*; both even have onstage bands.)

Marcela Breton clearly kept these difficulties in mind when she put together the anthology of jazz short stories she calls *Hot and Cool* (Plume). There are nineteen stories, arranged in rough chronological order. The earliest, by Rudolph Fisher, a novelist of the Harlem Renaissance, was published in 1930, and the most recent, by Martin Gardner, in 1987. Five of the stories deal directly with jazz. Six are largely taken up by racial matters, and six are about drugs and drinking. One is about a jazz fan, and one is a love story. The quality of the stories varies a good deal. "Mending Wall," by Willard Marsh, is set in Mexico and reads like an inept translation from the Spanish. Fisher's story, "Common Meter," is an engaging antique that is full of dated black slang and anthropomorphic musical descriptions: "Clarinets wailed, saxophones moaned, trumpets wept wretchedly, trombones laughed bitterly, even the great bass horn sobbed dismally from the depths." In Ann Petry's "Solo on the Drums," a jilted drummer makes his "big bass drum growl," and in "The Screamers" LeRoi Jones, using an arty epigrammatic prose, converts the music into Message: "The repeated rhythmic figure, a screamed riff, pushed in its insistence past music. It was hatred and frustration, secrecy and despair. It spurted out of the diphthong culture, and reinforced the black cults of emotion. There was no compromise, no dreary sophistication, only the elegance of something that is too ugly to be described."

These various excesses are nicely balanced by Terry Southern and Richard Yates and Langston Hughes. Southern writes with great subtlety about a white jazz lover who unwittingly becomes, in a black musician's disparaging words, a "professional nigger lover." Yates tells us of a black pianist who enrages two white admirers by Uncle Tomming with an important nightclub owner. Hughes, in his best jess-lissen style, deals with a rich white matron, Mrs. Ellsworth, who underwrites the classical training of a black woman pianist, Oceola Jones; in the end, Oceola marries and goes back to playing blues. ("Is this what I spent thousands of dollars to teach you?" Mrs. Ellsworth asks as Oceola makes "the bass notes throb like tom-toms deep in the earth.")

There are several funny stories in the book. In Peter De Vries' "Jam Today," which first appeared in *The New Yorker*, the narrator goes to a forties "platter party," at which each guest is asked to play his favorite 78-r.p.m. record. The party turns out to be made up of moldy figs who believe that no good jazz has been played since 1930, but the narrator brings a Benny Goodman big-band record. Embarrassed, he breaks the record and stuffs it into his overcoat pocket, then discovers when he leaves that he has put it in his host's pocket. Martin Gardner's "The Devil and the Trombone" deals with a professor returning home from a wearying evening meeting who stops in at a church to rest his mind and listen to the organ music he hears inside. The organist, dressed in a white robe, has wings folded at his sides, and he is playing unearthly music. Out of the blackness behind him comes a tall, hairy figure with swarthy skin and a forked-tail, who begins playing raucous tailgate trombone. The two jam together, and their music is so empyrean that the professor finds he suddenly understands the meaning of life—when the music stops, and the angelic figure tells him to go back to his pew and wake himself up. Donald Barthelme's ingenious "The King of Jazz," which also appeared in *The New Yorker*, is about the perfervid way that jazz has progressed in its ninety years, today's heroes trampling on yesterday's myths. It also attempts to solve the problem of how to describe the music—a problem that many writers have attacked with a metaphor in each hand. He gives us thirteen hilarious examples of how to approximate the sounds of jazz. Here are four: "That sounds like polar bears crossing Arctic ice pans? That sounds like a herd of musk ox in full flight? That sounds like male walruses diving to the bottom of the sea? That sounds like fumaroles smoking on the slopes of Mt. Katmai?"

Toni Cade Bambara's "Medley" is a dialect story told by a black beautician who walks out on the bass player she lives with. She describes him:

Larry Landers looked more like a bass player than ole Mingus himself. Got these long arms that drape down over the bass like they were grown special for that purpose. Fine, strong hands with long fingers and muscular knuckles, the dimples deep black at the joints. His calluses so other-colored and hard, looked like Larry had swiped his grandmother's tarnished thimbles to play with. He'd move in on that bass like he was going to hump it or something, slide up behind it as he lifted it from the rug, all slinky. He'd become one with the wood. Head dipped down sideways bobbing out the rhythm, feet tapping, legs jiggling, he'd look good. Thing about it, though, ole Larry couldn't play for shit.

Al Young's "Chicken Hawk's Dream" is short and nearly perfect. It begins: "Chicken Hawk stayed high pretty much all the time and he was nineteen years old limping down academic corridors trying to make it to twelfth grade." Chicken Hawk is a drug addict who lives in Detroit and dreams that he is walking around New York playing fantastic alto saxophone. He is so sure that the dream is true that he borrows a horn to practice on. But he can only make it squeak. He blames the horn, and drifts away with his friend Wine. Later, the narrator runs into Chicken Hawk on the street, and Chicken Hawk tells him that he is about to leave for New York to put together a band and make some records, as soon as he gets his horn out of hock.

Three stories in *Hot and Cool* move close to the heart of jazz. The longest, at sixty-three pages, is "The Pursuer," by the Argentine novelist Julio Cortázar. It was published in the late sixties, and is a thinly disguised account of the last months in the life of Charlie Parker, here called Johnny Carter. Cortázar moves inside Carter's complex, duplicitous, crazy head. Carter tells his Boswell, a critic named Bruno, about how he has been remembering his past: "It wasn't thinking, it seems to me I told you a lot of times, I never think; I'm like standing on a corner watching what I think go by, but I'm not thinking what I see. You dig?" Bruno decides not to alter the second edition of his biography of Carter, despite Carter's having told him that the book was fine except that he had been left out of it. Bruno explains with infuriating cool, "I decided not to touch the second edition, to go on putting Johnny forth as he was at bottom: a poor sonofabitch with barely mediocre intelligence, endowed like so many musicians, so many chess players and poets, with the gift of creating incredible things without the slightest consciousness (at most, the pride of a boxer who knows how strong he is) of the dimensions of his work."

Far more famous is James Baldwin's "Sonny's Blues," published in the late fifties. Baldwin was an exceptional essayist, but his fiction was often heated and clumsy. "Sonny's Blues" is about a drug addict who finds salvation—apparent salvation—by becoming a jazz pianist. The narrator, who is Sonny's straight older brother, goes to a club to hear him and, after the first set, sends a drink up to the bandstand for Sonny. (There are a number of gaffes in the stories, and this is one. Musicians rarely stay on the bandstand between sets.) Baldwin ends the story with a disastrous sentence: "For me, then, as they began to play again, [the drink] glowed and shook above my brother's head like the very cup of trembling."

In its handmade, assiduous way, Eudora Welty's "Powerhouse" may be the best fiction ever written about jazz. It first appeared in *The Atlantic*, in 1941, when she was a new writer, and it seems to be based on her having heard Fats Waller on the road in the South. (The central figure, Powerhouse, *is* Waller, and not "a pianist in the style of Albert Ammons and Meade Lux Lewis," as Marcela Breton claims in her introduction.) The story is an extraordinary mixture of surrealism and truth. It has a jittering comic surface, like Waller himself, that hides, as Waller's did, the heaviness and sadness most blacks carried around in this country fifty years ago—particularly if they were musicians from New York doing a string of one-night stands in the Deep South. The musicians play, have a beer at a nearby black café between sets, and play again. Here is some of Welty's exotic description of Waller: "You can't tell what he is. 'Nigger man'?—he looks more Asiatic, monkey, Jewish, Babylonian, Peruvian, fanatic, devil. He has pale gray eyes, heavy lids, maybe horny, like a lizard." Powerhouse tells his musicians that he has got a telegram from one Uranus Knockwood, saying that his wife is dead. He had talked to his wife on the telephone the night before, and she said she might jump out of the window. But no one knows who Uranus Knockwood is (a Welty conundrum, in which the despotic Greek god Uranus is guarded by Lady Luck), and the musicians begin to understand that perhaps Powerhouse is fantasizing and that his fantasy rests on the hope that expecting the worst might bring the opposite. Eudora Welty makes the reader see *and* hear Powerhouse. He is outsize in the story, but he is utterly human—a huge man, like Waller.

Virtuosos do not fit easily into jazz. The music revolves around improvisation, and jazz improvisers need only enough technique to play what they hear in their heads. (The drummer Sidney Catlett never considered himself a virtuoso, but he got off certain dazzling snare and cymbal patterns that not even the virtuosic Buddy Rich could match. Catlett's technique was an extension of his imagination; impossible figures popped into his head and instantaneously became real.) Too much technique saps improvisation: it causes floridity and grandstanding, and it tricks audiences into believing that bombast is music. Jazz has harbored two undeniable virtuosos (Rich may have been a third), but no one has ever known quite what to do with them. They are Sarah Vaughan, who died last spring at the age of sixty-six, and Art Tatum (1909–56), whose final recordings have been issued—with an hour of previously unreleased material—on six compact disks called "Art Tatum: The Complete Pablo Group Masterpieces."

Sarah Vaughan was born in Newark and joined Earl Hines' big band as a singer and second pianist when she was nineteen. She never had any formal training—she was a bebop baby. Charlie Parker and Dizzy Gillespie were in Hines' band, and so was the singer Billy Eckstine. Vaughan made her first recordings with Eckstine when he formed his own big band in 1944, and a year later she made a small-band record with Parker and Gillespie. By the end of the fifties, she had become a famous singer who moved easily between jazz and popular song. By the end of the sixties, she was a singer of operatic dimensions. She grew to diva proportions, and so did her voice. She had four octaves, each clear and spacious. She sang falsetto, and she could sound like a baritone. She could drop from soprano to baritone in the space of one word. Her low tones were cavernous and her high notes were silver peaks. She had several different vibratos, and when it pleased her she could sing without any vibrato at all. (Think of the Kate Smith singers of the thirties: their vibratos led them.)

In 1980, the composer, conductor, and critic Gunther Schuller introduced Vaughan at a recital she gave at the Smithsonian, and he said that she was "the greatest vocal artist of our century," a hosanna that he immediately complicated by adding that she was "the most *creative* vocal artist of our time." This was true. She was a wonderful embellisher and improviser, who never sang a song the same way twice. She remade her materials—generally, the songs of Rodgers and Hart, the Gershwins, Kern, Porter, and Arlen—in her own image. The cost to the songs was sometimes high. She altered melodic lines and harmonies, mislaid lyrics, and used so much melisma that the words became unintelligible. At her most unfettered, she became a horn singer. Yet her melodic lines were of such complexity and daring that no horn player could have played them. Ultimately, she became a kind of abstract singer, whose materials were inadequate for what she did but were all she had. She could, of course, also sing a song relatively straight. But the richness of her voice was always there, and, no matter how few melodic and harmonic alterations she made, this richness tended to overshadow the song, to lean over it, like a voluptuous woman reading a book.

Vaughan and Art Tatum revelled in their techniques. Vaughan liked to show off her intervals, her perfect pitch, her vibratos, and her range. Tatum liked to show off his touch (the envy of every pianist of the past fifty years), his startling speed, his two-handed runs, and his left hand, which could match his right. As Vaughan and Tatum grew older, they inevitably leaned more and more on their technical tricks. Vaughan shuttled between her registers, held notes so long they took on a life of their own, and pretended she was Joan Sutherland or Paul Robeson. Tatum released harmonic clouds, making his chords sound as if they had fifteen or twenty notes, and connected them with long runs—coils of sound that trapped the listener and freed Tatum of the burden of fresh improvisations. He gave the impression at such times that he was speeding luxuriously through the song; in reality, he was pedalling easily in place. Both Vaughan and

Tatum were worshipped by their audiences and by their fellow-musicians—for their bravura effects and for their musicianship—and they wore their mantles with a pleased arrogance.

Tatum's career didn't last much more than twenty years. (Vaughan's lasted forty-five years, an impressive length of time for any singer, and more impressive still when one realizes that her voice was even more resilient and powerful at the end of her career than at the beginning.) Tatum was recorded only fitfully until the early fifties, when the jazz impresario Norman Granz had him set down about two hundred numbers, more than a hundred of them solo efforts and the rest with various instrumentalists. (Would that Granz had filmed him at the same time; only three or four minutes of Tatum on film exist.) Granz got to Tatum when he was already showing signs of prolixity, but there are sufficient flashes of his old brilliance. This is particularly true of the group numbers, even though Tatum had spent most of his career as a solo pianist and found it difficult to squeeze himself into ensemble situations. He towered over musicians he was supposed to accompany, or else soloed so magnificently that he dwarfed everyone else.

Granz recorded Tatum with seven groups between 1954 and 1956. There were fourteen numbers with Benny Carter (on alto saxophone) and Louis Bellson; eight with Roy Eldridge, the bassist John Simmons, and the drummer Alvin Stoller; twenty-five with Lionel Hampton and Buddy Rich, augmented here and there by the trumpeter Harry Edison, the bassist Red Callender, and the guitarist Barney Kessel; ten with Callender and Jo Jones; eight with Buddy DeFranco, Callender, and the drummer Bill Douglass; and seven with the tenor saxophonist Ben Webster, Callender, and Douglass. Carter and Tatum got along well: Carter coasts easily over Tatum's polite waves, and Bellson is steady and swinging. Their best side is a medium-tempo "Blues in B Flat." In it, Tatum's four impassioned choruses amount to a short history of blues piano, and Carter's four come as close to being impassioned as he ever gets.

The Eldridge session doesn't quite work. The trumpeter, using a mute most of the time, buzzes along somewhere near Tatum, and his open horn is not as galvanic as it often was at this period. Tatum becomes irrepressible behind Eldridge's second chorus in "I Surrender Dear," when he looses an avalanche of notes that suggest a bad boy rolling down a hill in a barrel to get attention. Tatum, Hampton, and Rich recorded fifteen of their numbers at one session. Rich is heavy, and Hampton's vibes sound like nails being poured into a tin can. But Tatum has a good time. He drops some stride piano in behind Hampton on "Hallelujah," he solos behind Hampton's solo in "Body and Soul," and he reproduces Nat Cole's bridge from his trio recording of "What Is This Thing Called Love?" Harry Edison helps things along in the eight numbers he is in, but he is almost thrown in "Verve Blues" when Tatum plays some less than tonal tremolos behind him. The trio numbers with Red Callender and Jo Jones are just that—Tatum accompanied by bass and drums. Jones takes a couple of airy brush solos, and Tatum swings surprisingly hard in "Isn't It Romantic?" and "I Guess I'll Have to Change My Plans."

The Tatum-DeFranco-Douglass-Callender numbers are a lark. DeFranco, the most fluent of all jazz clarinettists, suits Tatum completely. They play tag, echo each other, parody each other, attempt to escape from each other, and turn each other's figures inside out. DeFranco once said of the session, "I was sick that day, but it wasn't an occasion I would have missed. It was a game between us of 'Can you top this?' He'd play some astonishing figure and laugh, or turn and make a face at me over one shoulder. Or he'd rest his right hand on his knee and play with just his left hand, making it sound like both hands. I think he could have outwitted Charlie Parker."

Tatum's date with Ben Webster was his last studio recording; he died two months after. It is an elegiac session. Webster, who idolized Tatum, plays with an enormous tone, and he doesn't growl, hit any clams, or coast. The two men rise up to meet each other, and in "Night and Day," "My Ideal," and "Where or When" they become one. Felicity Howlett, the Tatum wizard, has pointed out that Webster "considered 'Night and Day' to be his finest recorded performance." He is surely sitting on Tatum's right.

The Commodores _____

Mosaic Records, the jazz counterpart of the Library of America, decided several years ago to put out the huge Commodore catalogue (1938–54). Two volumes, each containing twenty-three LPs, have appeared, and the third and final volume, which will be somewhat smaller, is due soon.

Commodore was the first American all-jazz label. It was started by a shrewd, amiable, tireless jazz lover named Milt Gabler. Born in Harlem in 1911 of an American mother and an Austrian father, Gabler got into his lifework sidewise. He was taken into his father's radio shop after graduating from Stuyvesant High School; the shop was on Forty-second Street, opposite the Commodore Hotel. He had begun listening to jazz, and in due course he stocked jazz records. In the mid-thirties he started reissuing and selling out-of-print jazz records. The records were notable on two counts—they were the first jazz reissues, and they were the first recordings on which the personnel and the instrumentation were listed. Around the same time, Gabler began sitting in on recording sessions, and in 1937, dissatisfied with the way Victor, Columbia, and Decca were handling (or not handling) jazz musicians, he decided to make his own jazz records. The first session took place on January 17, 1938, the day after Benny Gooodman's Carnegie Hall concert. On hand were Bobby Hackett, Pee Wee Russell, George Brunies, and Eddie Condon, who were playing at Nick's, in the Village; Jess Stacy (who was with Goodman); Artie Shapiro (Joe Marsala); Bud Freeman (Tommy Dorsey); and George Wettling (Red Norvo).

Gabler produced his last Commodore session in 1950, and the last official Commodore record was made in 1954 by Leonard Feather and Danny Gabler, one of Milt's brothers. Gabler produced almost ninety Commodore dates, using over a hundred and fifty musicians and singers. Gilbert Millstein, in a Profile of Gabler published in the *The New Yorker*, quotes an anonymous musician. "There's a ray comes out of him," the musician said about Gabler. "You can't help doing someting the way he wants. Here is this guy can't read a note of music and he practically tells you what register you're going to play in just by the position of your head."

Gabler's tastes were not encyclopedic. He is still hale, and he says in an interview in the booklet for Volume I of the Mosaic reissue that the first jazz record to knock him out was "There'll Be Some Changes Made" and "I've Found a New Baby," by the Chicago Rhythm Kings. The record was made in 1928, when Gabler was seventeen, and three of the Rhythm Kings—Muggsy Spanier, Joe Sullivan, and Eddie Condon—would record again and again for him. (The music that teenagers like penetrates their bones.) The Rhythm Kings played a polyphonic small-band music that became known as Chicago jazz. It had improvised opening and closing ensembles and short solos often backed by organlike hums. A four-bar drum break followed by four more bars of ensemble often served as a coda. Sometimes the closing ensemble was delivered in a diminuendo-crescendo fashion, which gave the number a rampaging air. Chicago jazz, originally patterned after New Orleans jazz, was played by white musicians. After most of them moved to New York, in the early thirties, they revolved around the witty, hustling Condon. Their music could be heard from the late thirties to the late sixties at Nick's, at the various Eddie Condon clubs, and at both Jimmy Ryans.

Many of the sessions in the Commodore catalogue are given over to Chicago jazz. The rest are divided among the black swing musicians of the thirties and forties and fifties; such ancients as Jelly Roll Morton and Bunk Johnson; miscellaneous pickup groups; and solo pianists. (Gabler loved pianists, and he recorded—or reissued—solo sessions by Stacy, Joe Bushkin, Joe Sullivan, Willie the Lion Smith, Mel Powell, Teddy Wilson, and, again and again, the impenetrable George Zack.) Absent from the catalogue, though, is the whole bebop movement. There are no Charlie Parkers or Dizzy Gillespies, and Gabler is rueful about having missed them.

For all the Zacks, lacy Smiths, and plodding Chicago dates, there is brilliant music in the first two volumes of the Mosaic. (The second volume closes in 1945.) The best of the Chicago sides are the 1938 dates with Hackett, Jack Teagarden, and Max Kaminsky; the seventeen-minute 1940 "A Good Man Is Hard to Find" with Kaminsky, Spanier, Russell, and Stacy (originally spread out over four twelve-inch 78-r.p.m. sides); and the 1943 "That's a Plenty" session with Wild Bill Davison, Russell, Brunies, and Wettling. "That's a Plenty" and "Panama," made at the same session, are probably the greatest Chicago-style recordings ever made. Davison was a champion lead cornettist and a driving, emotional soloist, and the two numbers stomp and fly. The momentum built up in the final ensemble of "That's a Penty" is almost frightening. Russell is on a great many of the Chicago dates, and although he came to hate the music ("There's no room left in that music," he once said. "It tells *you* how to solo") he frequently plays with daring and originality. He teeters constantly on the edge of tonality, and he sometimes gets off patterns that would startle Ornette Coleman and Cecil Taylor. (He was once paired with Thelonious Monk at a Newport Jazz Festival concert, but when Russell soloed, Monk, puzzled or surprised, laid out.) His slow blues, particularly in the chalumeau register, are grieving *and* jubilant. Hackett is *juste* on most of his sides. And listen to Ernie Caceres, the unsung Texas baritone saxophonist, in the first take of Miff Mole's "Beale Street Blues." He begins his solo, in a "talking" fashion, in his high register, and he mostly stays there, making that ponderous instrument sound feathery and casual. Stacy sparkles in his half-dozen band dates. He plays a low, rocking figure behind Caceres in Hackett's "New Orleans" which gives the uncanny impression that he is backing Caceres on a second baritone saxophone.

Gabler's sessions with the swing musicians are full of beauties, too. Lester Young played his rare, lissome clarinet in all five numbers of the famous Kansas City Six date (Buck Clayton, Young, Eddie Durham, Freddie Green, Walter Page, Jo Jones), and six weeks later Gabler put Chu Berry (Cab Calloway's band) with Roy Eldridge (his own band) and Sidney Catlett (Louis Armstrong's big band). This was the first small-band record Catlett had done since 1933, and he makes Berry and Eldridge hum. Early in 1939, Billie Holiday set down her almost unbearable requiem "Strange Fruit" and her slow blues "Fine and Mellow." A year later, Gabler assembled Eldridge, Benny Carter, Coleman Hawkins, and Catlett for four numbers, including two complementary versions of "I Can't Believe That You're in Love with Me." The issued take is fast, and the alternate is in a rocking medium tempo. Both are classics. Early in 1942, Gabler recorded a superb Benny Goodman session, under Mel Powell's name. Present are Billy Butterfield, Goodman, George Berg, Powell, Al Morgan, and Kansas Fields. Goodman and Powell never swung harder than they do in "The World Is Waiting for the Sunrise." Late in 1943, Gabler mixed members of the Eddie Heywood Downtown Society Cafe band with members of Teddy Wilson's uptown band, and they did an indelible "The Man I Love" and a supreme, slow "Uptown Cafe Blues." And early in 1944 he recorded a Basie-oriented group including Lester Young and Dickie Wells, and the marvellous quarter Catlett had with Ben Webster, Marlowe Norris, and John Simmons.

Some of the miscellaneous recordings that turn up on the Mosaics were made for other labels and bought and released by Gabler. There are two creamy dates that were run by Leonard Feather—one with Hackett, Marsala, Pete Brown, and the stream-of-consciousness singer Leo Watson, and the other with Bill Coleman, Marsala, and Brown, accompanied only by bass and guitar. There is a handsome slow "Clarinet Blues" that

features Stacy, Butterfield, Eddie Miller, and the honeyed clarinettist Irving Fazola. There are twenty-five Jelly Roll Morton
numbers, made a year before Morton died. Twelve are rough-
neck band sides, and the rest are piano solos, several with
keening Morton vocals.

Mosaic does not do anything by halves. The surviving takes of
each number are given, with the issued version presented first.
Sometimes there are as many as four takes. Listening to them all
is like reading a novel in which all the early drafts are included.
In addition to the interviews with Gabler, the accompanying
booklets contain complete discographies, fresh photographs,
and indefatigable liner notes by Dan Morgenstern, who brings
this hybrid form close to perfection.